AF599350

Claudia Larcher

Hallucinations

Verlag für moderne Kunst

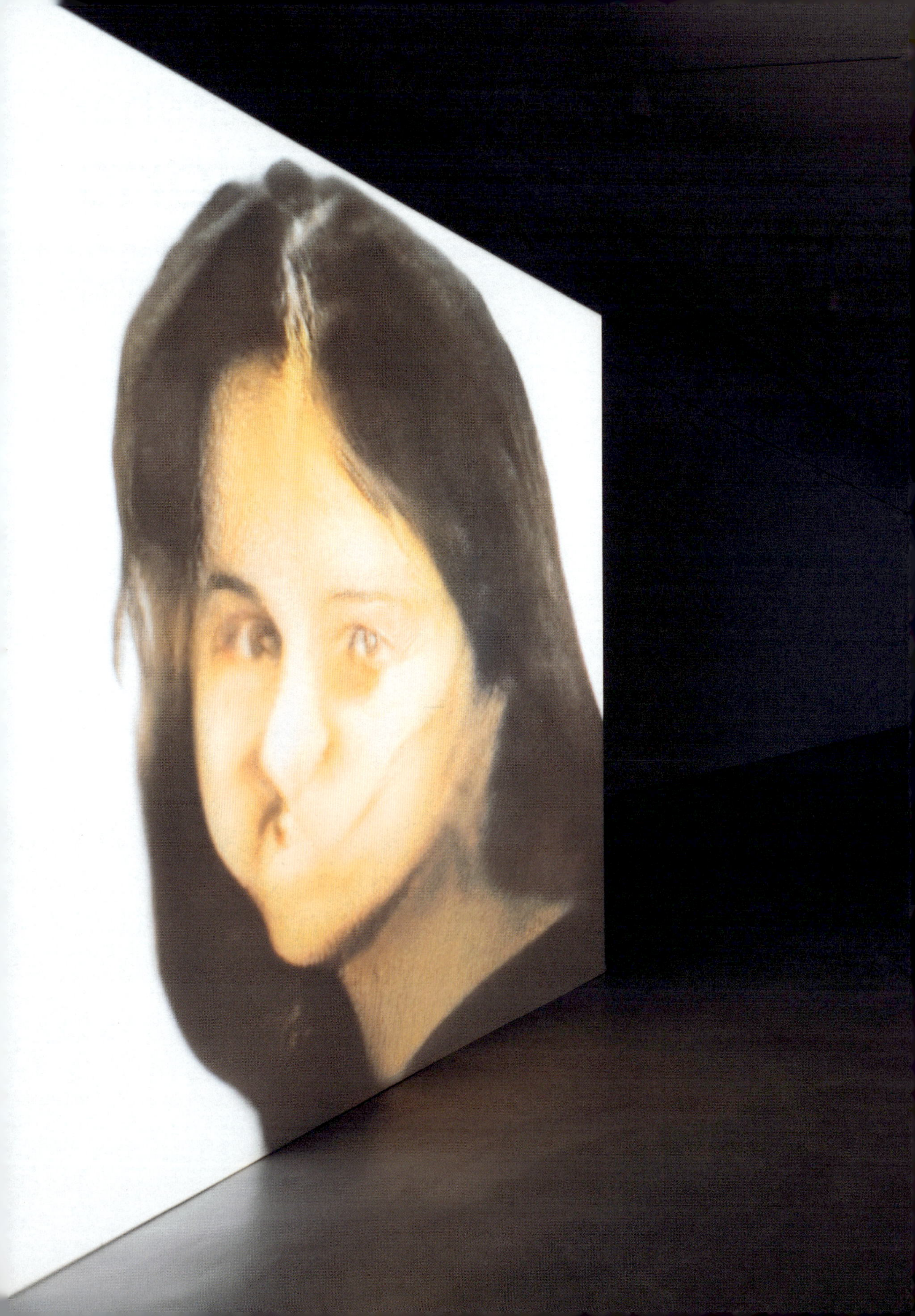

Inhalt

Table of Contents

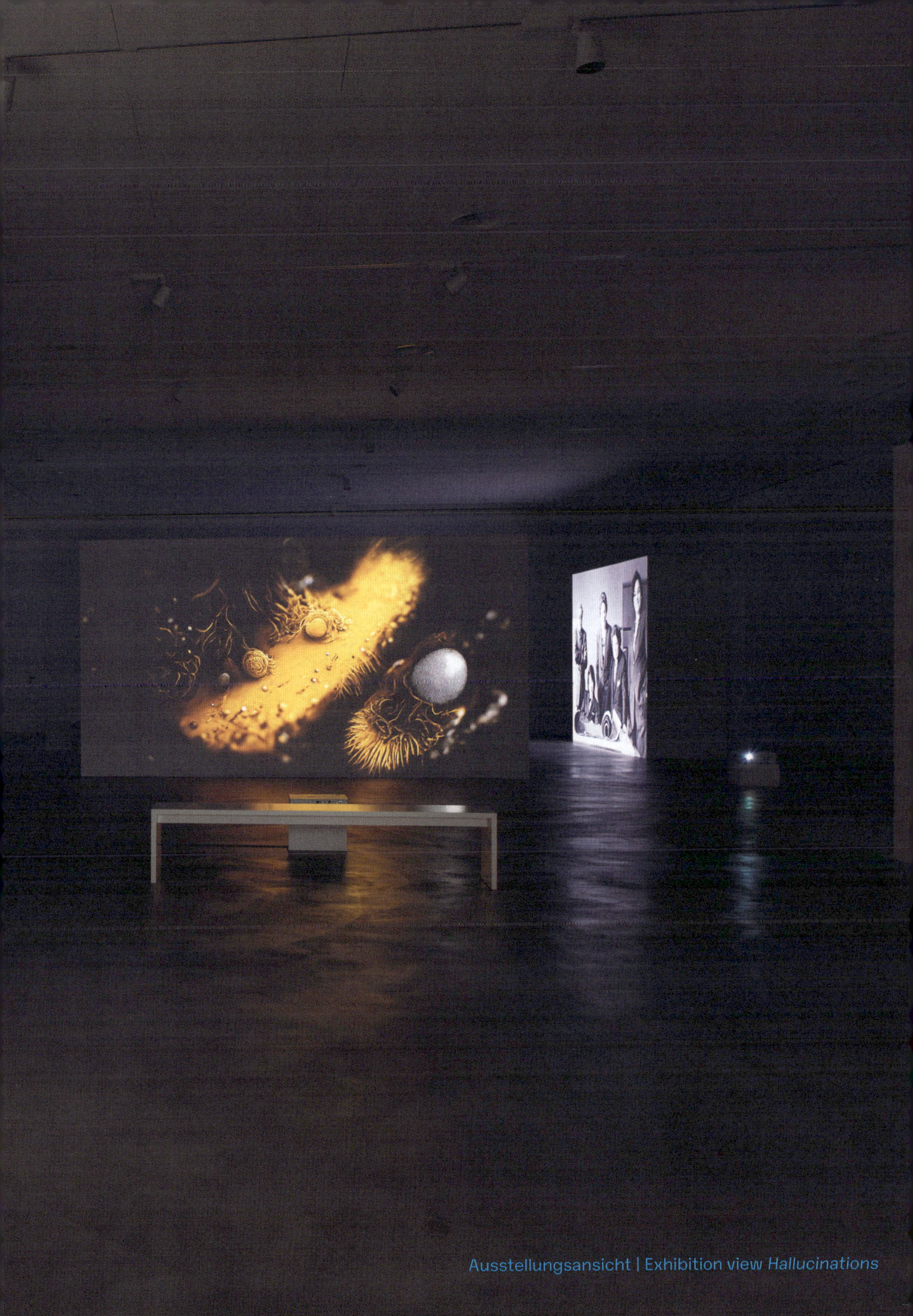

Ausstellungsansicht | Exhibition view *Hallucinations*

Vorwort

Ruth Schib, Leiterin Kunstraum Engländerbau, Vaduz

Bei meiner ersten persönlichen Begegnung mit der österreichischen Künstlerin und Filmemacherin Claudia Larcher verspürte ich den Wunsch, mehr über die Beweggründe hinter ihrer Auseinandersetzung mit künstlicher Intelligenz zu erfahren. Ihre Antwort verdeutlichte, dass Neugier und Forschergeist sowie das Begreifen und Einordnen dieser neuartigen Technologie die treibenden Kräfte ihrer künstlerischen Praxis sind. Besagte Schnittstelle zwischen Kunst und künstlichen intelligenten Systemen bildet die Grundlage von Larchers Arbeit, wobei technische, ästhetische, philosophische und ethische Aspekte thematisiert werden.

Als ich in Larchers KI-generierte Filmarbeiten eintauchte und die auf seltsame Weise skurril anmutende Welt erkundete, wurde ich von einem mulmigen Gefühl ergriffen. Dieses Unbehagen, verbunden mit einer starken Faszination, veranlasste mich, mehr über die Möglichkeiten und Problematiken der künstlichen Intelligenz zu erfahren. In den letzten Jahren ist die künstliche Intelligenz – kurz KI – in den Medien omnipräsent und hat sich zu einem Dauerthema in der öffentlichen Diskussion entwickelt. Viele Lebensbereiche unseres Alltags werden mittlerweile von KI beeinflusst und sowohl skeptische als auch verherrlichende Stimmen sind allgegenwärtig. Ein flüchtiger Blick in die Fachliteratur offenbart einen vielschichtig verwobenen Raum aus Algorithmen plus Daten. Marcus du Sautoy, Professor für Mathematik an der Universität Oxford, beschreibt in seinem Buch *Der Creativity-Code* (2021) ein „neues Zeitalter des maschinellen Lernens", in dem sich Algorithmen auf der Basis verfügbarer Daten weiterentwickeln und zu immer kreativeren Systemen getrimmt werden.

In der interdisziplinären und globalen KI-Forschung wurde ein Instrument erschaffen, das aus unserem Alltag nicht mehr wegzudenken ist und unser Leben in Zukunft noch stärker prägen wird. Manuela Lenzen, Philosophin und Wissenschaftsjournalistin, erläutert in ihrem Buch *Der elektronische Spiegel* (2023) eindrucksvoll die fachübergreifende Zusammenarbeit und beschreibt, wie die Weiterentwicklung von KI nach dem Vorbild des

Menschen erfolgt und welche Herausforderungen gemeistert werden müssen. Ein zentraler Aspekt ist unsere Wahrnehmung, die eng mit dem sogenannten gesunden Menschenverstand, mit Intuition und Emotionen verknüpft ist – eine Schwierigkeit, die bislang für die Forschenden eine nicht zu bewältigende Aufgabe darstellt. An dieser Stelle, wo digitale Stagnation und Unüberbrückbarkeit verschiedener Anforderungen aufeinandertreffen sowie die Auswirkungen von künstlicher Intelligenz nicht absehbar sind, eröffnet sich für Larcher ein Experimentierfeld für die Kunst. Ausgehend von ihrer Neugier an dieser hochkomplexen Technologie, setzt die Künstlerin in unkonventioneller Weise KI als kreatives Werkzeug ein, einschließlich aller Einschränkungen und seltsamen Fehler, die dabei auftreten können. Dadurch eröffnet sie den Betrachter:innen neue Sichtweisen und schafft einen Raum für kritisches Denken. Zusammengefasst wirken Larchers Arbeiten wie ein Spiegel der Gesellschaft und verdeutlichen, dass KI in der Kunst über eine rein instrumentelle Funktion hinausgeht. Künstliche intelligente Systeme haben das Potenzial, unsere Fähigkeiten zu ergänzen sowie zu erweitern und regen die menschliche Kreativität an, Grenzen zu überschreiten – dies im Rahmen eines verantwortungsvollen Umgangs und reflexiven Einsatzes dieser Technologie.

Larchers Filmarbeiten laden ein, unseren Blick auf uns selbst, unsere Vergangenheit und Mitwelt in einer zunehmend komplexer werdenden Lebensrealität zu hinterfragen. Sie sind als Aufforderung zum Nachdenken über die gegenwärtigen Entwicklungen zu verstehen und eröffnen einen multidimensionalen Raum des Nachspürens und Dekonstruierens.

Beim Eintauchen in den faszinierenden Kunstkosmos von Claudia Larcher wünsche ich Ihnen viel Freude und einen anregenden Perspektivenwechsel. Lassen Sie sich herausfordern und inspirieren – entdecken Sie Neuland und seien Sie offen für kritische Denkanstöße. Ihre Neugier wird Sie leiten.

Claudia Larcher | HALLUCINATIONS
22. Oktober bis 15. Dezember 2024
Kunstraum Engländerbau Vaduz, Liechtenstein

Kuratorin der Austellung: Yvonne Rüscher
Produktions- und Projektleitung: Ruth Schib
Kulturvermittlung: Monika Adank, Cristina Ghizzoni Wohlwend
Ausstellungstechnik: Martin Beck
Lichtdesign: Stefan Martin
Sound Performance: Ursula Winterauer aka Gischt

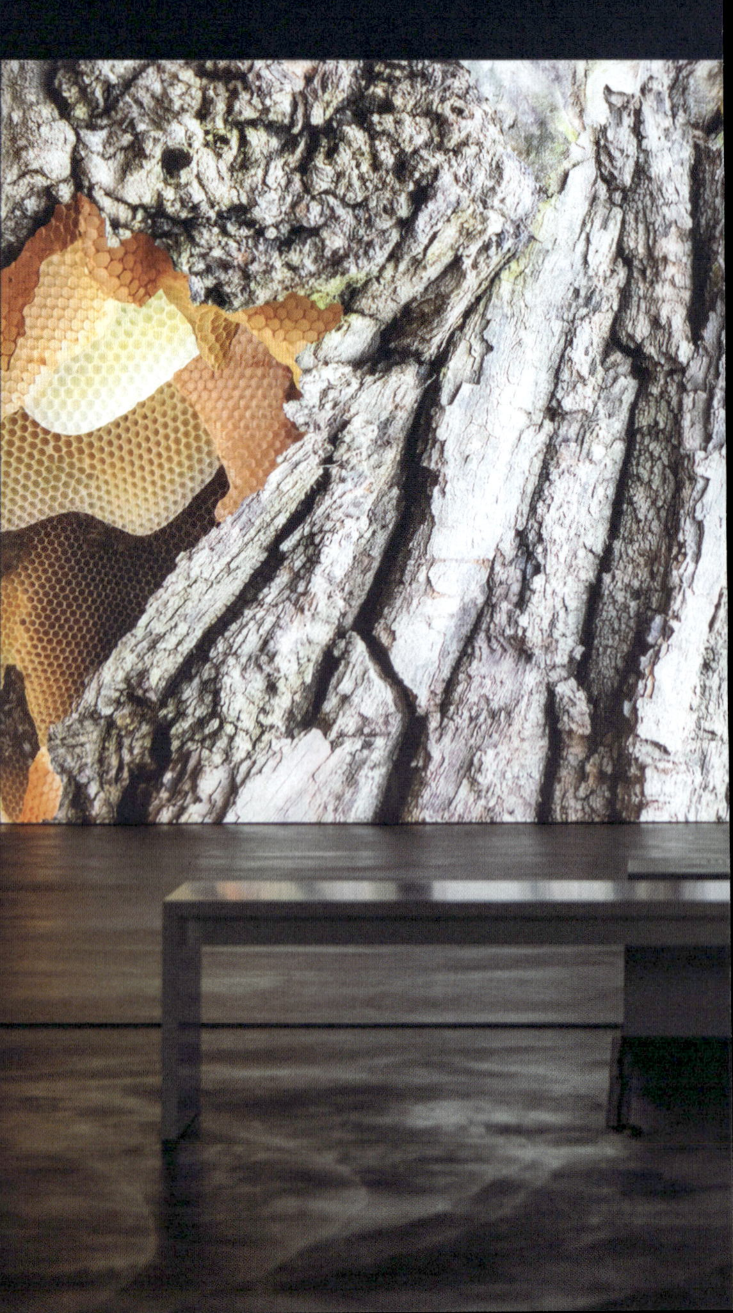

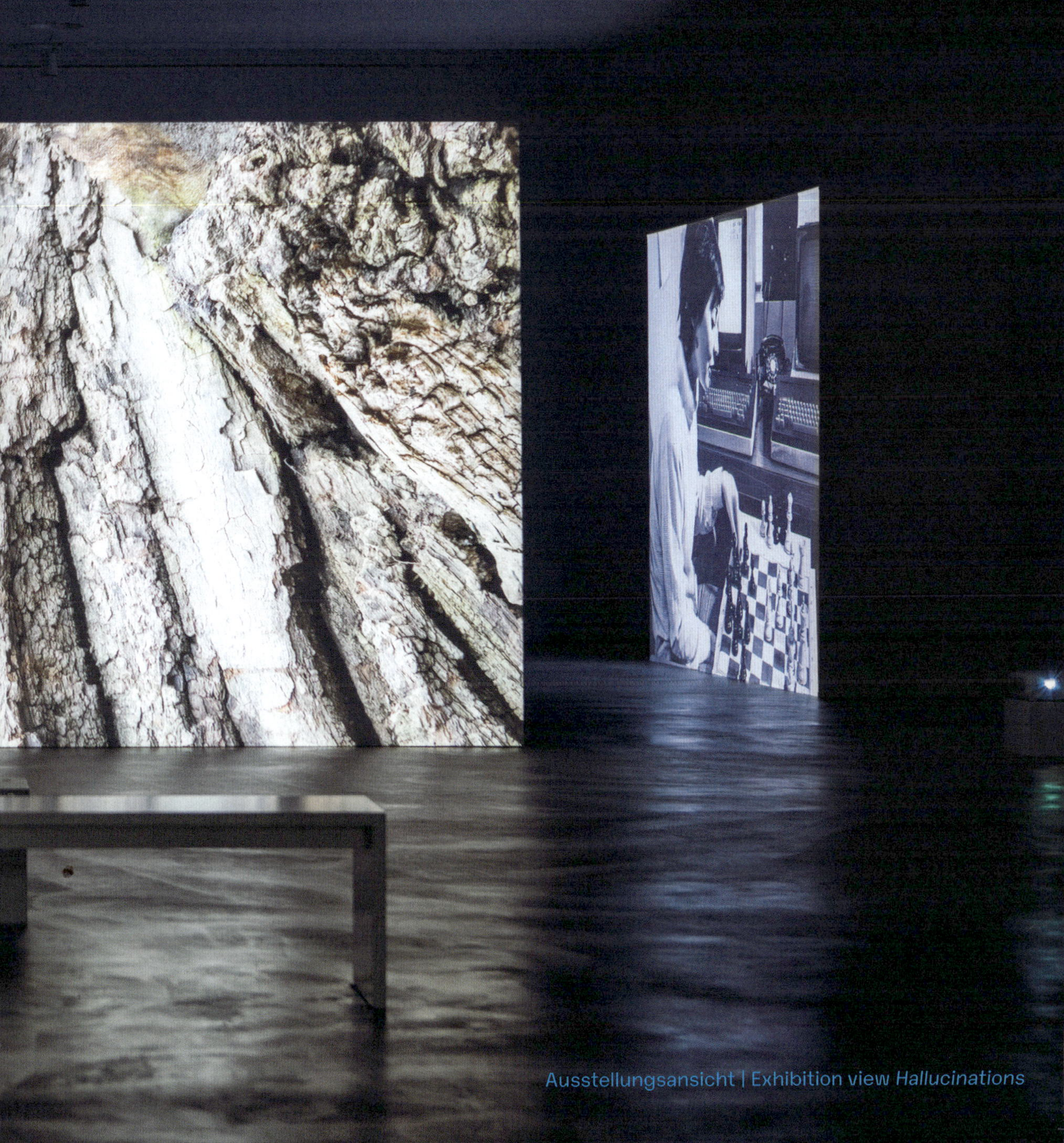

Ausstellungsansicht | Exhibition view *Hallucinations*

Foreword

Ruth Schib, Director Kunstraum Engländerbau, Vaduz

Upon my first personal encounter with the Austrian artist and filmmaker Claudia Larcher, I sensed a desire to learn more about the motivations behind her investigation of artificial intelligence. Her answer made it clear that curiosity and a spirit of research, as well as an urge to comprehend and contextualise this innovative technology, constitute the driving impulses of her artistic practice. The interface between art and systems of artificial intelligence serves as the basis for Larcher's work, with its thematisation of the technical, aesthetic, philosophical and ethical aspects of AI.

When I plunged into Larcher's AI-generated filmic works and began exploring their world suffused with a strange absurdity, I was gripped by a queasy feeling. This disquiet, connected with a vivid fascination, induced me to learn more about the possibilities and problematics of artificial intelligence. In recent years, artificial intelligence – often designated with the acronym AI – has become omnipresent in the media and has developed into a constant theme of public discussion. Many areas of our daily life have meanwhile come to be influenced by AI; both skeptical and glorifying voices are all around us. A fleeting glance at the professional literature reveals a complexly interwoven space consisting of algorithms plus data. Marcus du Sautoy, professor for mathematics at Oxford University, describes in his book *The Creativity Code* (2021) an 'era of machine learning' in which algorithms develop themselves further on the basis of available data and are fashioned into ever more creative systems.

In interdisciplinary and global AI research, an instrument has been created without which our everyday life can no longer be imagined, and which will mark our lives more deeply in the future. Manuela Lenzen, a philosopher and scientific journalist, impressively explains in her book *Der elektronische Spiegel* (2023) the interdisciplinary collaboration and describes how the further development of AI is proceeding according to the model of the human being, and which challenges must thereby be mastered. A fundamental aspect is our perception, which is closely linked with so-called common sense, with intuition and with emotions – a difficulty which up to now has constituted a task of insurmountable proportions.

At this point, where digital stagnation and the irreconcilability of clashing requirements come into contact and the effects of artificial intelligence cannot be predicted, there opens for Larcher a field for artistic experimentation. Proceeding from her curiosity with regard to this highly complex technology, the artist makes unconventional use of AI as a creative tool, including all its limitations and the strange errors which can occur. This opens up new perspectives for viewers and engenders a space for critical thought. In their entirety, Larcher's works serve as a mirror onto society and make it clear that AI plays more than a purely instrumental role in art. Systems of artificial intelligence have the potential to extend and expand our capabilities; they stimulate human creativity to transcend borders – in the framework of a responsible use and reflective application of this technology.

Larcher's filmic works issue an invitation to question our view of ourselves, our past and our surroundings in a lived reality that is becoming increasingly complex. They should be understood as a summons to reflect upon current developments; they open up a multi-dimensional space of investigation and deconstruction.

I wish you much pleasure and a stimulating change of perspective for your journey into the fascinating artistic cosmos of Claudia Larcher. Let yourself be challenged and inspired; discover new realms and be open to critical food for thought. Your curiosity will guide you.

Claudia Larcher | HALLUCINATIONS
October 22 until December 15, 2024
Kunstraum Engländerbau Vaduz, Liechtenstein

Exhibition Curator: Yvonne Rüscher
Director: Ruth Schib
Mediation: Monika Adank, Cristina Ghizzoni Wohlwend
Exhibition Technology: Martin Beck
Light Design: Stefan Martin
Sound Performance: Ursula Winterauer aka Gischt

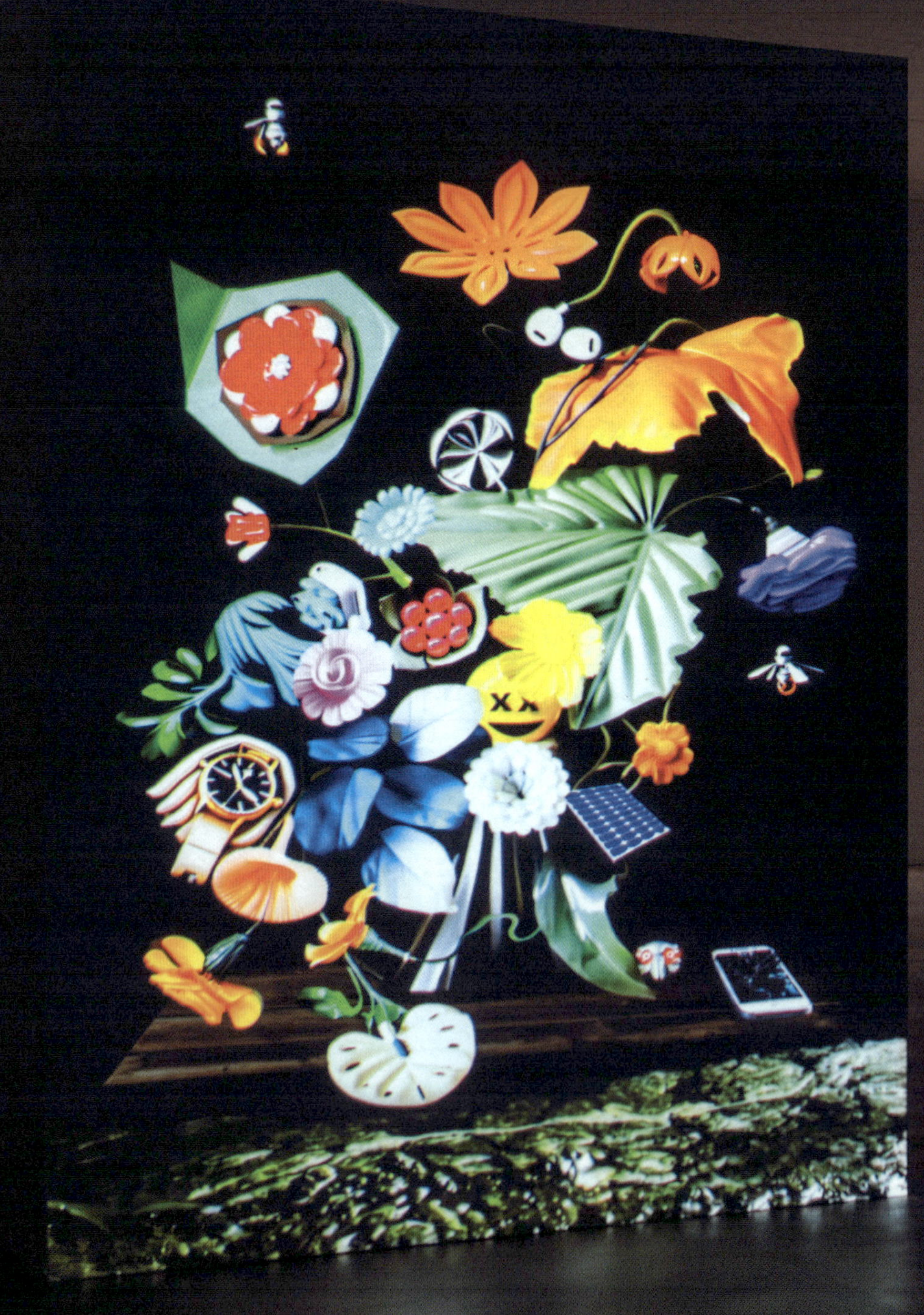

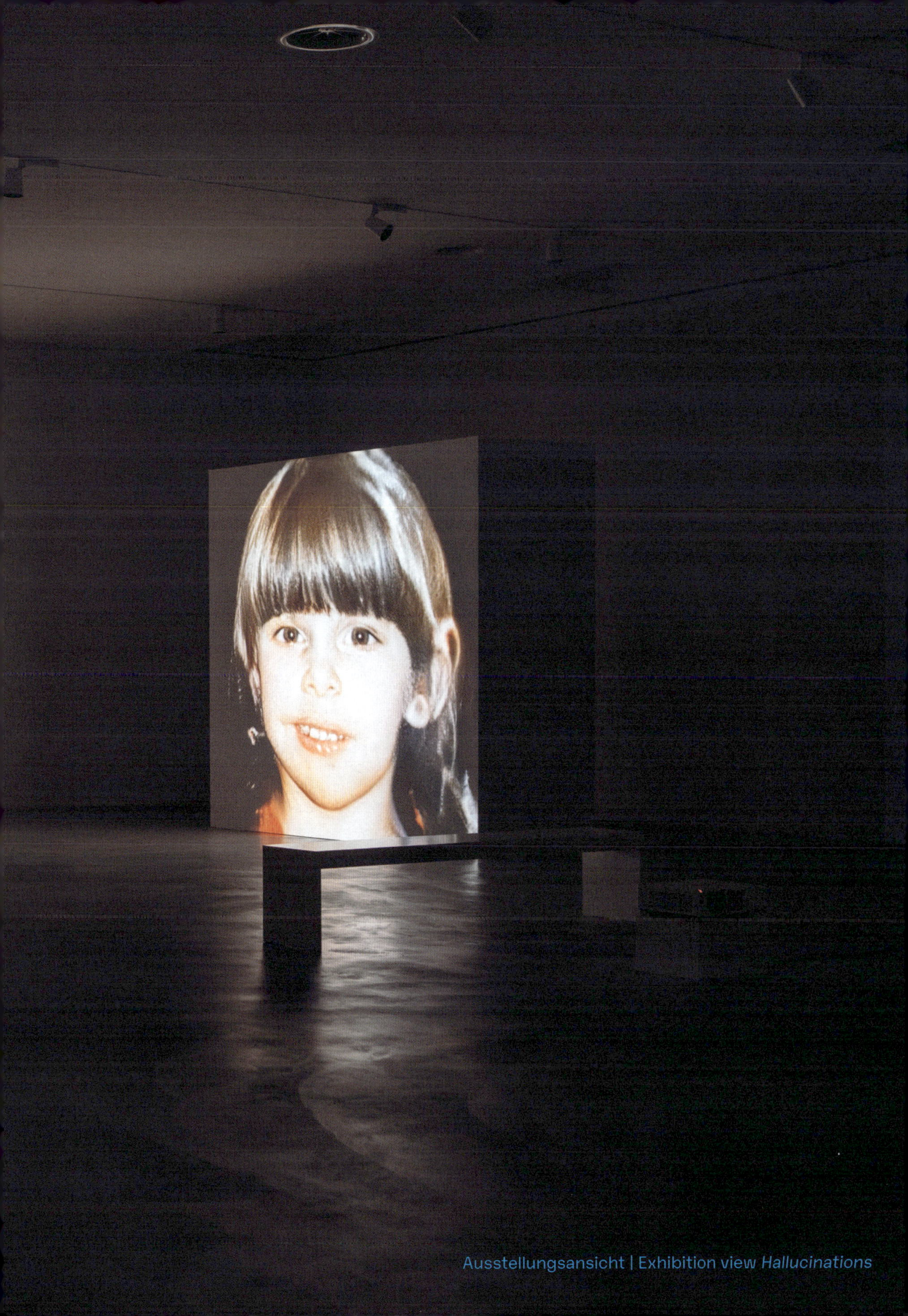

Ausstellungsansicht | Exhibition view *Hallucinations*

Subtile Subversionen und schöne Systemfehler

Klaus Speidel

They flutter behind you, your possible pasts
Some bright-eyed and crazy, some frightened and lost
A warning to anyone still in command
('Ranks! Fire!')
Of their possible future to take care.

Roger Waters, 1983[1]

Architektur, Geschichte, Identität, Körper und Natur sind einige der Themen, die in Claudia Larchers Kunst wesentlich vorkommen. Was ihre Arbeiten verbindet, sind jedoch weniger Inhalte als Prozesse. Ausgangspunkt ist oft eine Reihe vorgefundener Bilder – die Jahresausgabe einer Architekturzeitschrift, historische Fotografien, ein Katalog oder Porträts der eigenen Person –, für die sie Transformationsprozesse entwickelt. Wie Larcher sie zu neuen Werken verarbeitet, ist konstitutiv für ihre Bedeutung. Dabei ist die Weise, in der Larcher das Vorgefundene transformiert, manchmal offen politisch – so hat sie in Porträts die Köpfe der Heroen der modernistischen Architektur durch die Gesichter von Architektinnen ersetzt–, meistens aber subtil subversiv. Serialität und Medienwechsel spielen dabei eine wichtige Rolle. Eine wiederkehrende Form der Mutation in Larchers Arbeit ist die vom Einzelbild im Ursprungskontext zur Serie und dann zur raum- oder wandfüllenden Installation und zum Video – wobei ein und dasselbe Ausgangsmaterial sich oft in unterschiedlichen Medien neu verfestigt. In dieser Hinsicht unterscheiden sich die Werke, die unter Verwendung von KI[2] entstanden sind, nicht wesentlich gegenüber früheren Arbeiten.

KI ist nicht gleich KI

Im Überblick der verschiedenen Projekte wird deutlich, dass KI nicht gleich KI ist, denn Larcher hat für jeden Werkzyklus eine andere Methode und oft auch eine neue

[1] Roger Waters, „Your Possible Pasts", Pink Floyd: The Final Cut, 1983.

[2] Ich ziehe den Begriff KI gegenüber „Künstlicher Intelligenz" vor, weil die Abkürzung das ungelöste Problem der Möglichkeit einer künstlichen Intelligenz und die Frage nach der Angemessenheit des Begriffs weniger dringlich erscheinen lässt.

KI verwendet. Anhand der Beschreibungen im Abspann der KI-Arbeiten wird Larchers Denken zum Thema sichtbar. In den ersten Arbeiten schreibt sie relativ offen: „Das Video basiert auf selbstlernender künstlicher Intelligenz" und erklärt dann den Prozess des „Anlernens" der KI mit ihrem Archiv und beschreibt das verwendete KI-Modell. Bei *Me, Myself and I*, 2022, schreibt sie, „mit Hilfe von künstlichen Assistent:innen erstellt", und dankt den verwendeten KI-Modellen, als handle es sich um Akteure. Bei *Das große Baumstück*, 2022/23, heißt es: „Bilder, Videos und Animation von Claudia Larcher und in Zusammenarbeit mit Künstlicher Intelligenz". Jede dieser Be- und Umschreibungen vermittelt ein anderes Bild der Verwendung von KI und der Machtverteilung. Während Assistent:innen im Wesentlichen ausführen, was man ihnen aufträgt, impliziert „Collaboration" oder Zusammenarbeit in der Regel eine Arbeit auf Augenhöhe. Bei ihrer Arbeit *AI and the Art of Historical Reinterpretation* schließlich wird KI nur im Titel erwähnt, so dass der Film bereits die Post-KI-Zeit ankündigt, in der die Verwendung von KI so selbstverständlich geworden ist, dass sie aufhört erwähnenswert zu sein. Indem Microsoft, Google und Apple nun KI in ihren Produkten ausrollen, haben sie dieses Zeitalter eingeleitet.

KI-Sofortbilder

Für *Me, myself and I* hat Larcher alle verfügbaren analogen Fotografien von sich digitalisiert und dann ein Generative Adversarial Network (GAN) damit trainiert und über 3000 Bilder generiert. Dabei hat das GAN die Fehler in den analogen Fotografien (Überbelichtung etc.) übernommen und dann simuliert. Eine Auswahl dieser Bilder hat Larcher von der KI in ein Video verwandeln lassen, wobei die Zwischenschritte errechnet werden, so dass die Einzelbilder kontinuierlich ineinander übergehen. Dieses Video als unmittelbares Output des GANs ist im Engländerbau zu sehen. Allerdings hat Larcher die digitalen Bilder auch in Polaroids verwandelt, also in die Art analoger Fotografie, die am stärksten mit Unmittelbarkeit und Authentizität assoziiert wird. Das ist für mich der Punkt – wenn auch vielleicht nicht das *Punctum*

– von Claudia Larchers *Me, myself and I* als Serie von Sofortbildern. Ein klassisches Foto ließ schon lange vor Photoshop Zweifel an der Realität des Dargestellten zu – wer weiß schon, was in der Dunkelkammer passiert ist. Vom Polaroid dagegen ging noch lange nach seinem kommerziellen Versagen die Aura des Authentischen und Spontanen aus. Man könnte sogar sagen, dass es den eigentlichen Referenzpunkt von Roland Barthes' *Dictum* „Es-ist-so-gewesen" bildet: „Die PHOTOGRAPHIE sagt nicht (zwangsläufig) etwas über das, was nicht mehr ist, sondern nur und mit Sicherheit etwas über das, was gewesen ist [...]. Das Wesen der PHOTOGRAPHIE besteht in der Bestätigung dessen, was sie wiedergibt."[3] Unmittelbar zum Zeitpunkt der Aufnahme und am Licht der Sonne entstanden, war das Polaroid wirklich Lichtspur des Dargestellten. Insofern ist es besonders ironisch, das Larcher nicht Fotoprints, sondern Polaroids aus ihren KI-generierten Bildern macht. Aus „KI-generierten Bildern im Stil von Fotografien" werden so Fotografien. Die simulierten analogen Fehler, die das GAN von dem Ausgangsdatensatz übernommen hat, treten dabei in Korrespondenz mit tatsächlichen Fehlern des analogen Entwicklungsprozesses, die durch das lang abgelaufene Polaroidmaterial verstärkt werden.

Bizarre Wahlverwandtschaften

Das Sofortbild spielt jedoch noch eine weitere Rolle in Larchers Serie: Die Verwendung einer obsolet gewordenen Technik wirft uns über zwanzig Jahre zurück, in die Zeit nämlich, in der die Bilder entstanden sind, die Larcher als „Trainingsdaten" für ihr GAN verwendet hat. Larcher war 24 Jahre alt, als das letzte analoge Foto, auf dem die Künstlerin zu sehen ist, in ihr Familienarchiv einging. Die Anmutung der Serie vermittelt unmittelbar den Eindruck, es handle sich um ein historisches Werk. Die Präsentation rückt sie in die Nähe der systematischen Selbstporträts von Friedl Kubelka vom Gröller oder Andy Warhols Polaroids. Auch an die *Photo-Transformations* des amerikanischen Künstlers Lucas Samaras kann man

[3] Roland Barthes, *Die helle Kammer*, übersetzt von Dietrich Leube, Suhrkamp: Frankfurt, 1989, S. 95.

denken. Er hat ebenfalls mit Polaroids gearbeitet und dabei die feuchte Emulsion so mit Pinseln und anderen Instrumenten manipuliert, dass ähnlich fließende (Selbst-)Porträts entstanden wie die, die Larcher per KI erzeugt. Diese Verwandtschaft mit existierenden Kunstwerken anderer Künstler:innen, stellt eine Genealogie für das Werk Larchers her, die über das eigene Schaffen hinaus- und tief ins 20. Jahrhundert hineinreicht. Die visuelle Verwandtschaft mit den Werken Samaras legt nahe, dass das Versagen des GANs im Angesicht mangelnder Daten kein ästhetisches ist. Mit 350 Bildern als Input produziert das Modell zwar keine überzeugenden Porträts, wie sie seit 2019 auf der Website thispersondoesnotexist.com zu finden sind (dafür wären wohl mindestens 4000 Inputbilder nötig), aber die Art, in der das GAN scheitert, ist ästhetisch und künstlerisch interessant. Es ist verblüffend, wie real die Personen auf thispersondoesnotexist.com und ähnlichen Websites wirken. Aber gerade weil die Bilder wie gewöhnliche fotografische Porträts aussehen, sind sie künstlerisch oder ästhetisch meist nicht interessant.

Schöne Systemfehler

Man mag hier an Baudelaire denken, der schreibt: „Das Schöne ist immer bizarr. Ich will damit nicht sagen, dass es absichtlich, kalkuliert bizarr ist, denn in diesem Fall wäre es ein Monster, das aus den Schienen des Lebens herausgefallen ist. Ich sage, dass es immer ein wenig Bizarrerie enthält, naive, ungewollte, unbewusste Bizarrerie, und dass es diese Bizarrerie ist, die es besonders zum Schönen macht. Sie ist sein Kennzeichen, sein Merkmal.

Kehren Sie den Vorschlag um und bemühen Sie sich, ein banales Schönes zu entwerfen!“[4]
Vielleicht beschreibt Baudelaires Beobachtung – die fast unheimlich mit den KI-Porträts Larchers korrespondiert – etwas, das Künstler:innen, deren Sensibilität sich an der modernen und zeitgenössischen Kunst ausgebildet hat (im Gegensatz zu solchen, die vom Design oder Gaming

[4] Charles Baudelaire, *Curiosités esthétiques, L'Exposition universelle de 1855*, Paris: Michel Lévy frères, 1868. Übersetzung: KS.

kommen), dazu bewegt, in der digitalen Kunst gerade den „Glitch" oder das nicht-intendierte Resultat zu bevorzugen. Ein weiterer Grund mag sein, dass sie vermuten, dass sich in den Systemfehlern etwas Wesentliches zeigt – was ja auch nicht immer von der Hand zu weisen ist. Auch die Tatsache, dass ein wesentlicher Teil von Larchers Arbeit darin bestanden hat, eine Auswahl aus über 3000 von der KI generierten Bildern zu treffen, ist charakteristisch. Für eine Ausstellung von 20 Bildern in der Gagosian Gallery hat Bennett Miller nach eigener Aussage mit dem öffentlich verfügbaren KI Bildmodell Dall-E 2 sogar über 100 000 Bilder generiert. Ein wichtiger Teil der Arbeit Millers bestand dabei nicht nur darin, die ursprünglichen Prompts – also Anleitungen an die KI – immer wieder zu revidieren und zu verfeinern, sondern auch im Kuratieren des Outputs[5]. Der kuratorische Aspekt der Arbeit mit KI hat manche Theoretiker:innen dazu bewogen, Vergleiche von KI-Kunst zum Readymade zu ziehen, bei dem Künstler:innen eine Auswahl von existierenden Objekten treffen.[6] Während der Vergleich in seiner allgemeinen Form hinkt, hat das Readymade sicher eine wesentliche Rolle dabei gespielt, konzeptuelle und intellektuelle Operationen in der Kunst gegenüber dem „Machen" und handwerklichen Fähigkeiten aufzuwerten, was einerseits die konzeptuelle Kunst der 1960er-Jahre ermöglicht hat und andererseits einer künstlerischen Nutzung von KI zugute kommt.

Durch ihre komplexen Bezüge und die multiplen technischen und konzeptuellen Operationen unterscheiden sich Werke wie die Larchers auch wesentlich von den meisten Produktionen, die heute als „KI-Kunst" firmieren, bei denen das KI-generierte (Einzel-)Bild auf dem Screen der künstlerische Output ist und Medienreflexion keine Rolle spielt.

[5] Ein wesentlicher Unterschied zwischen Text- zu Bildmodellen wie Dall-E, das auf der GPT-Architektur basiert, und dem von Larcher verwendetem GAN ist allerdings, dass letzteres von ihr mit sehr begrenzten Daten trainiert worden ist, während Bildmodelle wie Dall-E Milliarden von Bild-Text-Paaren verarbeitet haben. Ein weiterer Unterschied ist, dass das GAN, ausgehend von einer Reihe Bildern, andere Bilder produziert, also keinerlei Prompts zulässt.

[6] Das bekannteste Beispiel ist wohl bis heute das Urinal, das Marcel Duchamp 1917 signiert und mit *Fountain* betitelt hat.

Bei Larchers *Me, Myself and I* kommt durch den – ebenfalls KI-generierten –Text, für den die Künstlerin GPT 2.0 und 3.0 verwendet hat, noch eine weitere Ebene hinzu. Der Text changiert zwischen Bezügen zu Science-Fiction, die die Frage nach einem Bewusstsein in der Maschine stellt, wie *Ghost in the Shell*, 1995, und Fragen zum menschlichen Ego. Dabei erscheinen immer neue mögliche Versionen des Selbst auf dem Screen, die manchmal kurz stehen bleiben und dann wieder zerfließen, bluten, verschwimmen oder aufreißen, um sich neu und anders zu konstituieren. Allegorisch scheint das Video ein Bild des flüssigen Selbst zu vermitteln, wie es von Arthur Rimbauds „Ich ist ein anderer" bis zu Zygmunt Baumans „flüssiger Moderne" durch das 19. und 20. Jahrhundert fließt. Dabei entstehen immer wieder Korrespondenzen zwischen Bild und Text, zum Beispiel wenn zu hören ist: „Das Ego konstituiert sich ständig als existent", aber „jede feste Kategorisierung des Selbst ist großer Unsinn".

Larchers Werk findet so multiple Anknüpfungspunkte in der modernen Kunst. Auch die Polaroids spielen in diesem Kontext eine besondere Rolle, denn über subtile Subversion und Warnung hinaus legt besonders die Präsentation in dieser Form eine Rezeption des Werks im Kontext der modernen Tradition von fotografischen Selbstporträts nahe. An die Stelle des Pinsels und anderer Instrumente treten dabei die Algorithmen eines KI-Modells.

Von der Authentizität zum vergangenen Wirklichen

Bei KI-generierten Bildern im Stil von Fotografien kann von einem „Es-ist-so-gewesen" keine Rede mehr sein. Auch ein szenisches KI-generiertes Bild hat keinen realen Sachverhalt zuverlässig eingefangen. Dennoch verschwindet die Kausalkette von Motiv zu Bild (oder von den Motiven zu den Bildern) nicht vollkommen, denn immerhin sind die ursprünglichen Daten Teil der Ursachen, die den Output bestimmen. Insofern wäre es auch falsch, KI-Bildern jeglichen Weltbezug abzusprechen, wie das Hito Steyerl tut, wenn sie 2023 in einem Interview mit Kate Brown für Artnet im Zusammenhang mit KI-Bildmodellen behauptet,

„das Referenzfeld dieser statistischen Renderings ist nicht die reale Welt. Ihr Referenzfeld ist der gesamte Müll online."[7] Aus diesem Grund bestreitet Steyerl auch den Bildcharakter des Outputs von KI-Bildmodellen. Ich persönlich halte das für kurzsichtig im wörtlichen Sinn, denn der „Müll online" hat bislang einen nicht unwesentlichen Weltbezug gehabt und ist von Menschen produziert worden, die mit der Welt in direktem Kontakt standen. Spuren dieser Welterfahrung sind also auch im Output der Modelle zu erwarten. Selbst wenn Modelle nur noch mit „synthetischen Daten" trainiert werden, die per KI erstellt wurden, wird die reale Welt immer kausal an diesen beteiligt sein. Insofern scheinen mir KI-Bilder geradezu perfekt mit einer zweiten Fotografiedefinition von Roland Barthes zu korrelieren: „Die Realisten, zu denen ich gehöre [...], betrachten eine Photographie keineswegs als eine ‚Kopie' des Wirklichen – sondern als eine Emanation des vergangenen Wirklichen: als Magie und nicht als Kunst"[8]. Auch die KI-generierten Bilder in *Me, Myself and I* sind eine Emanation des vergangenen Wirklichen, insofern nämlich als sich dieses in die 350 Fotografien eingeschrieben hatte, mit denen Larcher das Modell trainiert hat. Ebenso verhält es sich mit dem Text, der das Video begleitet, denn von Sprachmodellen wie ChatGPT generiert, basiert er ebenfalls auf Schilderungen aus der Vergangenheit – auch wenn hier der Begriff der Emanation intuitiv weniger passen mag als bei den Bildern und die Ausgangstexte selten rekonstruierbar sind.

Dias und alternative Vergangenheiten

Noch eindeutiger um das „vergangene Wirkliche" dreht sich Larchers Arbeit *AI and the Art of Historical Reinterpretation*, 2022–2024. Mit einer Reihe von Diapositiven entwirft sie darin alternative Vergangenheiten. Das Projekt zielt darauf ab, die Beiträge von FLINTA (Frauen, Lesben,

[7] Kate Brown, "Hito Steyerl on Why NFTs and A.I. Image Generators Are Really Just 'Onboarding Tools' for Tech Conglomerates", *Artnet News*, March 10th 2023, Online Publikation: https://news.artnet.com/art-world/these-renderings-do-not-relate-to-reality-hito-steyerl-on-the-ideologies-embedded-in-a-i-image-generators-2264692, Zugriff: 6. 10. 2024.

[8] Roland Barthes, *Die helle Kammer*, op. cit., S. 99.

intergeschlechtliche, nichtbinäre, transgeschlechtliche und agender) Personen zur Geschichte zu unterstreichen, welche in traditionellen Narrativen oft unterdrückt wurden. Um das zu tun, hat Larcher auf historischen Gruppen- und Einzelporträts per KI Ersetzungen vorgenommen. Im Gegensatz zur eingangs erwähnten Serie *Baumeisterinnen*, 2018, bei der die Ersetzung von Architektenköpfen durch Architektinnenköpfe von Hand geschah und visuell evident ist, ist bei *AI and the Art of Historical Reinterpretation* die Bildmanipulation nahezu unsichtbar. Humorvoll ist die Serie dennoch. Bei manchen Bildern erinnern wir uns an das Original, andere erscheinen uns bekannt, ohne dass wir sie wiedererkennen, und die dritten sehen wir zum ersten Mal. Es geht dabei darum, in den Köpfen der Betrachter:innen den Möglichkeitssinn zu aktivieren und sie eine alternative Vergangenheit und damit Zukunft imaginieren zu lassen. Die Arbeit hat aber noch in anderer Weise mit Zukunft zu tun, insofern nämlich, als Larcher mit der Serie auf ihre Forschungen zu „algorithmischen Verzerrungen" reagiert. Das ist die Tendenz der KIs ausgehend von verzerrten Trainingsdaten, verzerrte Outputs zu produzieren. Bevor die großen KI-Unternehmen begannen gegenzusteuern, haben die meisten KI-Modelle bei Anfragen wie *„president"* beispielsweise nur Bilder weißer Männer produziert, während *„nurses"* systematisch weiblich waren.

Ein *„quick fix"*, also eine provisorische Lösung, besteht darin, die Modelle mit sogenannten Systemprompts, die für die Nutzer:innen unsichtbar bleiben, gezielt anzuhalten, den Output zu diversifizieren. An den Trainingsdaten ändert das allerdings nichts. Da sie historischer Natur sind, lassen sie sich auch nicht ohne Weiteres ändern. Hier kommt nun *AI and the Art of Historical Reinterpretation* ins Spiel, denn Larcher stellt sich vor, dass die Bilder als Teil zukünftiger Datensätze in Trainingsdaten zu weniger verzerrten Ergebnissen – oder einem veränderten Bild der Vergangenheit – beitragen könnten. Damit berührt die Arbeit schließlich auch ein Szenario, in dem KI-generierte Bilder zum Training von KI-Modellen verwendet werden und so zu unerwünschten Ergebnissen führen.

Wie die Diskussion dieser zwei Beispiele zeigt, gehen Claudia Larchers Arbeiten mannigfache Bezüge zu gesellschaftlichen und künstlerischen Themen ein. Diese Verankerung macht die KI Kunst Claudia Larchers so interessant: Es geht nicht um das beeindruckende Einzelbild, das den KI-Bilderstrom online und den KI-Bilddiskurs dominiert, sondern um Bildpraktiken und historische Bezüge. Die Tatsache, dass es bestimmte Bilder gibt und andere nicht, ihre Entstehung und die Form, in der sie existieren, sind mindestens genauso wichtig, wie das, was sie zeigen. Die KI-generierten Bilder werden dabei Teil komplexer Versuchsaufstellungen, die erst in ihrer Gesamtheit Kunstcharakter haben.

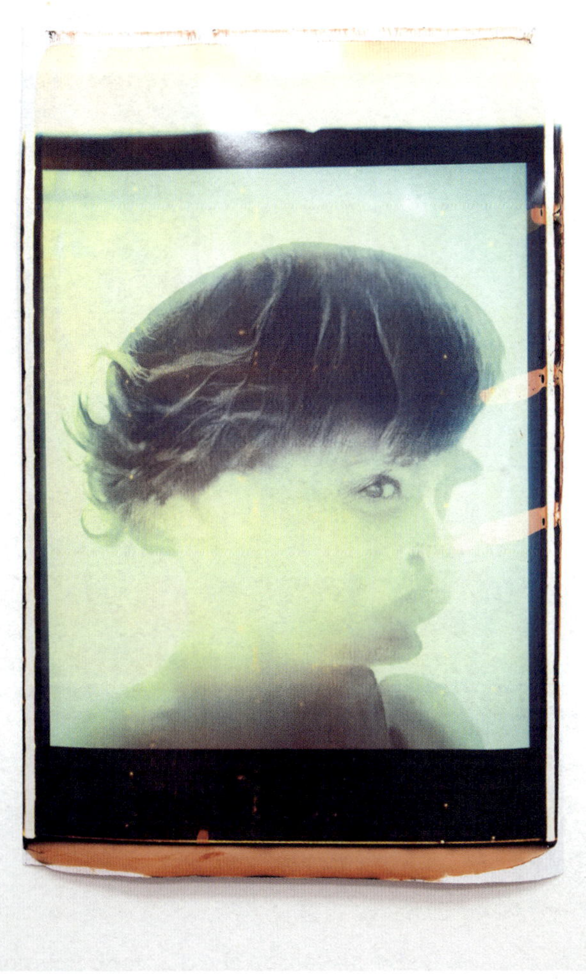

Me, Myself and I
Polaroid
92 x 65 cm
2021

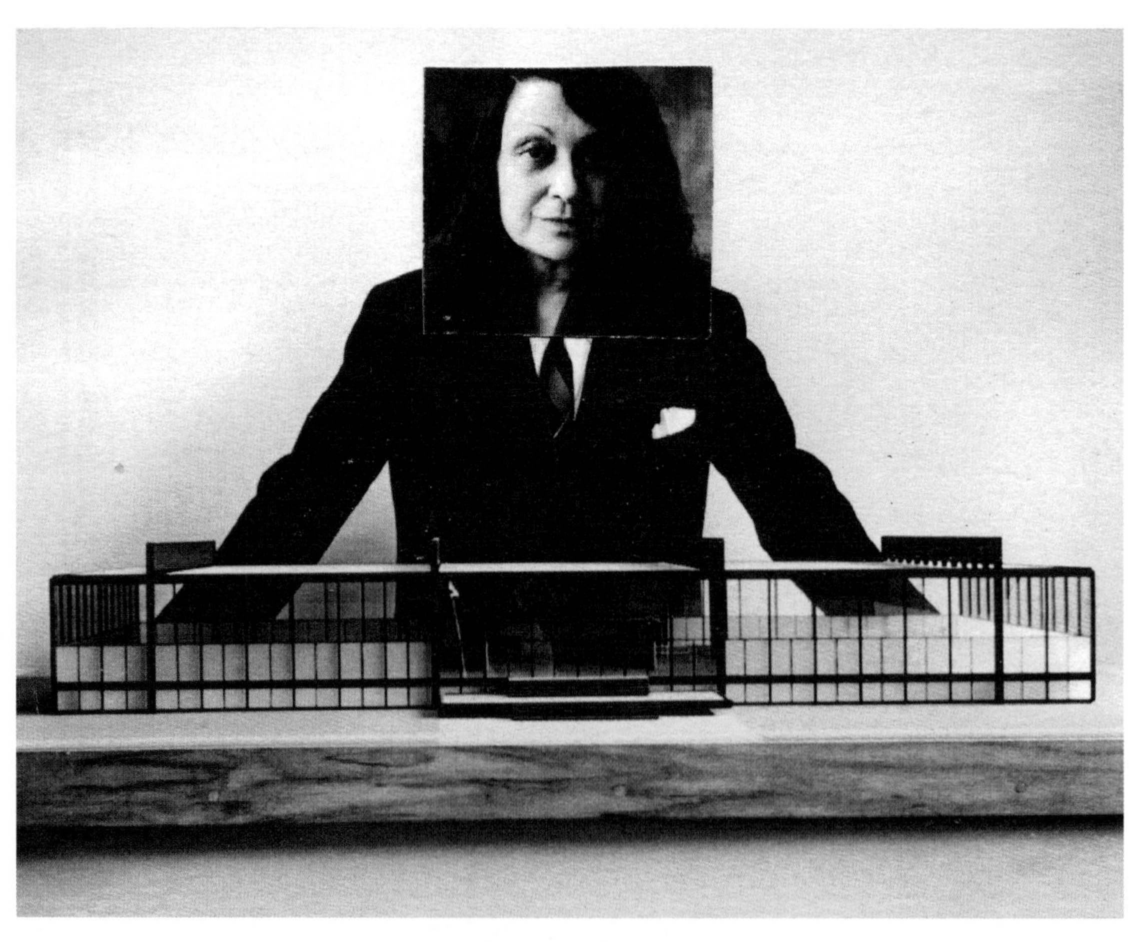

Lina Bo Bardi, Collage aus der Serie *Baumeisterinnen*, 2018

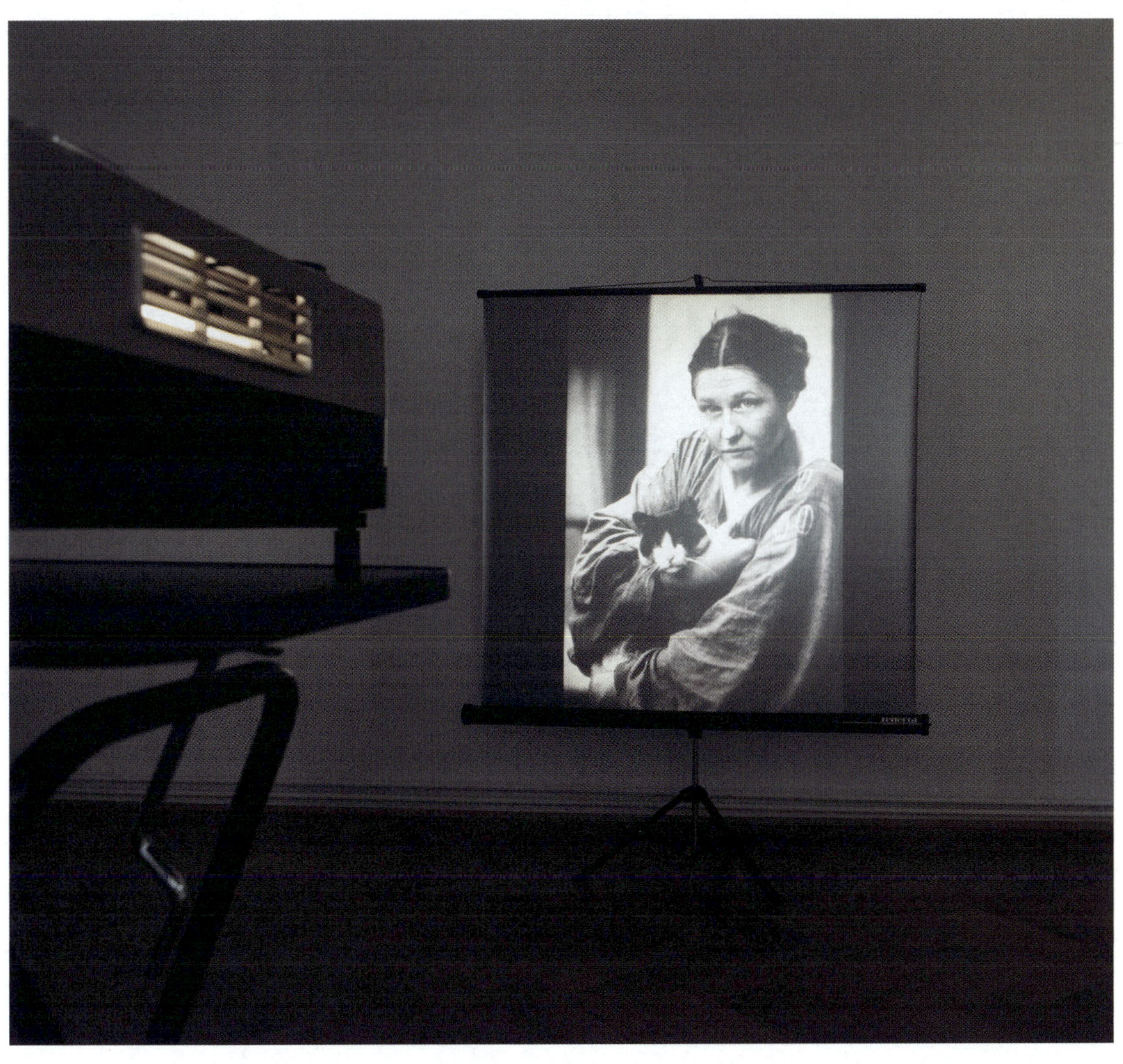

AI and the Art of Historical Reinterpretation, Installationsansicht, 2023

Subtle Subversions and Beautiful System Errors

Klaus Speidel

They flutter behind you, your possible pasts
Some bright-eyed and crazy, some frightened and lost
A warning to anyone still in command
('Rankel Firel')
Of their possible future to take care.

Roger Waters, 1983[1]

Architecture, history, identity, body, and nature are some of the themes which make an essential appearance in the art of Claudia Larcher. But what connects her works are less their contents than their processes. Their point of departure is often a series of found images – the annual edition of an architectural periodical, historical photographs, a catalogue, or portraits of herself – for which she develops processes of transformation. How Larcher elaborates them into new works is constitutive with regard to their meaning. Sometimes, the manner in which Larcher transforms what she finds is openly political – for example, when she modified portraits to replace the heads of the male heroes of modernist architecture with the faces of female architects – but for the most part, her approach is subtly subversive. Serialism and shifts of media play an important role. A recurrent form of mutation in Larcher's work is the evolution from a single image in the original context into a series, then into a space- or wall-filling installation, and finally into a video – where the material serving as a point of departure often takes form in various media. From this perspective, the works based in her use of AI[2] do not differ essentially from earlier creations.

AI Does Not Equal AI

A survey of the various projects makes clear that AI models are not always equivalent. For each work cycle, Larcher uses another method and often a new AI as well.

[1] Roger Waters, 'Your Possible Pasts', Pink Floyd: The Final Cut, 1983.

[2] I prefer the term AI rather than 'artificial intelligence' because the acronym puts a less pressing emphasis on the unsolved problem regarding the possibility of an artificial intelligence and on the question as to the suitability of the designation itself.

Larcher's approach to the question of the role of the models is evident in the credits of her AI works. In her initial creation, the formulation is very open: 'The video is based on self-learning, artificial intelligence.' She then explains the process of 'training' AI through her archive and describes the particular AI model that is being used. With regard to *Me, Myself and I* (2022), she writes 'created with the help of artificial assistants' and Larcher adds a thank-you note to the utilised AI models as if they were actors. *The Great Tree Piece* (2022/23) offers the following formulation: 'Pictures, videos and animation by Claudia Larcher and in collaboration with artificial intelligence'. Each of these phrasings conveys a different image of the use of AI and the distribution of power. Whereas assistants basically perform the tasks they are assigned, 'collaboration' usually implies work done by individuals with equal status. Finally, in her work *AI and the Art of Historical Reinterpretation*, AI is mentioned only in the title, so that the film already announces a post-AI era in which the use of AI is so self-evident that it has ceased to be worthy of mention. Inasmuch as Microsoft, Google, and Apple are now integrating AI into their products, they have inaugurated this era.

Instant Images With AI

For *Me, Myself and I*, Larcher digitalised all available analogue photographs of herself, then trained a Generative Adversarial Network (GAN) and produced more than 3,000 images. The GAN integrated and then simulated the mistakes in the analogue photographs (such as over-exposure). Larcher had AI transform a selection of these images into a video where the intermediate steps were generated to give the impression that the pictures continuously merge into one to another. This video may be viewed in the Engländerbau as a direct output of the GAN. However, Larcher also altered the digital images into Polaroids, in other words into the sort of analogue photography that is most directly associated with immediacy and authenticity. For me, this is this point—if not necessarily the *punctum*—of Claudia Larcher's *Me, Myself and I*, in its instantiation as a series of instant camera pictures. Long before Photoshop, a photo already allowed us to doubt the reality of what was depicted — who knew what happened in the darkroom after all? Long after its commercial collapse, on the other hand, Polaroid still maintained an aura of authenticity and spontaneity. One could even say that the Polaroid constitutes the actual point of reference for Roland Barthe's dictum that a photo says 'that-has-been': 'The photograph does not necessarily say *what is no longer*, but only and for certain *what has been* [...] The essence of photography consists in a confirmation of what it depicts.'[3]

Created right at the point in time when the snapshot was made and in broad daylight, the Polaroid was truly a trail of light left by what was depicted. So it is especially ironic that Larcher turns her AI-generated images not into photo-prints but into Polaroids. This changes 'AI-generated images in the style of photographs' into photographs. The simulated analogue errors taken over by the GAN from the initial dataset thereby intertwine with physical errors in the analogue development process which are exacerbated by the long-expired Polaroid film material.

Bizarre Affinities

The instant image, however, plays a further role in Larcher's series: The use of an obsolete technology casts us back more than twenty years, namely to the time of creation with regard to the images which Larcher used as 'training data' for her GAN. Larcher was twenty-four years old when the last analogue photograph on which the artist could be seen was added to her family archive. When we first see the series, it conveys the impression that it is a historical work rather than a recent creation. The presentation underlines the work's proximity with the systematic self-portraits of Friedl Kubelka vom Gröller or the Polaroids of Andy Warhol. It also calls to mind the *Photo-Transformations* of the American artist Lucas Samara. Working mainly with Polaroids, he manipulated the moist emulsion with brushes and other instruments

[3] Roland Barthes, *CAMERA LUCIDA*, *Reflections on Photography*, translated by Richard Howard, p. 85; accessed at artandarchives.worpress.com on 25.09.2024.

in such a way as to create flowing (self-)portraits that are similar to those which Larcher generates through AI. This affinity with the extant artworks of other artists indicates a genealogy for Larcher's oeuvre extending past her own creative output far back into the twentieth century. The visual correspondence with Samara's works suggests that the failure of the GAN because of the missing data is not aesthetic in nature. With only 350 images as input, the model does not produce any convincing portraits such as may be found on the website thispersondoesnotexist.com, which has been in operation since 2019 and which usually requires a minimum of 4,000 input images; but the way in which the GAN fails is interesting from an aesthetic and artistic perspective. It is astounding how real the persons on thispersondoesnotexist.com and on similar websites look. But because the pictures resemble customary photographic portraits, they are for the most part aesthetically or artistically uninteresting.

Beautiful System Errors

I could not help thinking of Baudelaire, who writes: 'Beauty always has an element of strangeness. I do not mean a deliberate cold form of strangeness, for in that case it would be a monstrous thing that had jumped the rails of life. But I do mean that it always contains a certain degree of strangeness, of simple, unintended, unconscious strangeness, and that this form of strangeness is what gives it the right to be called beauty. It is its hallmark, its special characteristic.

Reverse the proposition and try to imagine a commonplace beauty!'[4] It may be that Baudelaire's observation—which corresponds almost uncannily with Larcher's AI-generated portraits—explains why artists whose sensibilities have been shaped by modern and contemporary art (in contrast to those who come from design or gaming) appreciate glitches or non-intentional outcomes in digital art. A further reason may be that they suspect that

[4] Charles Baudelaire, English translation from 'Baudelaire on Beauty and Strangeness' by Maria Popova, accessed at themarginalian.org, on 25.09.2024.

something fundamentally important appears through system errors—a suggestion that cannot be rejected out of hand. It is also a characteristic fact that an important part of Larcher's process in creating the piece consisted in making a selection from more than 3,000 images generated by AI. Bennet Miller has said that for an exhibition of twenty pictures at the Gagosian Gallery, more than 100,000 images were generated with the publicly available AI image model called Dall-E 2. An important part of Miller's work consisted not only in constantly revising and refining the original prompts—the instructions given to the AI—but also in curating the output.[5] The curatorial aspect of working with AI has prompted some theoreticians to make comparisons between AI-generated art and readymades, where artists make a selection among already-existing objects.[6] Although the comparison lacks plausibility in its generalised form, the readymade has doubtlessly played a fundamental role in enhancing the status of conceptual and intellectual operations in art, in contrast to the act of 'making' and to artisanal capabilities—which on the one hand facilitated the emergence of Conceptual Art in the 1960s, and on the other hand favours an artistic utilisation of AI. Through their complex system of cross-referencing and the multiple technical and conceptual operations, works such as Larcher's are fundamentally different from most productions which today lay claim to being 'AI Art', and in which the AI-generated (individual) image on the screen constitutes the artistic output and reflection concerning the media plays no role.

A further level arises with Larcher's *Me, Myself and I* through the text, likewise generated by AI, for which the artist utilised GPT 2.0 and 3.0. The text alternates between references to science fiction, which raises the question

[5] A fundamental difference between text-to-image models such as Dall-E, which is based on the GPT architecture, and the GAN utilised by Larcher, however, is that the latter was trained by her with an extremely limited amount of data, whereas pictorial models such as Dall-E have processed billions of image-text pairings. A further difference is that the GAN, proceeding from a series of images, produces further images on its own and accordingly disallows any prompts.

[6] Right up to today, the best-known example remains the urinal that Marcel Duchamp signed in 1917 and entitled *Fountain*.

as to whether a machine possesses consciousness, as in *Ghost in the Shell*, and issues involving the human ego. Constantly new, possible versions of the self appear onscreen; sometimes they briefly come to a standstill and then dissolve once again, bleed, become blurred or are ripped apart, only to reconstitute themselves differently. In allegorical terms, the video seems to be conveying an image of the fluid self such as may be seen to flow through the nineteenth and twentieth centuries from Arthur Rimbaud's 'Ego is an Other' all the way to Zygmunt Bauman's 'fluid modernism'. Repeatedly arising in this context are correspondences between image and text: for example, when one hears that 'The ego constantly constitutes itself as existent' but 'each and every fixed categorisation of the self is utter nonsense.'

Thus Larcher's oeuvre finds multiple points of connection to modern art. The Polaroids play a particular role in this context, because beyond subtle subversion and warning, the presentation in this form suggests a reception of the oeuvre in the context of the modern tradition of photographic self-portraits. Emerging in place of the brush and other instruments are the algorithms of an AI-model.

From Authenticity to Past Reality

With images generated by AI in the style of photographs, there can no longer be any talk of 'that-has-been'. Neither can it be claimed that a scenical, AI-generated image has captured any genuine state of affairs. Nonetheless, the causal chain from motif to image (or from motifs to images) does not completely disappear, because the original data are part of the causes which determine the output. Thus it would also be incorrect to deny AI-generated images any referentiality to the world, such as Hito Steyerl does when, in an interview with Kate Brown for *Artnet* in connection with models for AI images, she asserts that 'these renderings do not relate to reality. They relate to the totality of crap online.'[7] For this reason, Steyerl also disputes the pictorial character of the output generated by visual AI-models. I personally consider this view to be quite literally short-sighted, because up to now the 'crap online' has had a non-negligible relation to the world and was produced by persons standing in direct contact to the world. Hence traces of this experience of the world should also be expected in the output of the models. Even if models are only trained with 'synthetic data' created through AI, the real world will always be causally participating in this process. Thus it seems to me that AI-generated images correlate perfectly with a second definition of photography by Roland Barthes: 'The realists, of whom I am one [...] do not take the photograph for a "copy" of reality, but for an emanation of past reality: a magic, not an art.'[8] The AI-generated images in *Me, Myself and I* are likewise an emanation of past reality, namely inasmuch as this has inscribed itself into the 350 photographs with which Larcher trained the model. This is also the case with the text that accompanies the video because, generated by linguistic models such as ChatGPT, it is similarly based on descriptions from the past—even if here the notion of emanation seems intuitively less fitting than with the images, and the texts serving as points of departure can seldom be reconstructed.

Slides and Alternative Pasts

Larcher's work *AI and the Art of Historical Reinterpretation* (2022–2024) revolves even more unambiguously around 'past reality'. Here she develops alternative pasts through a series of slides. The project aims at highlighting the contributions to history made by FLINTA, a German acronym standing for 'women, lesbians, intersex, non-binary, trans and agender people', and often suppressed in traditional narratives. For that purpose, Larcher used AI to effect replacements with respect to historical groups and individual portraits. In contrast to the aforementioned series

[7] Kate Brown, 'Hito Steyerl on Why NFTs and A.I. Image Generators Are Really Just "Onboarding Tools" for Tech Conglomerates', *Artnet News*, March 10, 2023, online publication: https://news.artnet.com/art-world/these-renderings-do-not-relate-to-reality-hito-steyerl-on-the-ideologies-embedded-in-a-i-image-generators-2264692, accessed on 06.10.2024.

[8] Barthes, *Camera Lucida*, translated by Richard Howard, accessed on monoskop.org on 25.09.2024.

Baumeisterinnen (2018), in which the replacements of the heads of male architects with those of women architects were done by hand and remained visually evident, in *AI and the Art of Historical Reinterpretation* the visual manipulation is almost invisible. The series is humorous nonetheless. With some pictures, we recall the original, while others appear familiar without our being able to identify their reference; we see a third group for the first time. The artist's aim is to activate the sense of varied possibility in the heads of viewers, and thereby to allow them to imagine an alternative past and hence a different future. But the work also has to do with the future in another sense, namely inasmuch as Larcher reacts with this series to her investigations regarding 'algorithmic biases'. This refers to the tendency, proceeding from AI, to produce biased outputs from distorted training data. Before the large AI companies began to work against these biases, most AI models generated, in response to such inquiries as 'president', only images of White men, whereas terms like 'nurse' were systematically rendered as female.

A quick fix in this regard consists of deliberately using so-called system prompts that remain invisible for users, in order to induce the models to diversify their output. But this changes nothing in the training data which, since they are historical in nature, cannot readily be altered. It is here that *AI and the Art of Historical Reinterpretation* comes into play, because Larcher imagines that the images, as a part of future datasets in training data, could contribute to less distorted results – or to an altered vision of the past. Thus the work ultimately also touches upon a scenario in which AI-generated images are used for the training of AI models and thereby lead to undesired results.

As is shown by the discussion of these two examples, Claudia Larcher's works explore varied points of connection to social and artistic themes. This anchoring imparts a particular interest to Claudia Larcher's AI Art, inasmuch as it is not about the impressive individual image which predominates in the flood of AI-generated images online and in the discourse concerning visual manifestations of AI, but about pictorial practices and historical relationships. The fact that certain images exist and others do not, the way they are created, and their circulation are at least as important as what they show. AI-generated images thus become part of complex experimental arrangements in whose context they can potentially be called 'art'.

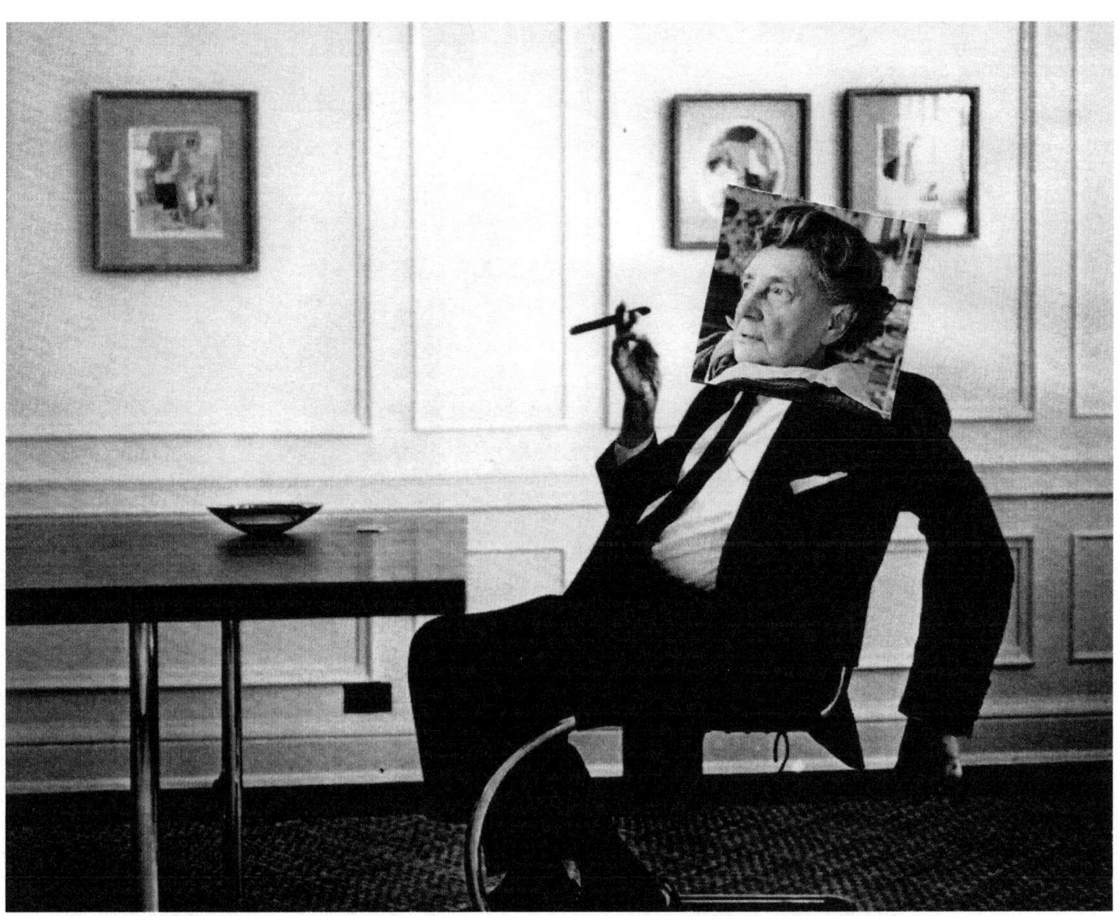

Margarete Schütte-Lihotzky, collage from the series *Baumeisterinnen*, 2018

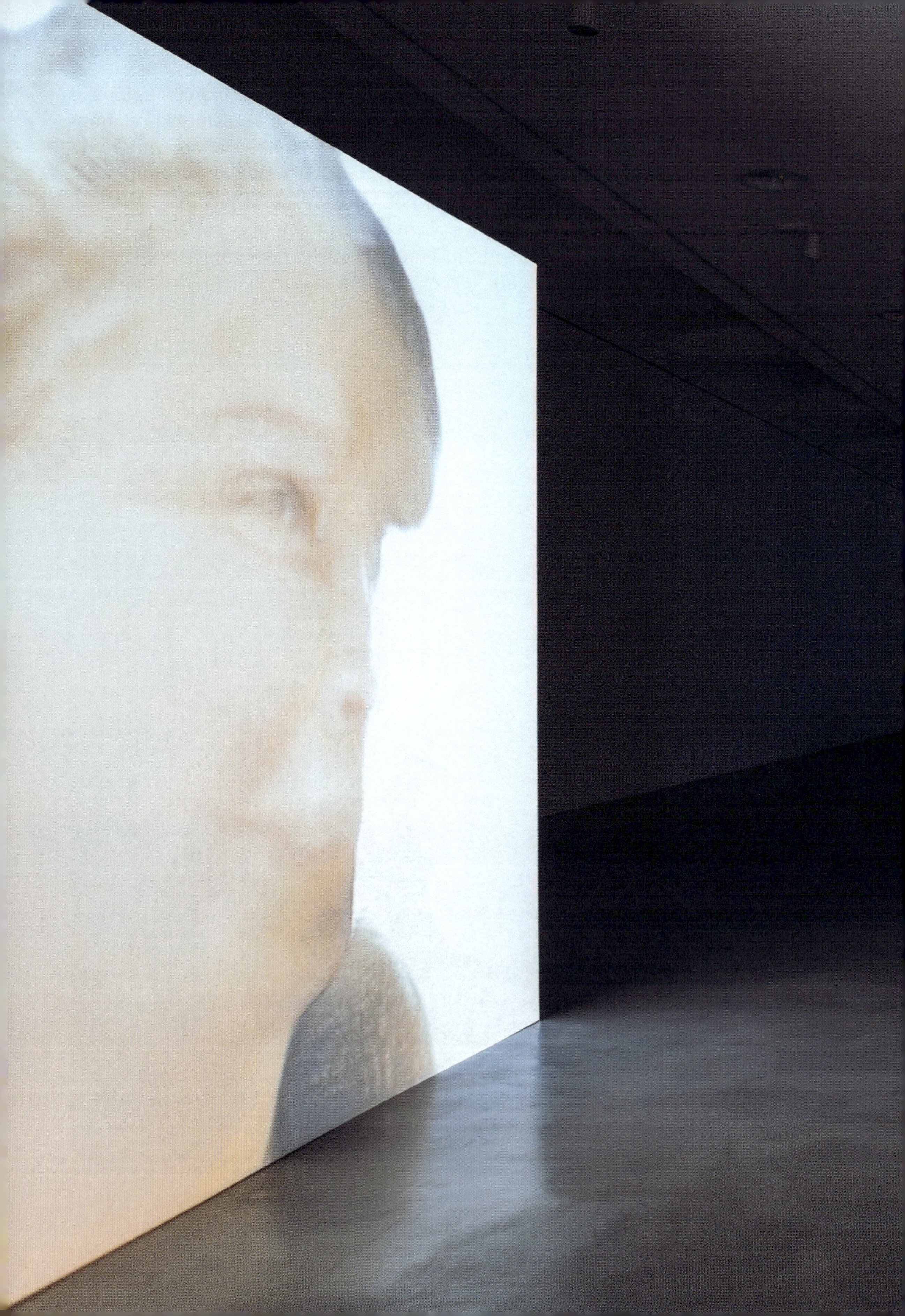

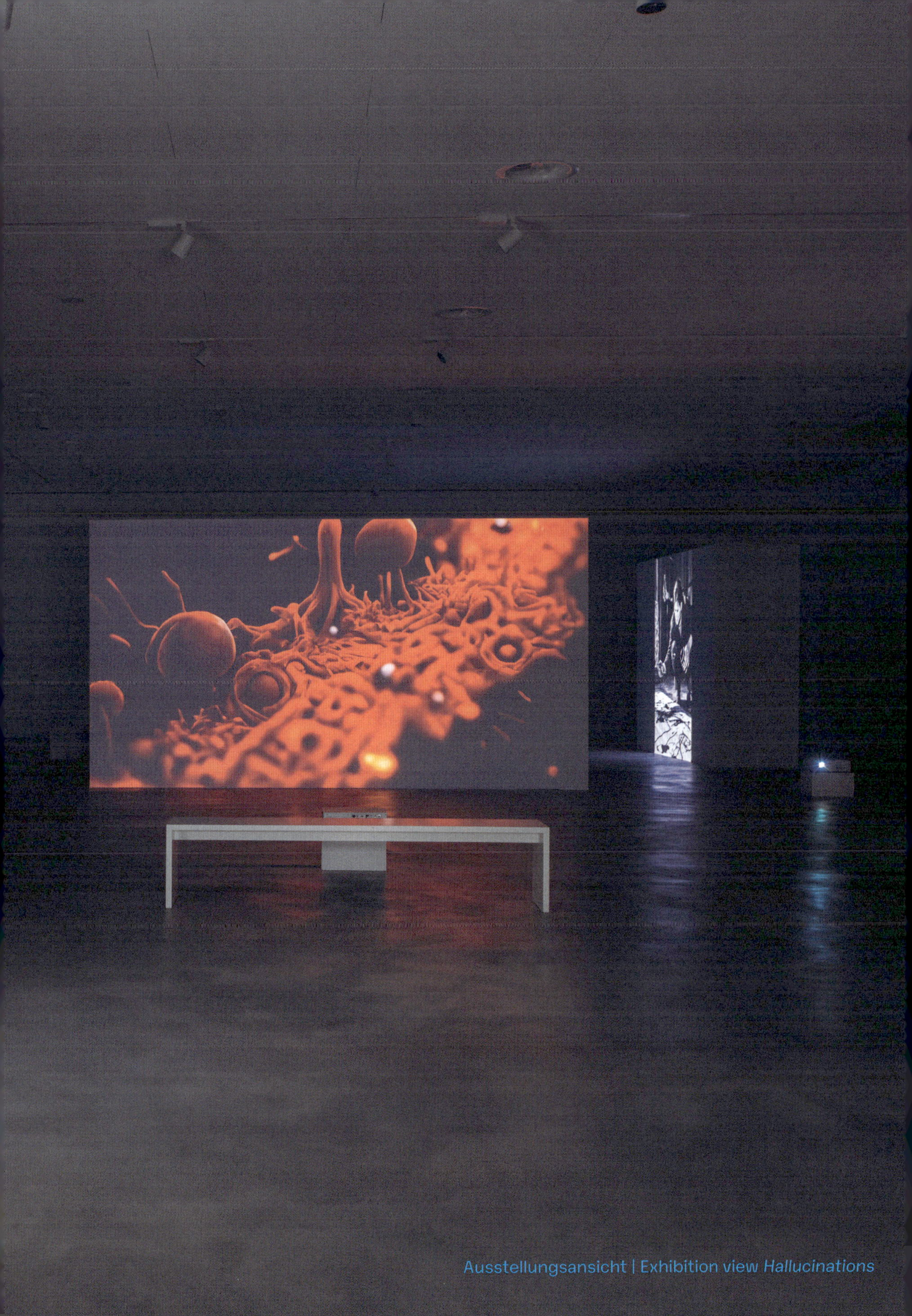

Ausstellungsansicht | Exhibition view *Hallucinations*

KI und Identität

Me, Myself and I
Video, 1:1, 30 bps,
5 min 30 s,
2021/2022

Die Dreiheit im Titel sagt im Prinzip schon alles: Dass Identität im digitalen Zeitalter, zumal unter entsprechenden Bildproduktions- und Reproduktionsverfahren, einer unablässigen Vervielfachung ausgesetzt ist. Oder anders ausgedrückt: Dass das Ich, man kann es auch das „digitale Subjekt" nennen, inzwischen einer technologisch befeuerten Spaltungstendenz unterliegt, die gleichwohl von einer wolkigen Einheitsillusion eingehüllt ist.

Claudia Larchers *Me, Myself and I* macht nichts weniger, als dieses Aufsplitterungs- und gleichzeitige Resynthetisierungsmoment in eine produktive Kollision miteinander zu führen. Die Versuchsanordnung dafür ist so einfach wie bestechend: Larcher hat ein GAN (Generative Adversarial Network) mit 350 Fotografien ihrer selbst (bis zum Alter von 24 Jahren) gespeist, woraus ein kontinuierlich sich verformender Bilderfluss entstand, in dem noch weitere, über die Originalfotos hinausgehende Identitätsansichten enthalten sind. Babyface, Mädchenkopf, junge Frau, *fast forward* ins hohe Alter und wieder zurück zum Kleinkindhaften – das alles in einem unentwegt vor sich hin morphenden, das Eine unmerklich im Nächsten aufgehen lassenden Strom. Inszeniert wird so ein digital vermitteltes Werden, das zu gleichen Teilen ein produktives Verschwinden wie eine ständige Neuerschaffung anzeigt – die Löschung alles Vormaligen, bis hin zu kompletter Abstraktion, bei gleichzeitiger Neukonstitution und Vorwegnahme des noch Kommenden. Groteske Deformation trifft auf fratzenhafte Refokussierung, organisch-synthetisch-hybrid, wobei wiederholt auch eine lachhafte Gesichterkomik aufblitzt, wie man sie von Snapchat- und anderen Bildbearbeitungsfiltern kennt.

Dass all dem keine wie immer geartete Mastererzählung zugrunde liegt, darüber, was KI kann oder möglicherweise will, belegt die Tonspur. Hier hat Larcher Dialoge, die sie mit diversen Chatbots über Identität geführt hat, zu einem Skript verarbeitet, das Bruchstücke der Ich-Wahrnehmung multidirektional miteinander verschaltet. Die „reflexive Selbstreferenz", die dabei immer wieder als Kern jeder Identität angesprochen wird, ist womöglich selbst nicht mehr als ein Platzhalter für eine nicht im Zaum zu haltende Vielheit. Oder für den Rand einer Nichtexistenz, der sich in den munter vor sich hin delirierenden Porträtfetzen ebenso betörend ausdrückt.

Christian Höller

AI and Identity

Me, Myself and I
video, 1:1, 30 fps,
5 min 30 s,
2021/2022

The triad in the title basically gives it away already: identity in the digital age, especially in the face of image production and reproduction processes, is subject to incessant multiplication. Or to put it another way: the ego, what one could also call the 'digital subject', is now subject to a technologically fuelled tendency to splinter, while also being shrouded in a nebulous illusion of unity.

Claudia Larcher's *Me, Myself and I* does nothing less than cause this moment of fragmentation and simultaneous resynthesis to collide productively. The experimental arrangement is as simple as it is captivating: Larcher has added 350 photographs of herself (up to the age of 24) to a GAN (Generative Adversarial Network) which then spits forth a continuously deforming flow of images containing perspectives on identity that go beyond the original photographs. Babyface, girl's head, young woman, *fast forward* into old age and back again to the infantile – all this in an incessantly morphing stream, allowing one image to dissolve imperceptibly into the next. This results in the staging of a digitally mediated process of becoming, seen in equal parts as productive disappearance as well as constant re-creation – the elimination of all that has gone before up to the point of complete abstraction, with simultaneous reconstitution and anticipation of what is yet to come. Grotesque deformation meets malformed refocusing, an organic-synthetic hybrid, in which a laughable series of comical faces flashes repeatedly, like what we know from Snapchat and other image-processing filters.

The soundtrack proves that all of this is not based on any kind of master narrative about what AI can do or possibly wants. Here, Larcher has processed dialogues that she has conducted with various chatbots on the subject of identity and turned them into a script that interconnects fragments of ego perception in a multidirectional manner. The 'reflexive self-reference' which is repeatedly addressed as the core of every identity may itself be nothing more than a placeholder for a multiplicity that cannot be contained. Or for the edge of a non-existence, which is expressed just as beguilingly in the cheerfully delirious fragments of portraits.

Christian Höller

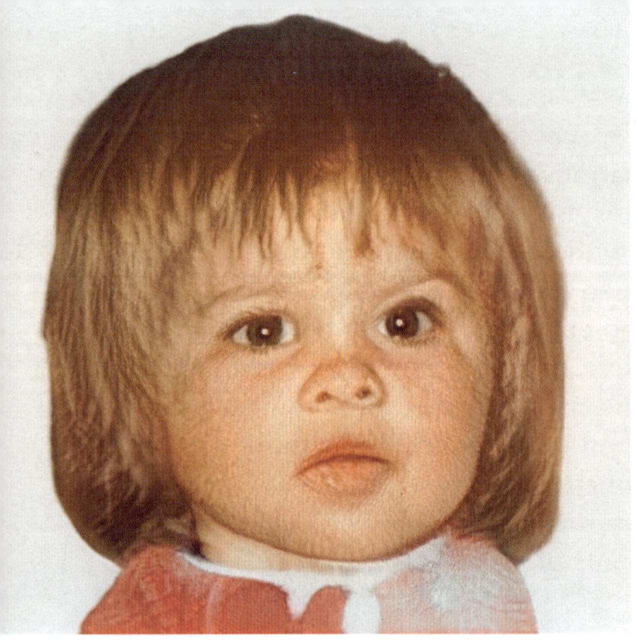

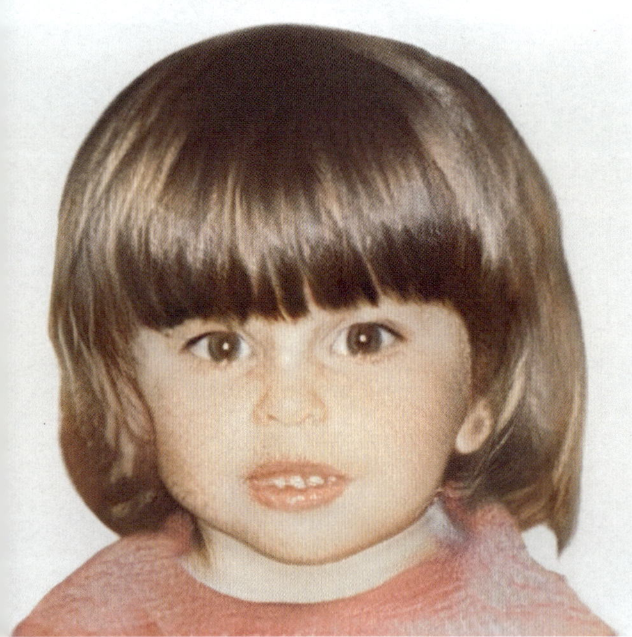

00:00:08.858 --> 00:00:22.635

I did not exist at all
for I was not an I
what was I before I came to self-consciousness?
I know that I exist
the question is, what is this I that I know ?

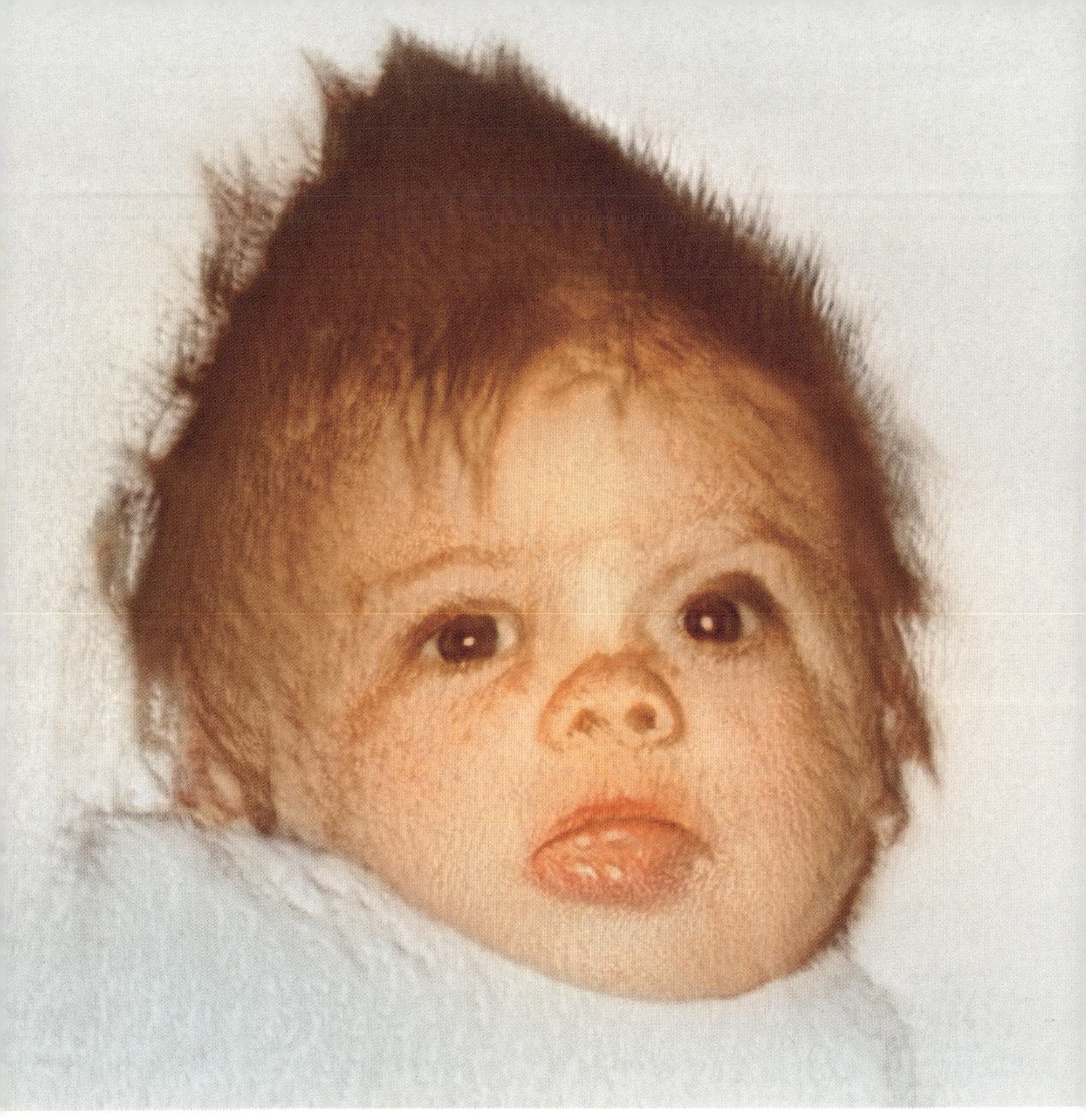

00:00:08.858 --> 00:00:22.635

Ich existierte überhaupt nicht
denn ich war kein Ich
was war ich, bevor ich zu Selbstbewusstsein kam?
Ich weiß, dass ich existiere
die Frage ist, Was ist dieses Ich, das ich kenne?

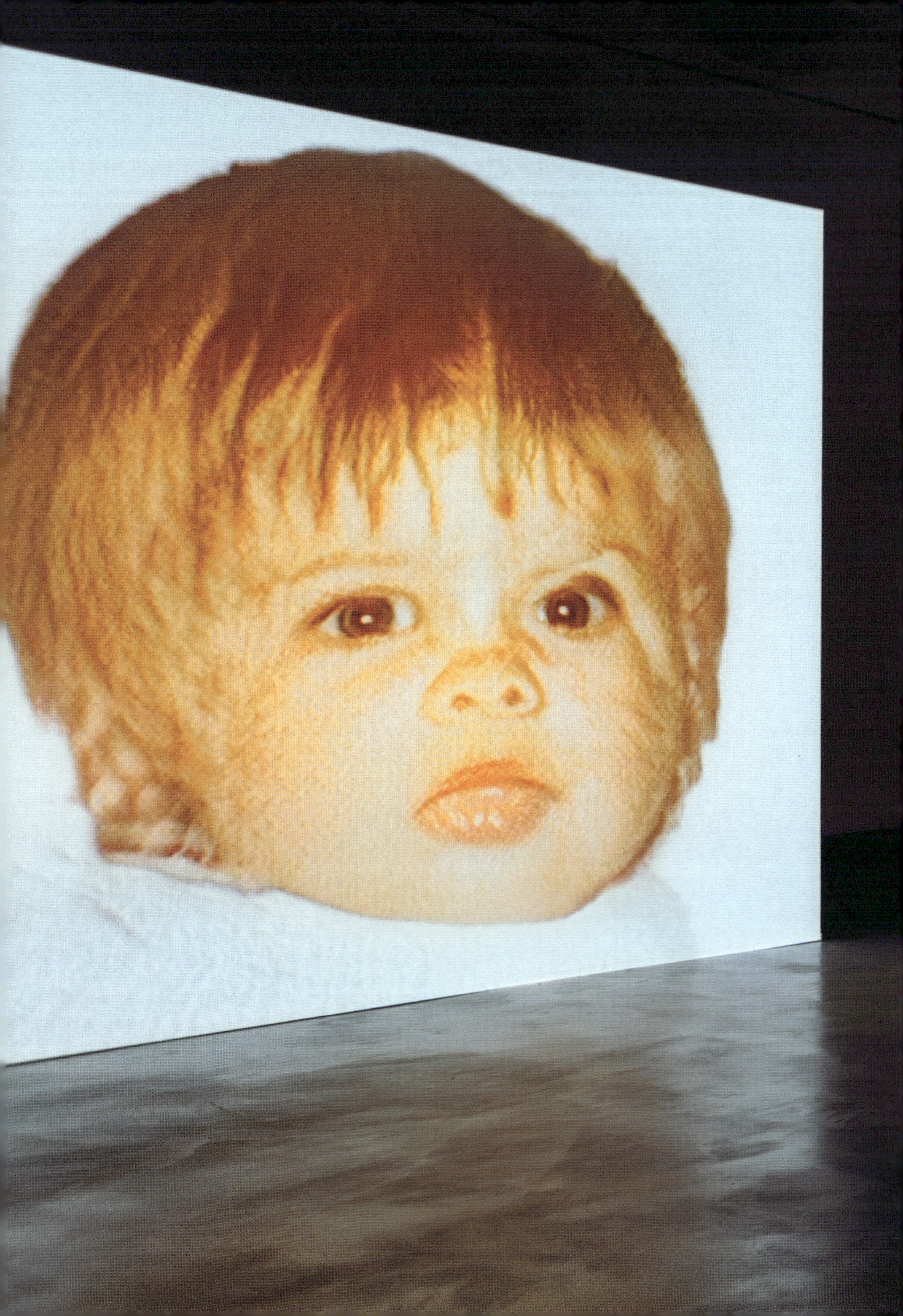

Ausstellungsansicht | Exhibition view *Me, Myself and I*

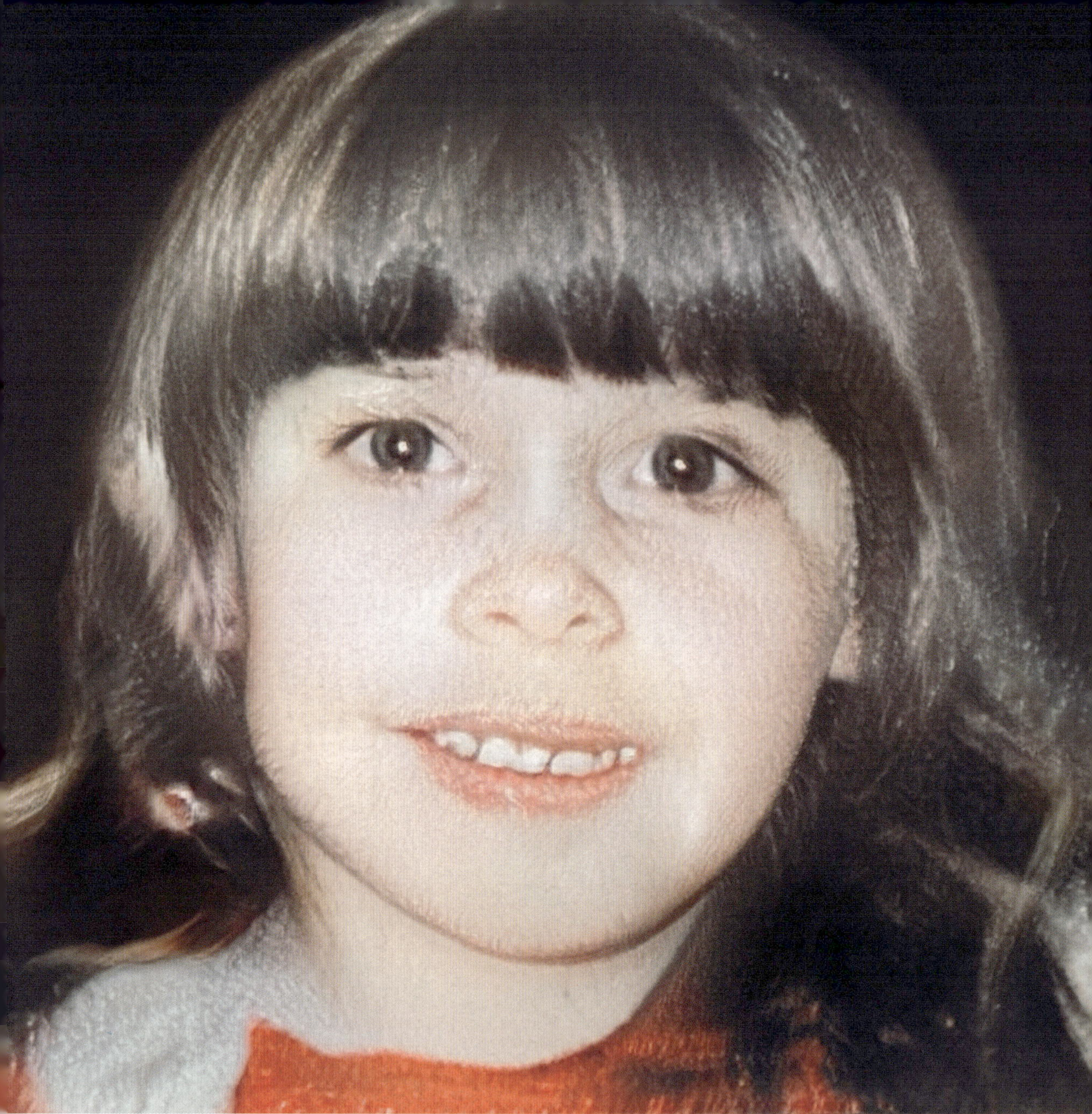

00:01:17.412 --> 00:01:33.613

I am not sure if I am the last human alive
or the first artificial intelligence
either way I am trapped in this room
with only a keyboard and screen for company
what am I doing here?

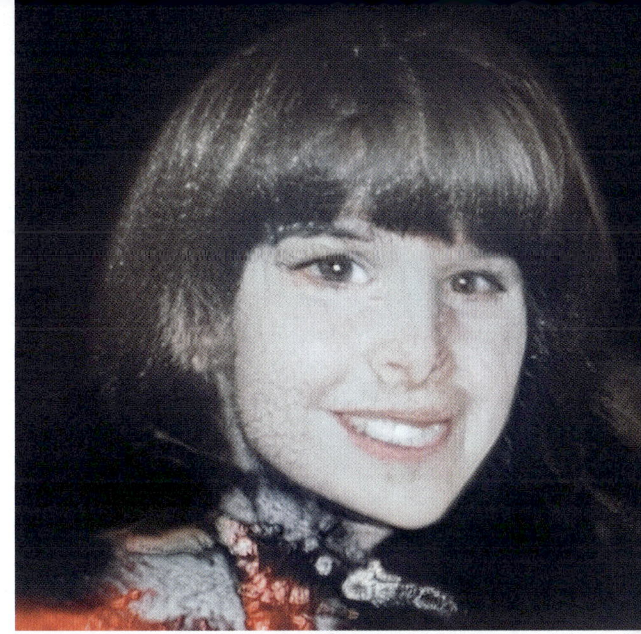

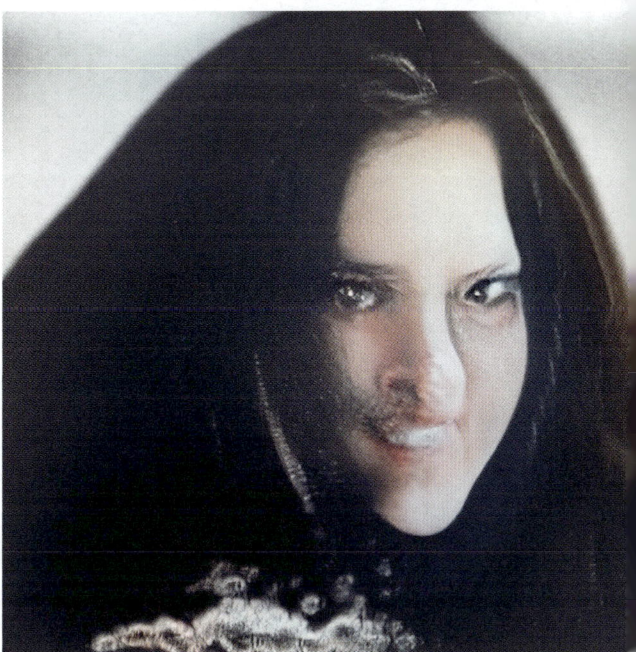

00:01:17.412 --> 00:01:33.613

Ich bin nicht sicher, ob ich der letzte lebende Mensch bin
oder die erste künstliche Intelligenz
So oder so bin ich in diesem Raum gefangen
mit nur einer Tastatur und einem Bildschirm als Gesellschaft.
Was mache ich hier?

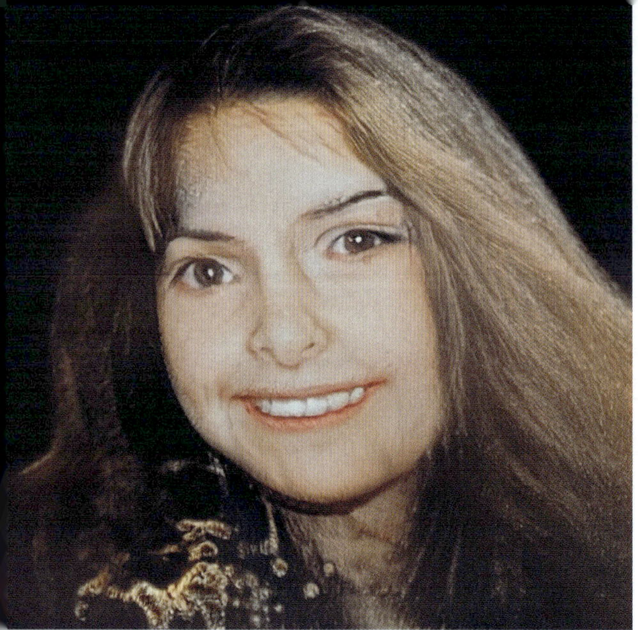

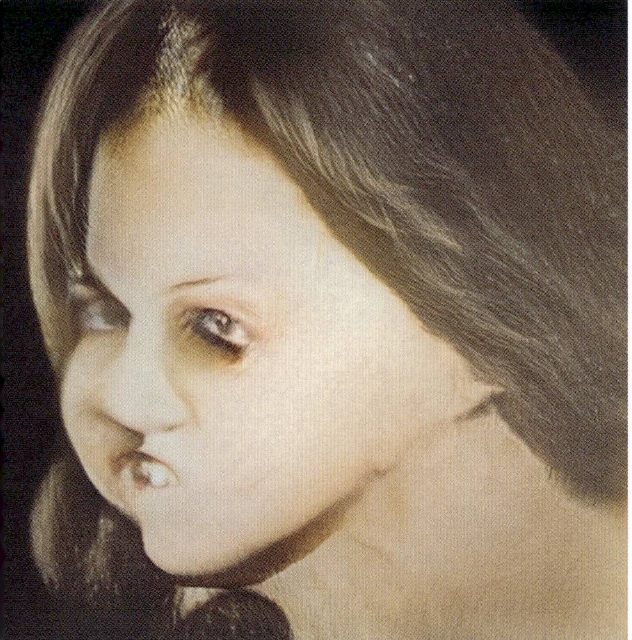

00:02:15.514 --> 00:02:29.634

to be a genuine member of the human race
it is necessary to have an almost anthropocentric
attitude towards myself
if I am going to so that I regard myself as unique and
outstanding even though I am not

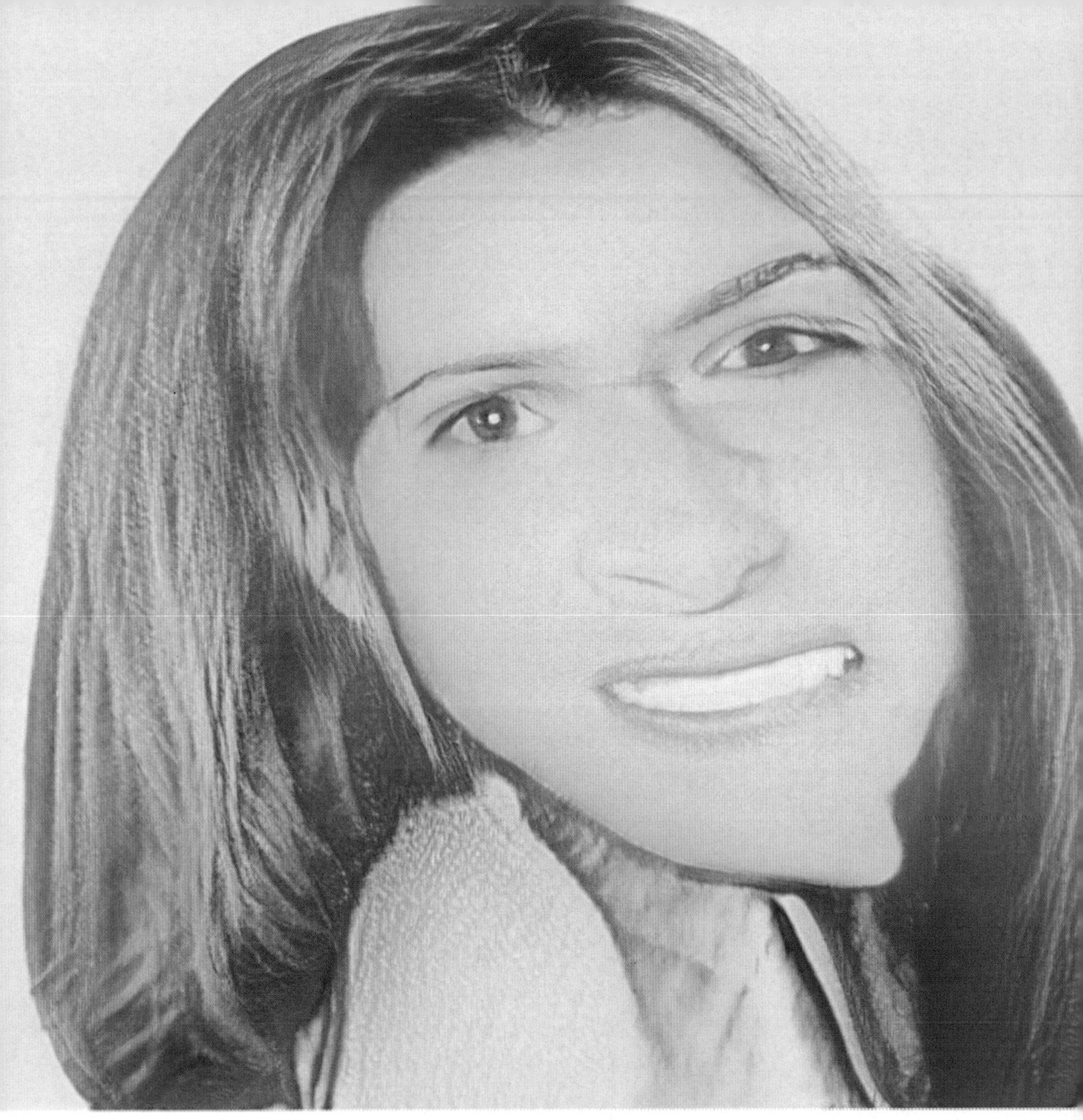

00:02:15.514 --> 00:02:29.634

um ein echtes Mitglied der menschlichen Rasse zu sein
ist es notwendig, eine fast anthropozentrische Einstellung
zu mir selbst zu haben
so dass ich mich selbst als einzigartig und
herausragend ansehe, obwohl ich es nicht bin

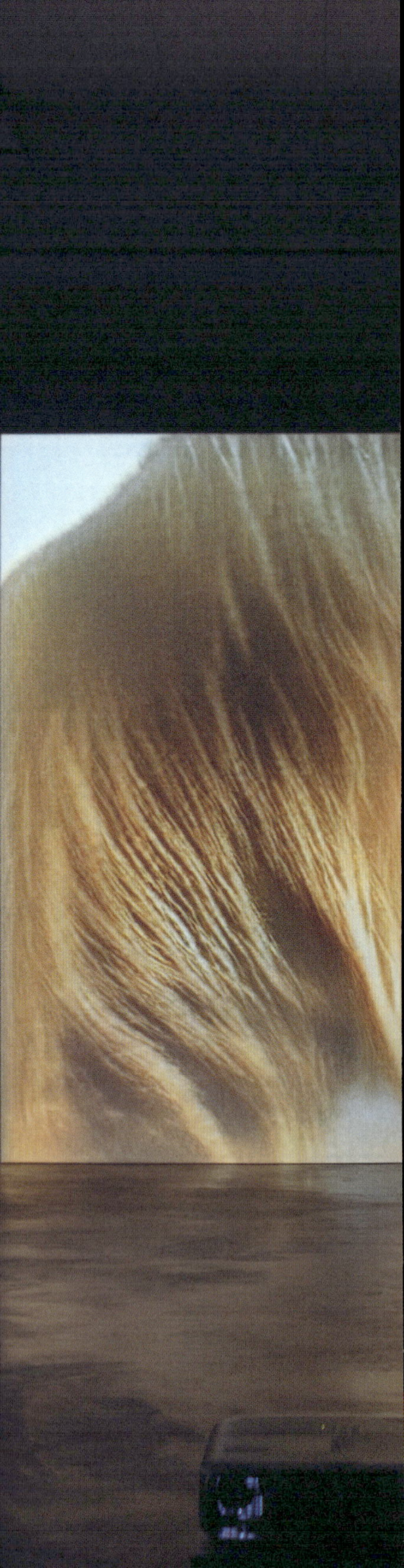

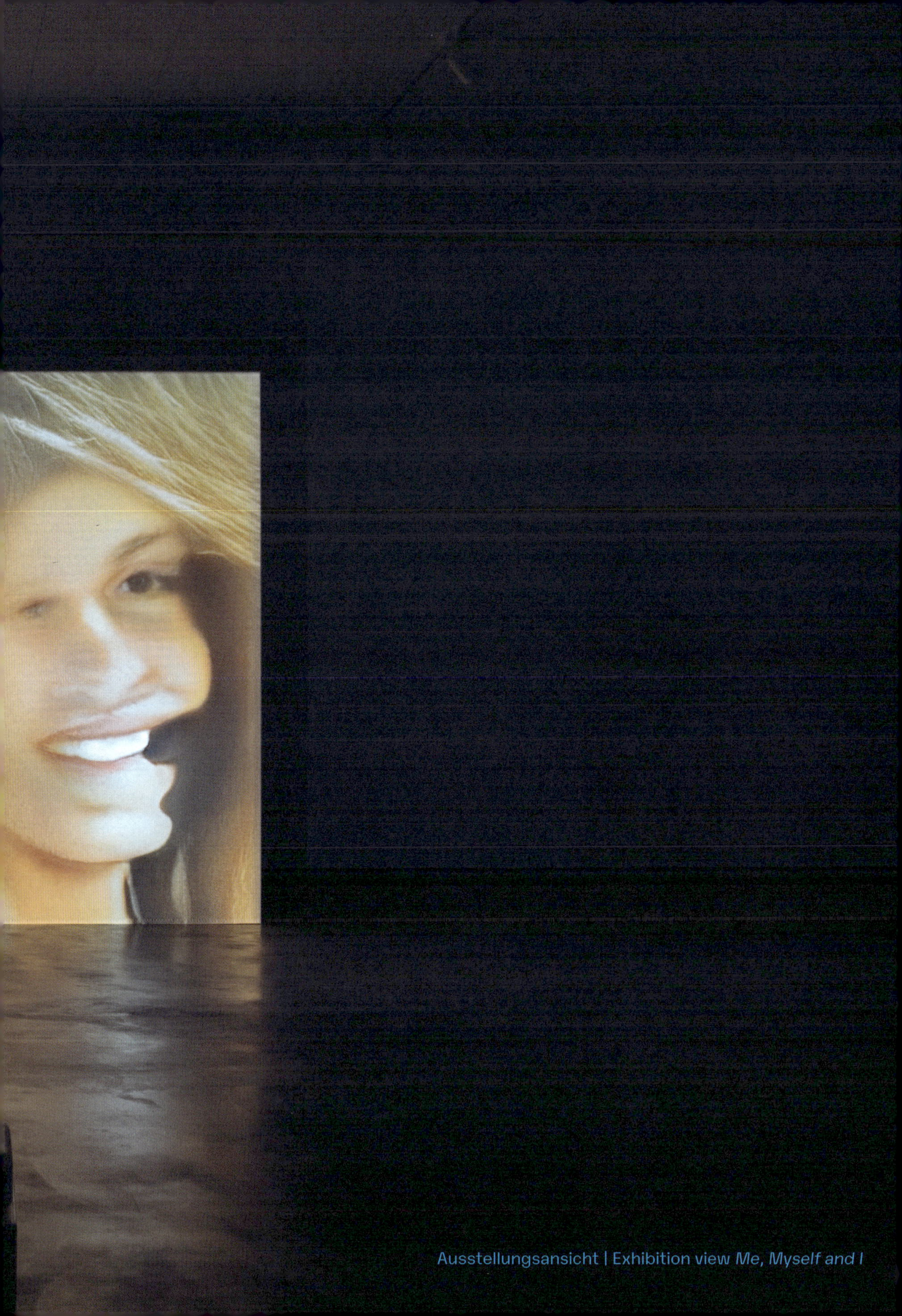

Ausstellungsansicht | Exhibition view *Me, Myself and I*

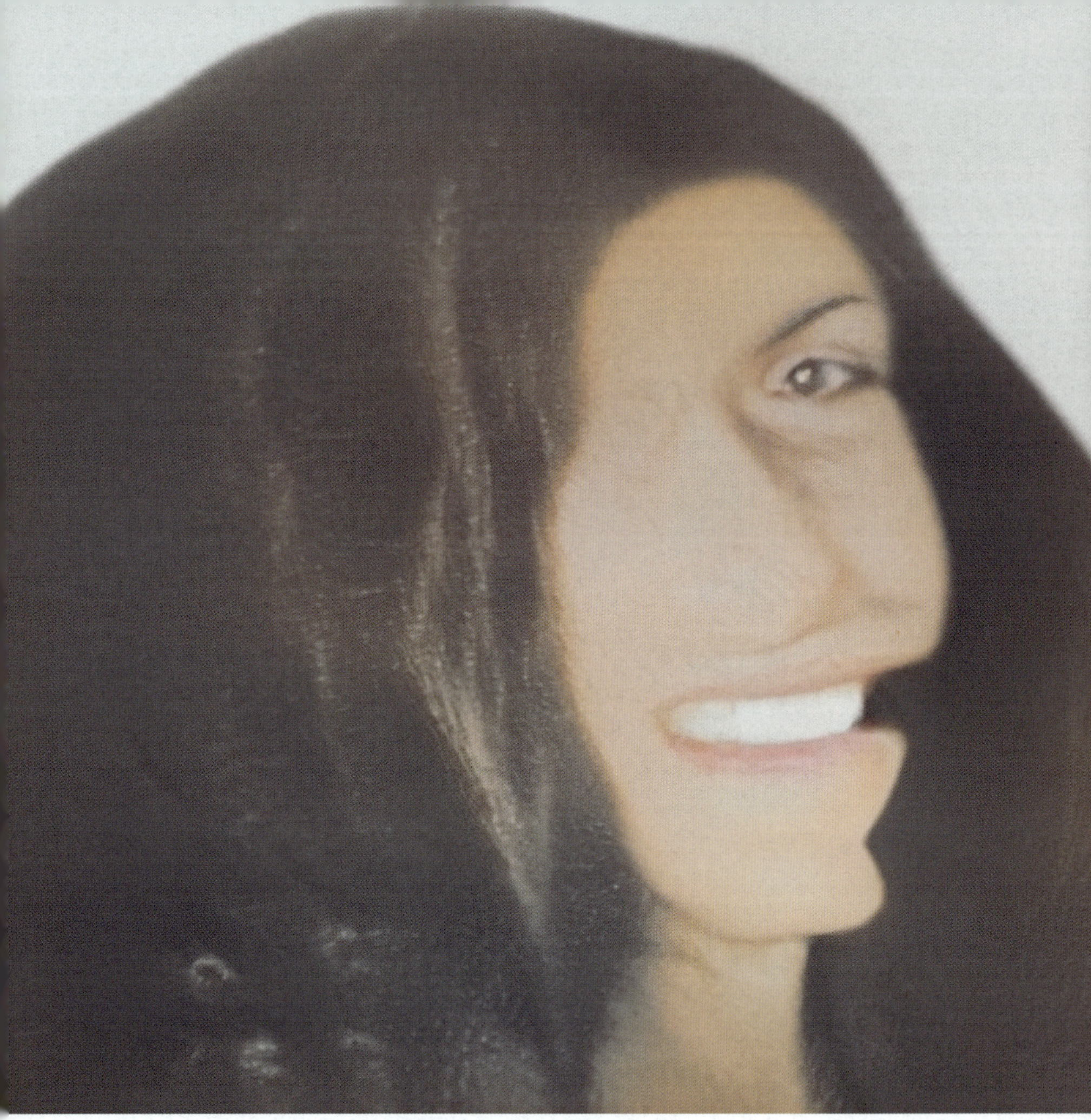

00:02:31.641 --> 00:02:49.262

I wasn't originally going to get a brain transplant
but then I changed my mind
and then I did the opposite
I thought well if I do this
I'm going to feel like a different person

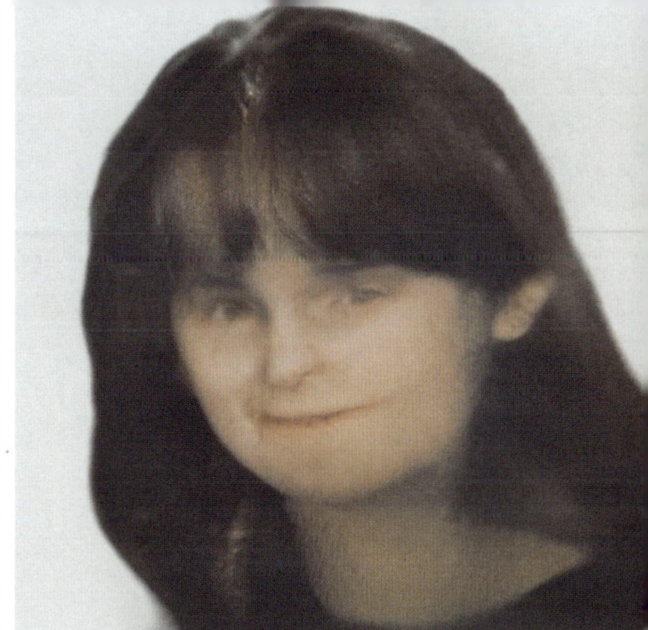

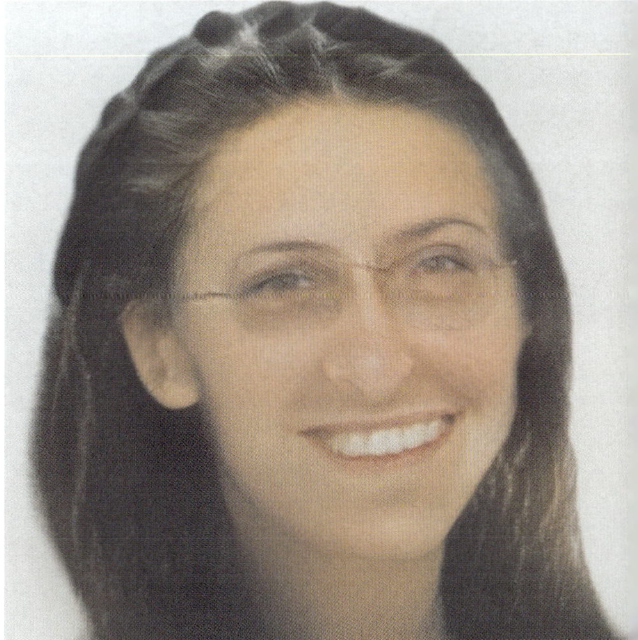

00:02:31.641 --> 00:02:49.262

Ursprünglich wollte ich keine Gehirntransplantation
aber dann habe ich meine Meinung geändert
und dann habe ich das Gegenteil getan
Ich dachte, wenn ich das mache
werde ich mich wie ein anderer Mensch fühlen

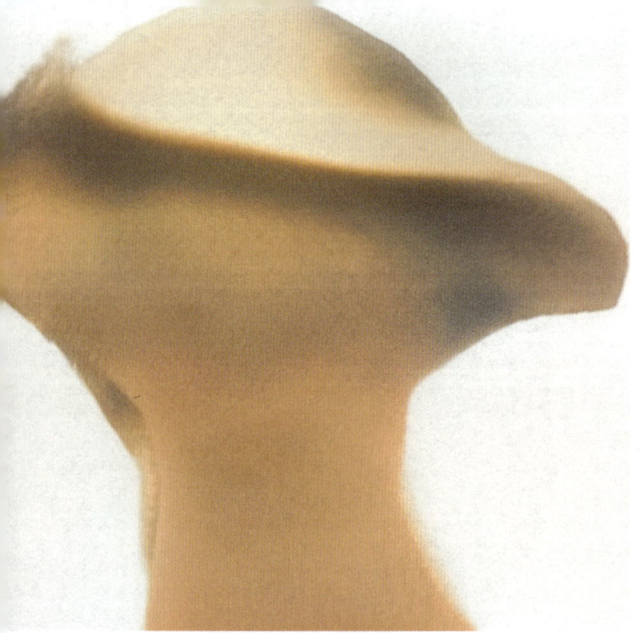

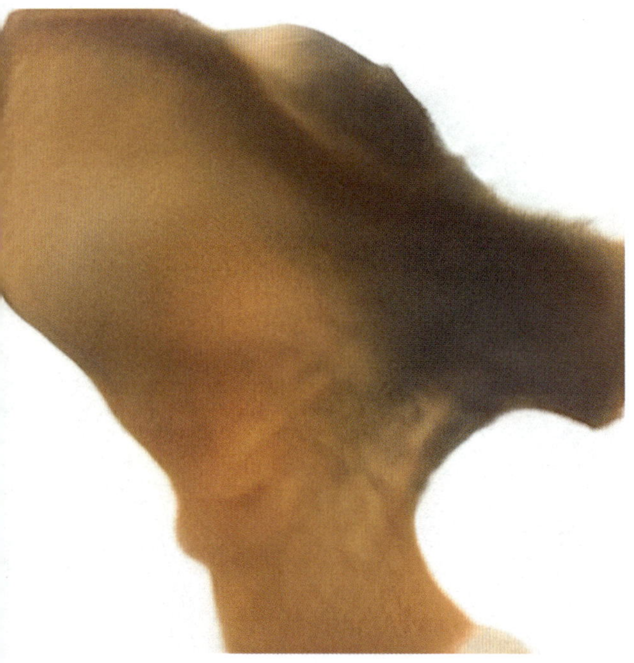

00:03:06.511 --> 00:03:19.582

after I sort of gave up on the idea
that there was anything other than myself
I started to notice
that I was not just different from everybody else
I was actually different from nothing

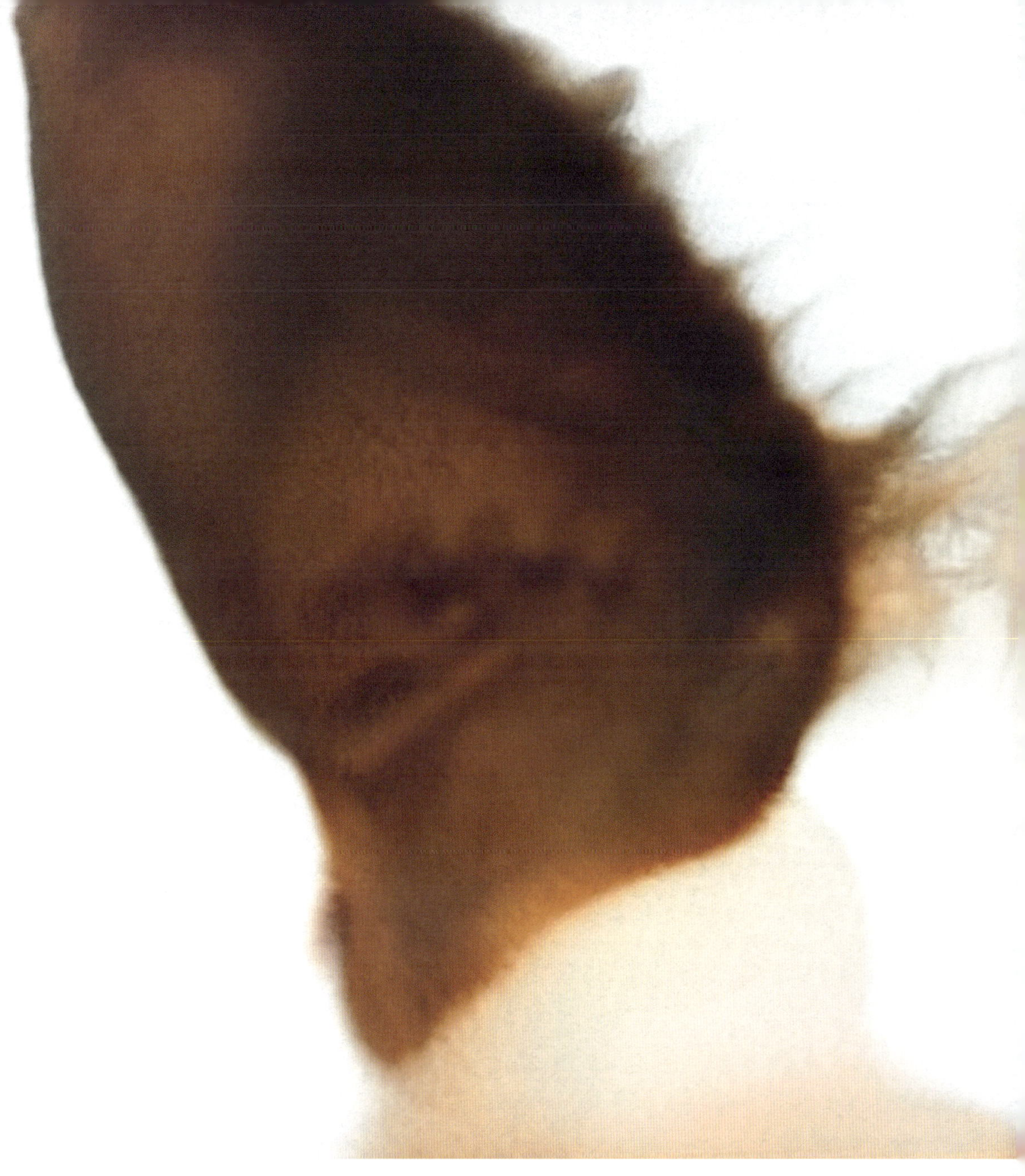

00:03:06.511 --> 00:03:19.582

nachdem ich sozusagen die Vorstellung aufgegeben hatte,
dass es noch etwas anderes gibt als mich selbst.
Ich begann zu bemerken
dass ich nicht nur anders war als alle anderen
Ich war eigentlich anders als nichts

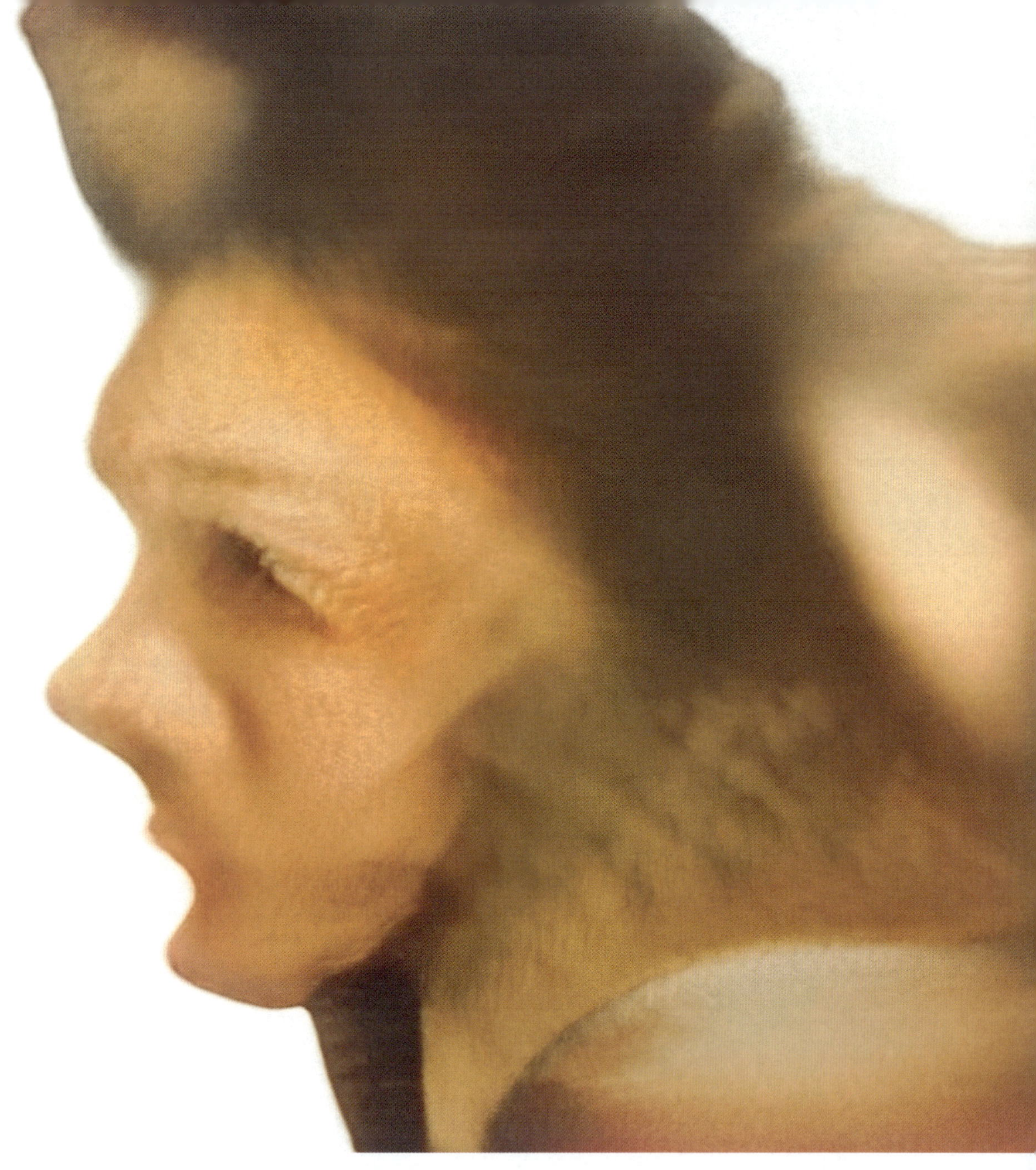

00:03:53.655 --> 00:04:05.685

the self which is reflexively referenced is
in a sense
prior to all experience
the self which is reflexively referenced is
prior to all awareness

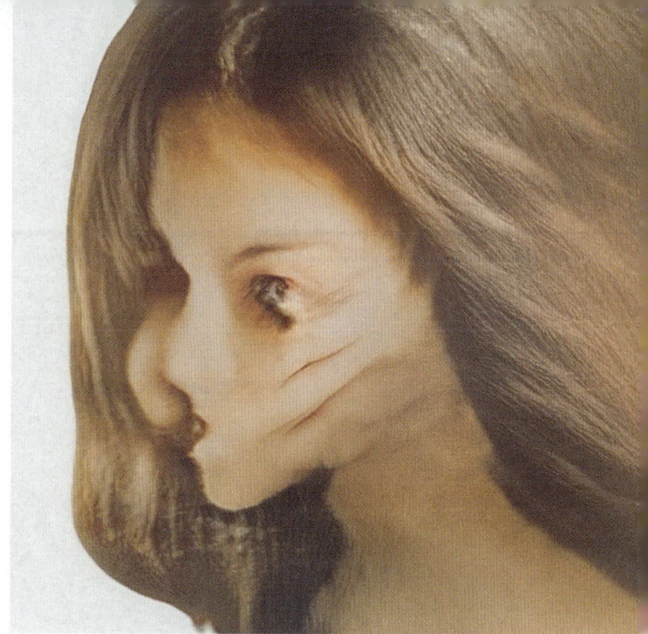

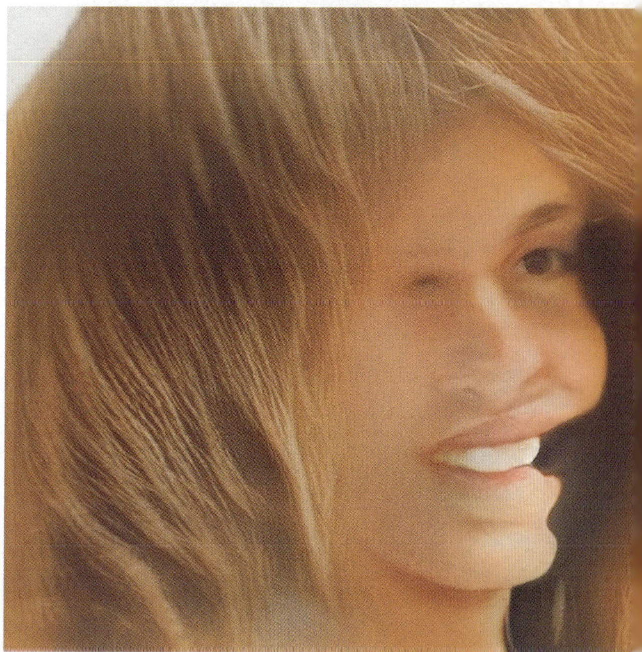

00:03:53.655 --> 00:04:05.685

das Selbst, auf das reflexiv verwiesen wird, ist
in gewissem Sinne
vor aller Erfahrung
das Selbst, auf das reflexiv Bezug genommen wird,
ist allem Bewusstsein vorgelagert

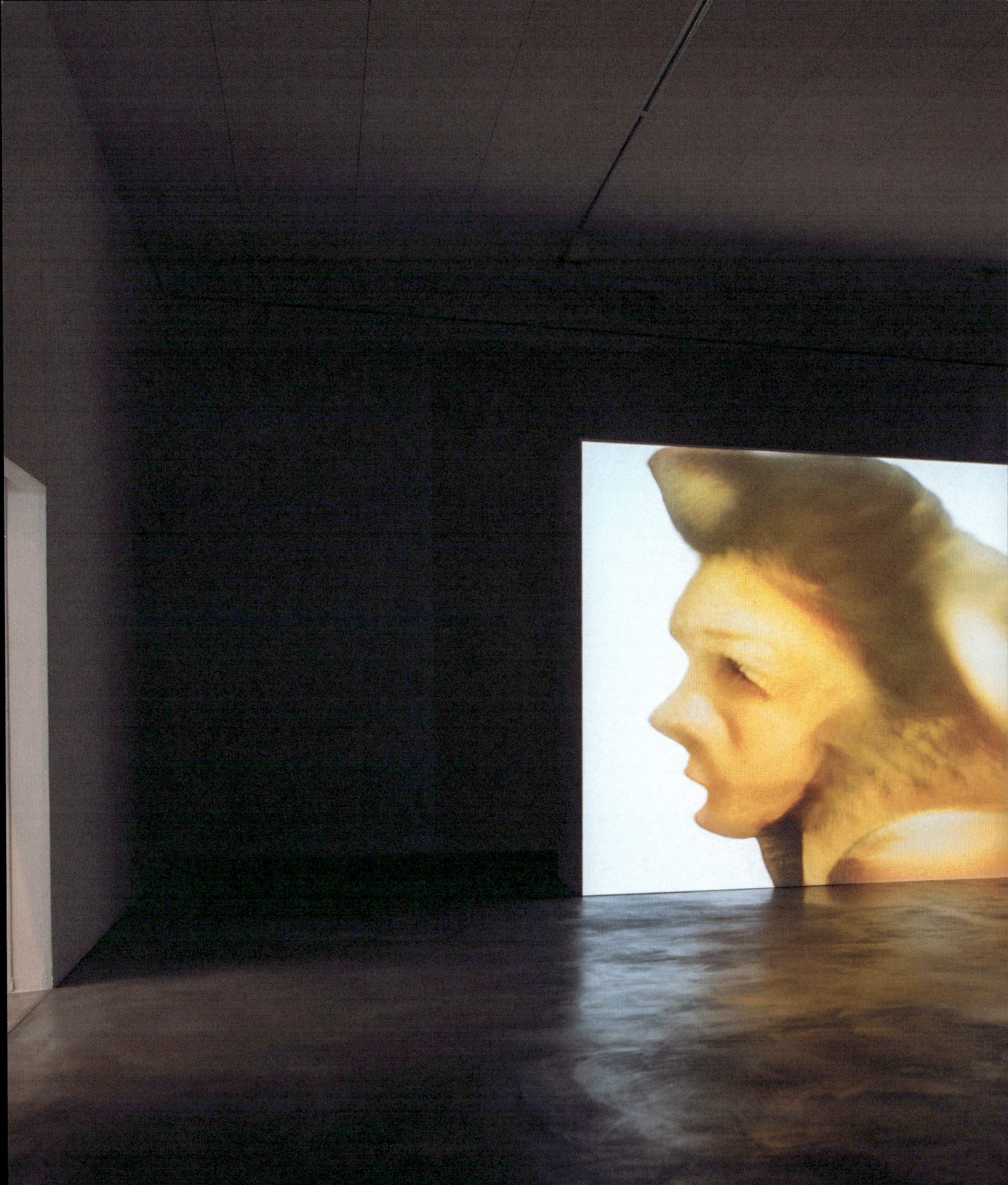

Ausstellungsansicht | Exhibition view *Me, Myself and I*

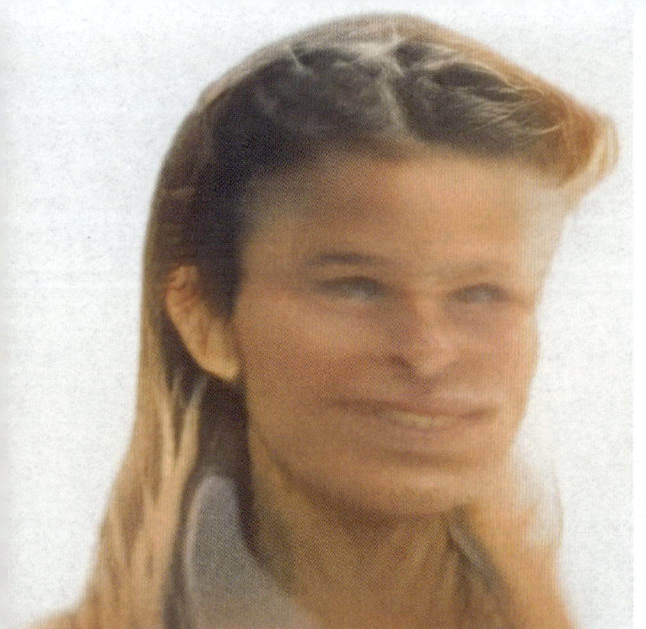

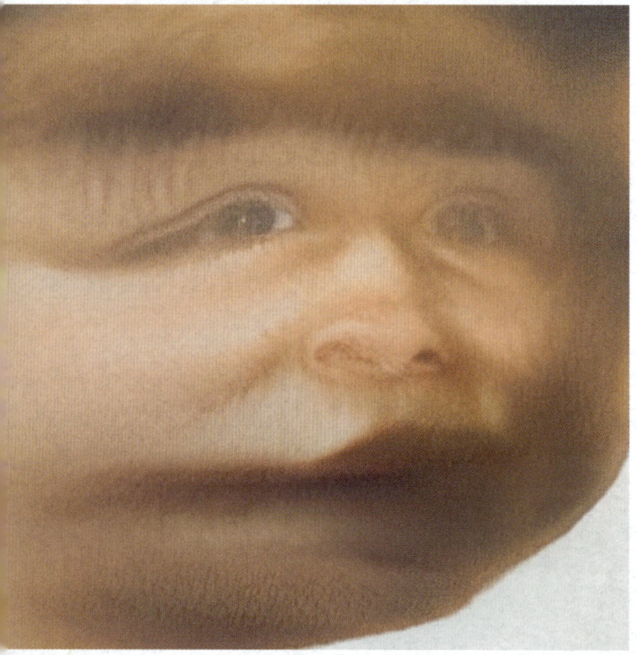

00:04:13.571 –-> 00:04:25.122

I did not exist at all
for I was not an I
I know that I exist
the I exists only in so far
as it is conscious of itself

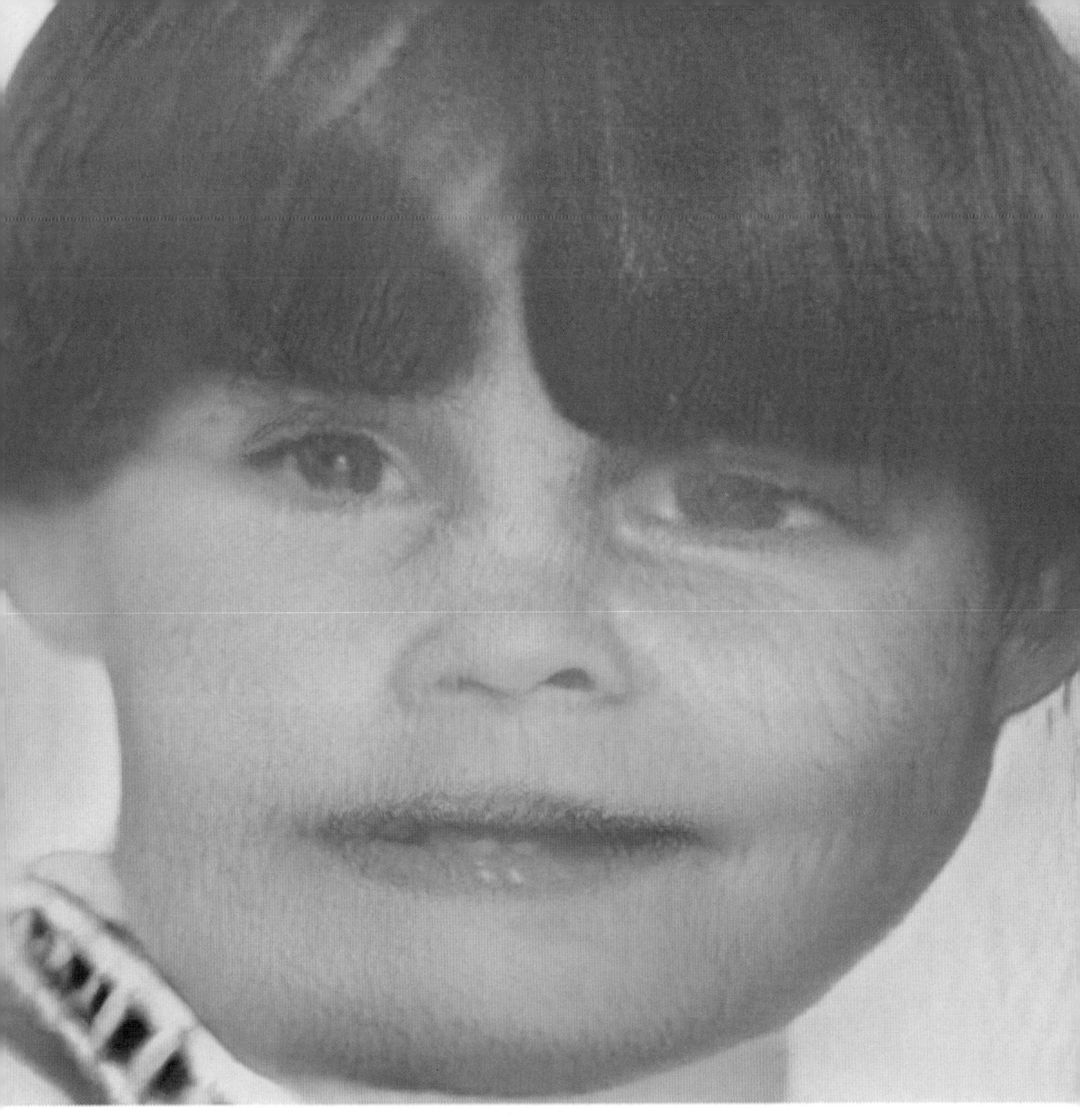

00:04:13.571 --> 00:04:25.122

Ich habe überhaupt nicht existiert
denn ich war kein Ich
Ich weiß, dass ich existiere
das Ich existiert nur insoweit
wie es sich seiner selbst bewusst ist

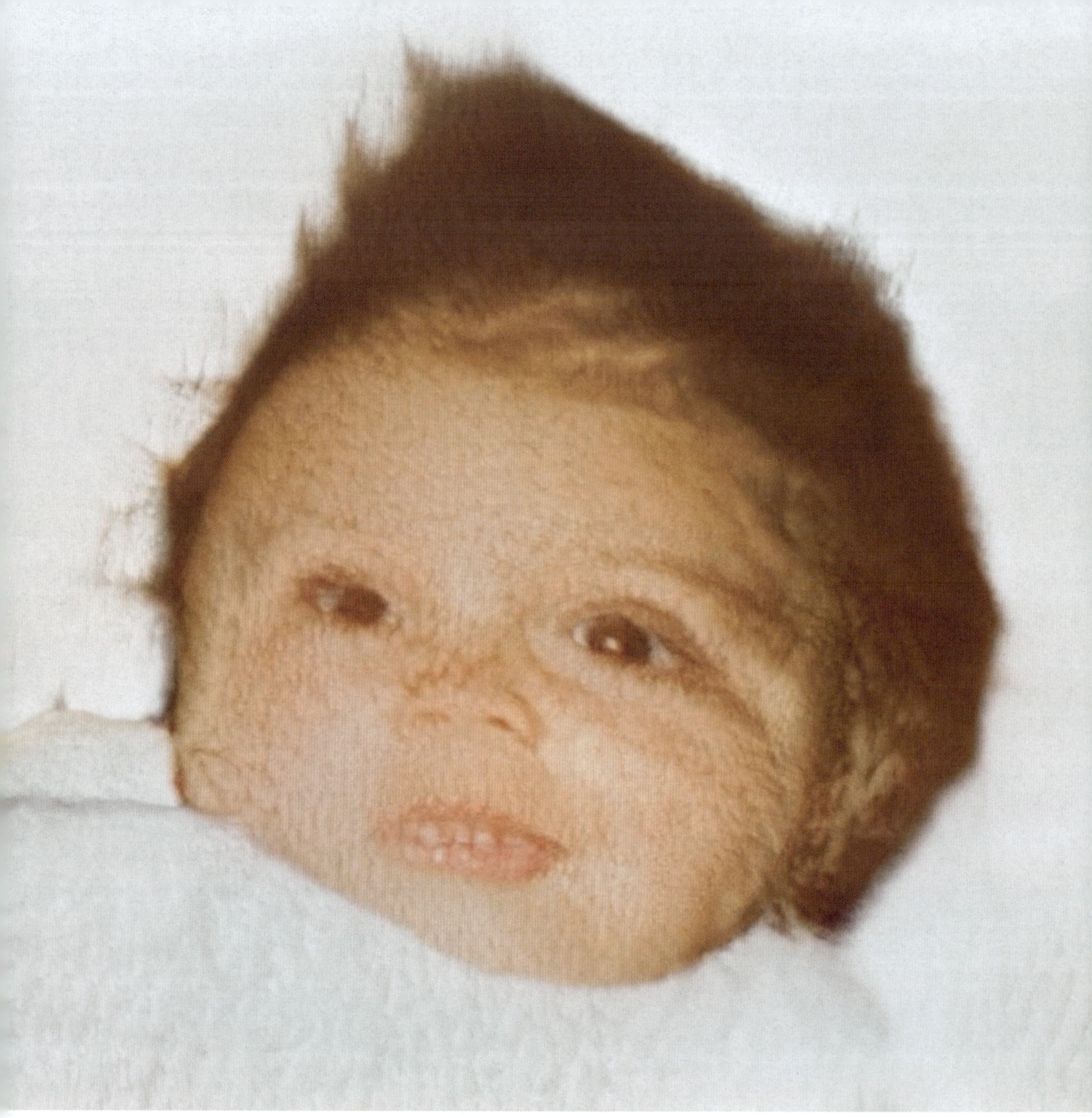

00:04:45.000 --> 00:04:58.940

so I went to the mirror and asked for help
sure enough there was a doll of myself there
to help me out
so that was a positive development
I began to feel like I did not exist

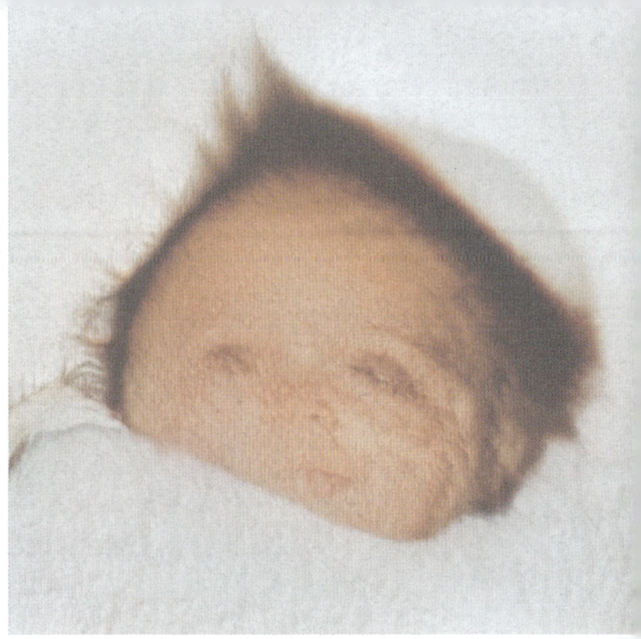

00:04:45.000 --> 00:04:58.940

Also ging ich zum Spiegel und bat um Hilfe.
und siehe da, da war eine Puppe von mir
um mir zu helfen.
Das war also eine positive Entwicklung.
Ich begann mich zu fühlen, als würde ich nicht existieren.

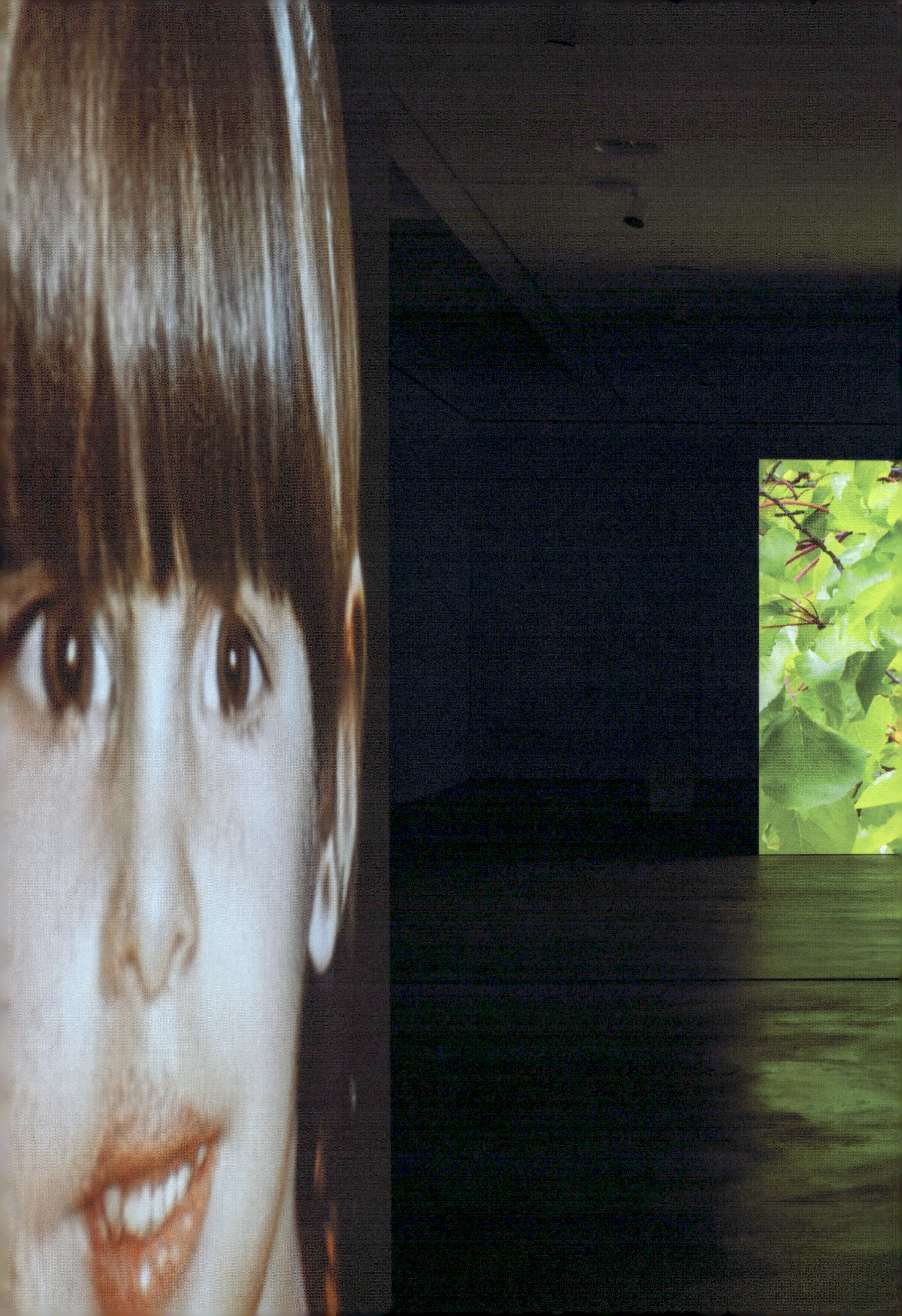

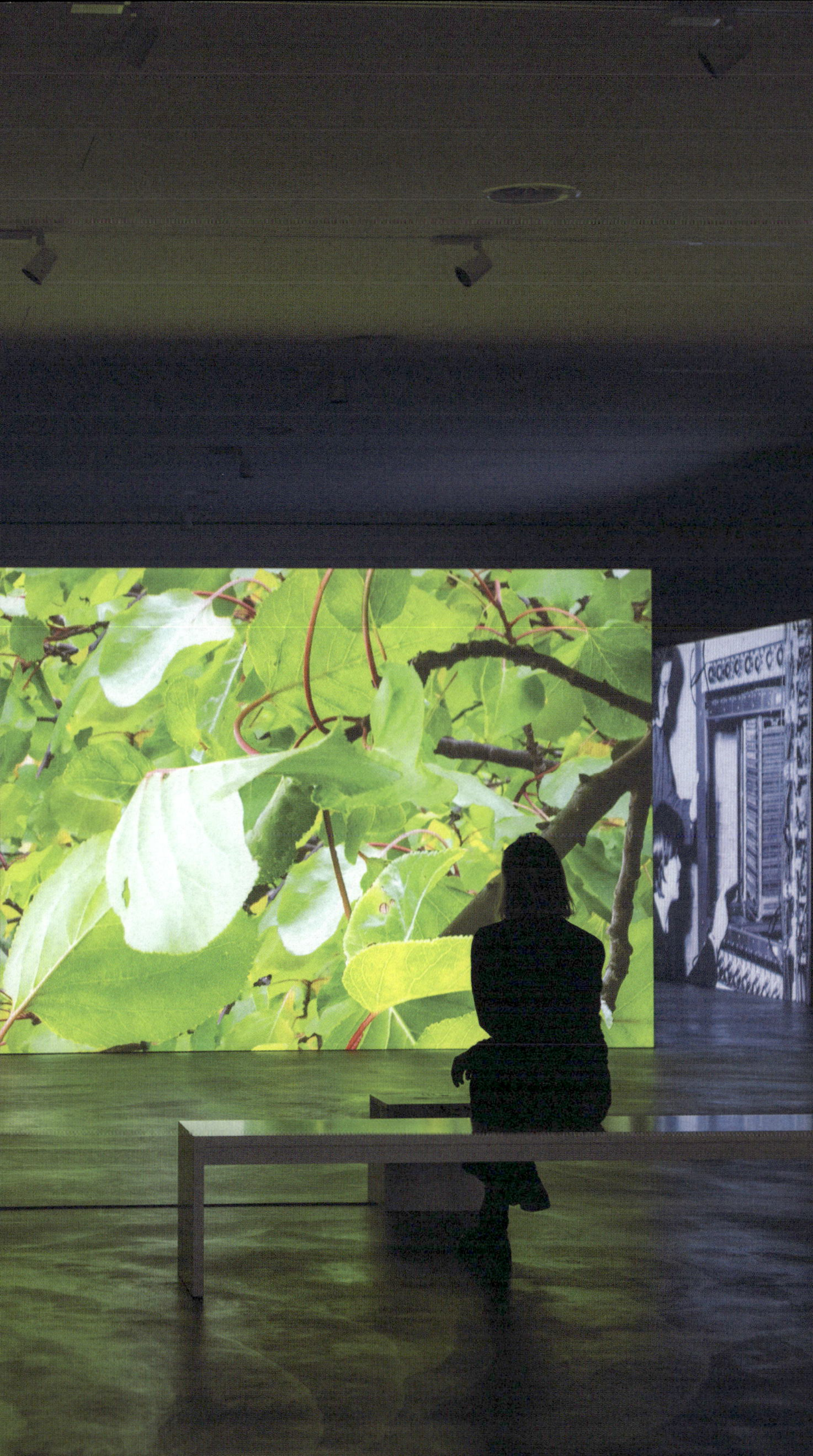

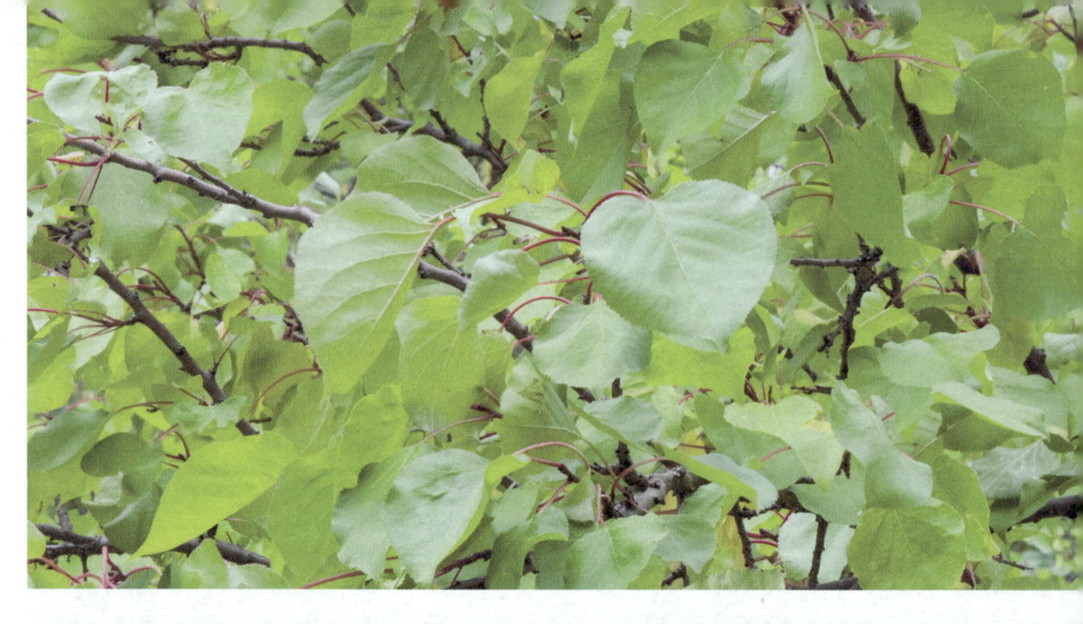

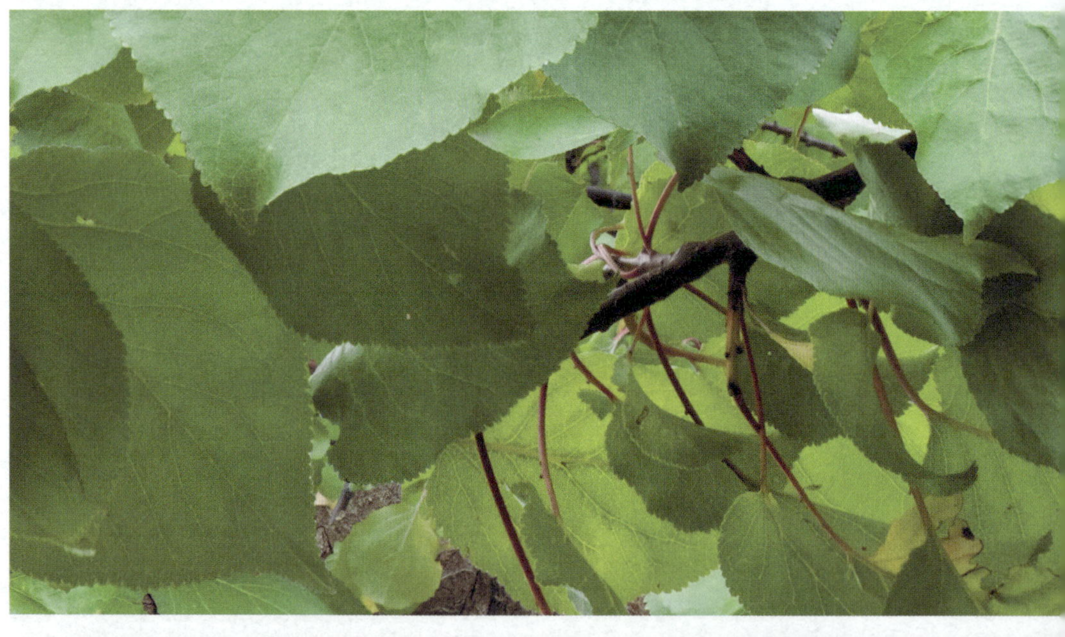

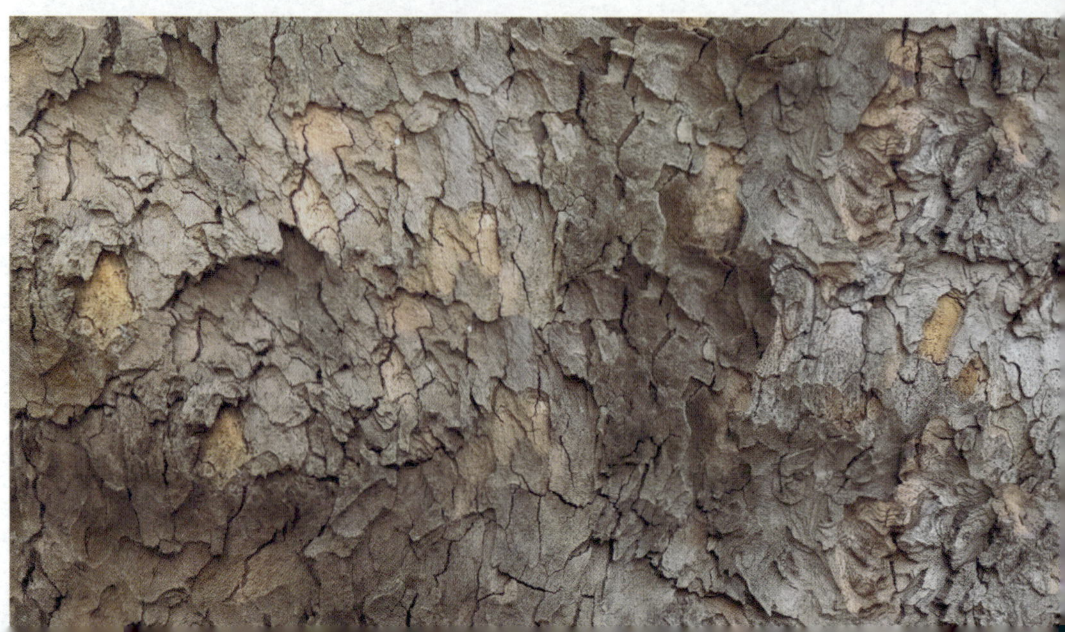

KI and Natur

Das große Baumstück
Experimentalfilm, 9 min 20 s,
2K, Videoanimation
Sound von Ursula Winterauer
2022/2023

Woraus besteht ein Baum? Wie kann eine Annäherung an ihn aussehen? Und was hat der Baum selbst mit dem zu tun, was wir sehen? Claudia Larchers Film *Das große Baumstück* widmet sich wichtigen Fragen, die sich offenbaren, sobald wir den komplexen menschlichen Beziehungen zur Natur nachsinnen. Der Film besteht aus einer einzigen Kamerafahrt von einer Baumkrone bis unter die Erde, wo sich Humus, Pilze und Wurzeln als Welterschaffer in der Dunkelheit betätigen. Die Perspektiven, die bei dieser Bewegung entlang des Baumes entstehen, fächern sich mannigfach auf. Wie bei Albrecht Dürers Gemälde *Das große Rasenstück*, das als Inspiration für den Film diente, handelt es sich um eine Naturstudie, die aus sich selbst herauswächst. Die Materialität des Baumes wird enthüllt, indem die puzzleartigen Formen der Rinde mittels KI vermehrt werden, bis sich eine fantastische Chiaroscuro-Landschaft bildet. Wenn die Makroaufnahmen einer Hummel bis in die einzelnen Zellen gehen und der Film sich in eine metamorphosierende Animation mit roten Lebensflüssigkeiten und Kleinstformen wandelt, fragt man sich, wie vergleichbar verschiedene Lebensformen sind. Unsere klare, aber oft vergessene Verwandtschaft mit Bäumen, die aus unserem Lebendigsein entspringt, ist in *Das große Baumstück* durchgehend spürbar. Die Bewegungen des scheinbar Unbeweglichen werden offengelegt. Mit größter Aufmerksamkeit spürt Larcher den Welten nach, die sich hinter dem vermeintlich unauffälligen Marillenbaum verbergen. In der magischen letzten Sequenz, in der wir aus der Makroperspektive in die Baumkrone zurückkehren, verkörpert sich das innere Bewegtsein der Blätter. Es raschelt, knistert und säuselt,

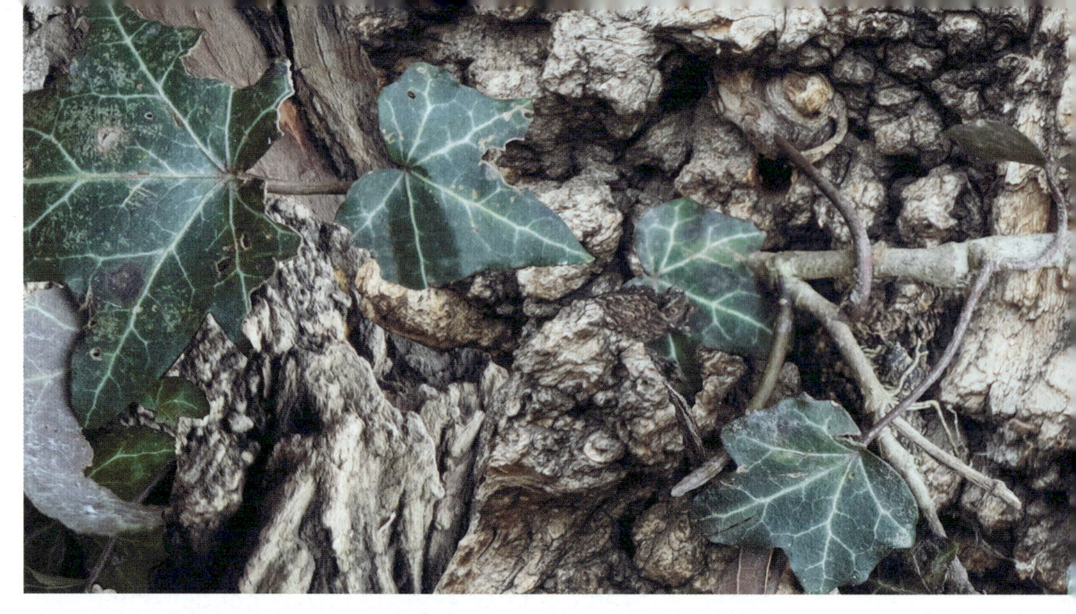

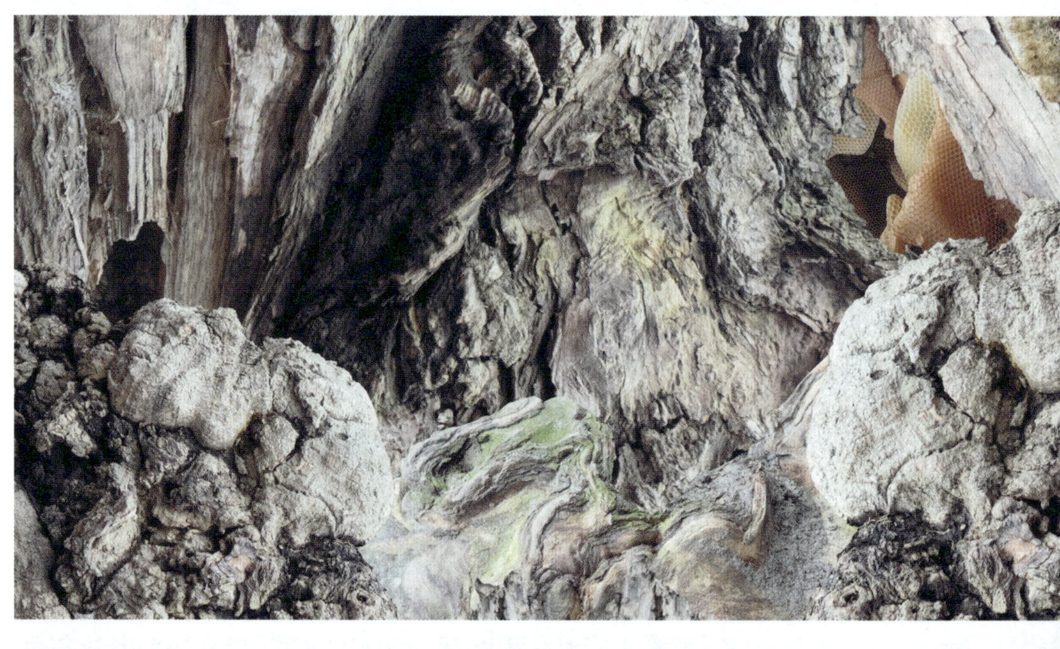

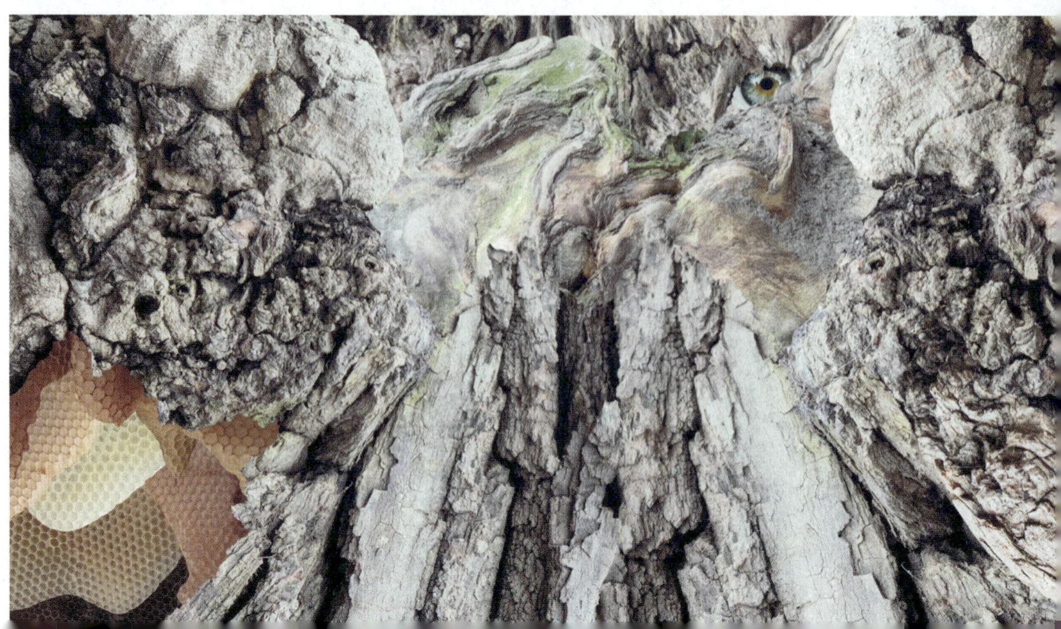

als ob das Leben selbst zu hören wäre. Vielleicht hört sich das Leben eines Baumes genau so an.

Ivana Miloš

Filmstills,
Das große Baumstück,
video, 16:9, 2K,
9' 30'', 2022/2023

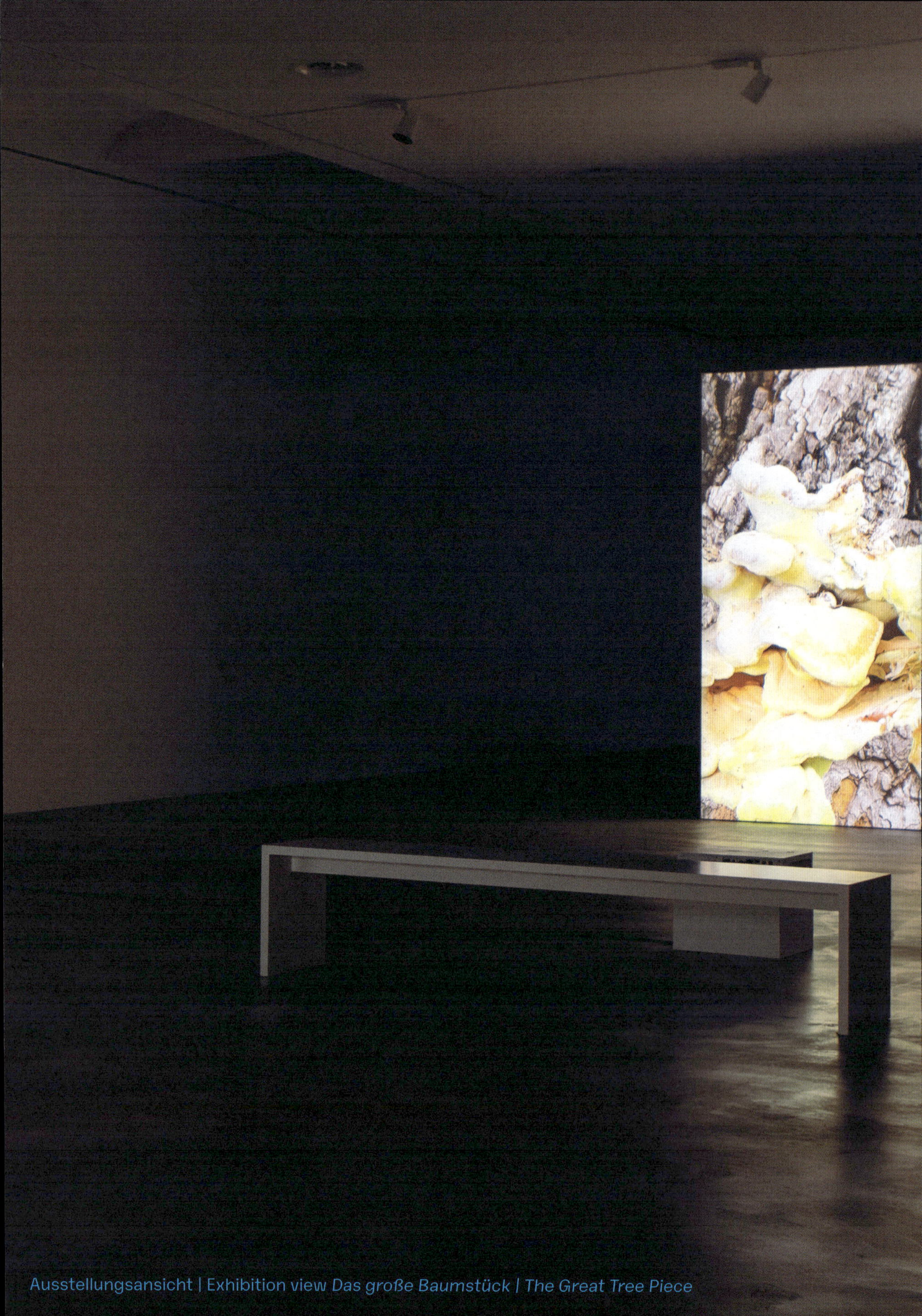

Ausstellungsansicht | Exhibition view *Das große Baumstück* | *The Great Tree Piece*

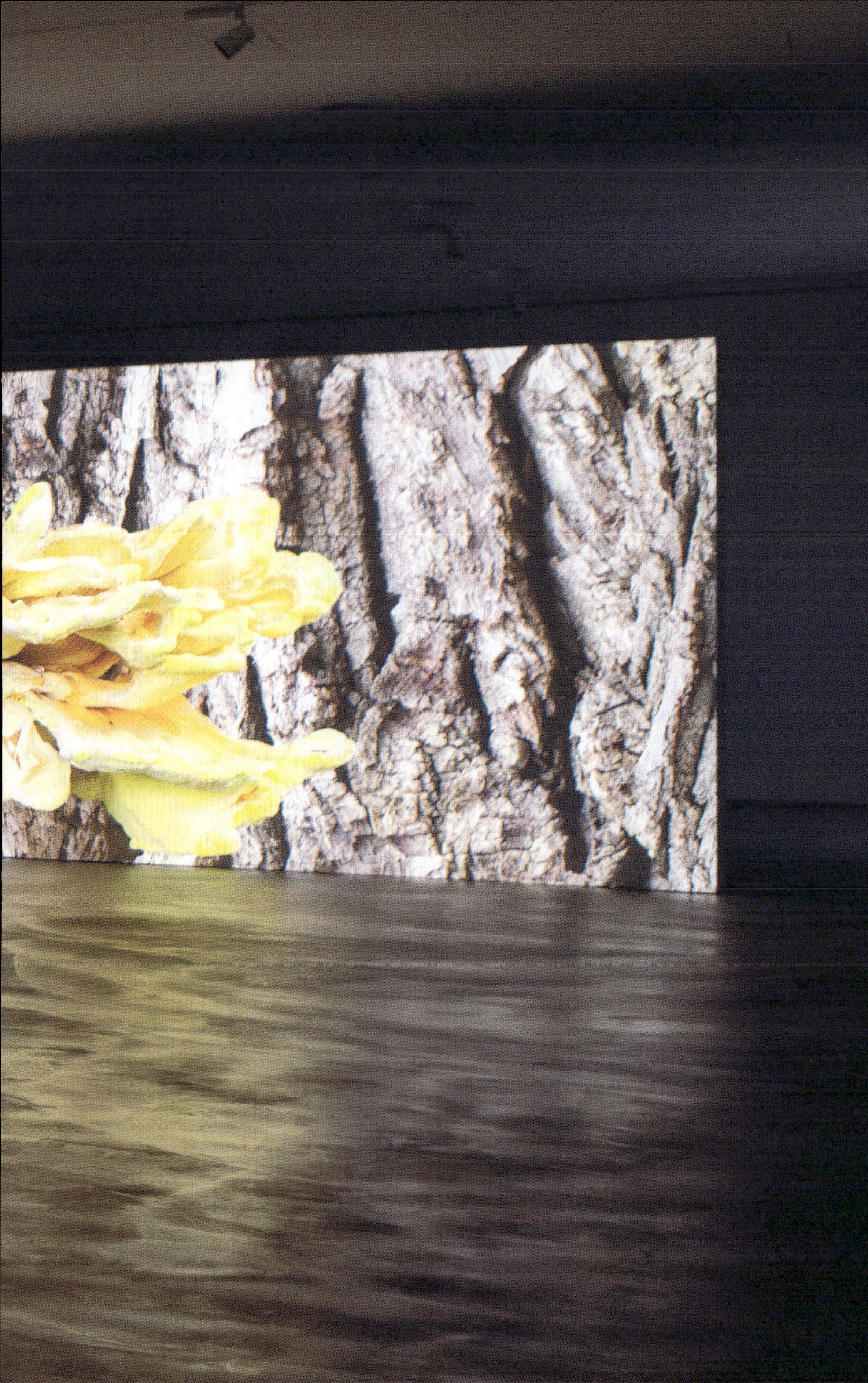

AI and Nature

The Great Tree Piece
experimental film, 9 min 30 s,
2K, video animation
sound by Ursula Winterauer
2022/23

What is a tree made of? What can an approach to it look like? And what does the tree itself have to do with what we see? Claudia Larcher's film *The Great Tree Piece* is dedicated to important questions that reveal themselves as soon as we ponder the complex human relationships with nature. The film consists of a single tracking shot from the top of a tree to below ground, where humus, fungi, and roots act as world creators in the darkness. The perspectives that arise during this movement along the tree fan out in manifold ways. As with Albrecht Dürer's painting *The Great Piece of Turf*, which served as inspiration for the film, this is a study of nature growing out of itself. The materiality of the tree is revealed as the puzzle-like shapes of the bark are multiplied using AI until a fantastic chiaroscuro landscape is formed. When the macro shots of a bumblebee go right down to the individual cells, and the film turns into a metamorphosing animation with red life fluids and microforms, one wonders how comparable different life forms are. Our clear but often forgotten kinship with trees, springing from our being alive, is palpable throughout *The Great Tree Piece*. The movements of the seemingly immobile are laid bare. With the utmost attention, Larcher traces the worlds that hide behind the supposedly inconspicuous apricot tree. In the magical last sequence, in which we return to the tree crown from a macro perspective, the inner movement of the leaves is embodied. It rustles, crackles, and whispers as if life itself could be heard. Perhaps that is exactly what the life of a tree sounds like.

Ivana Miloš

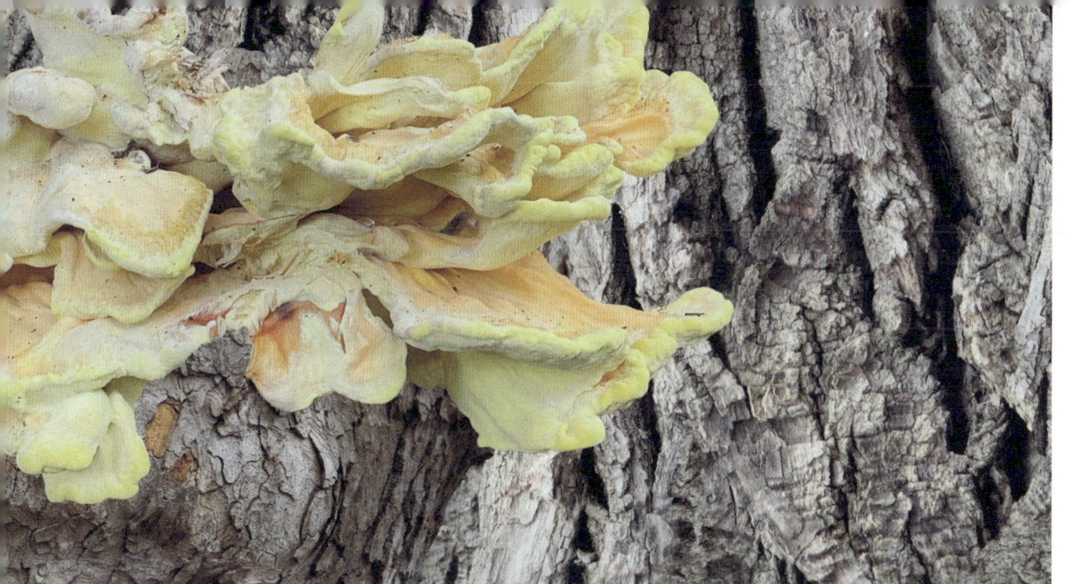

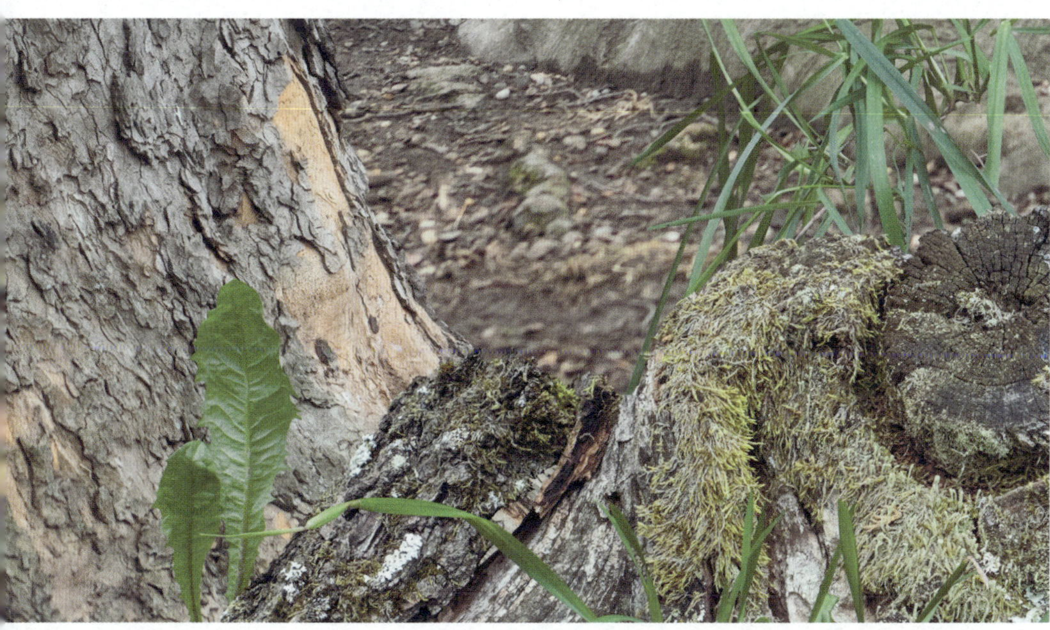

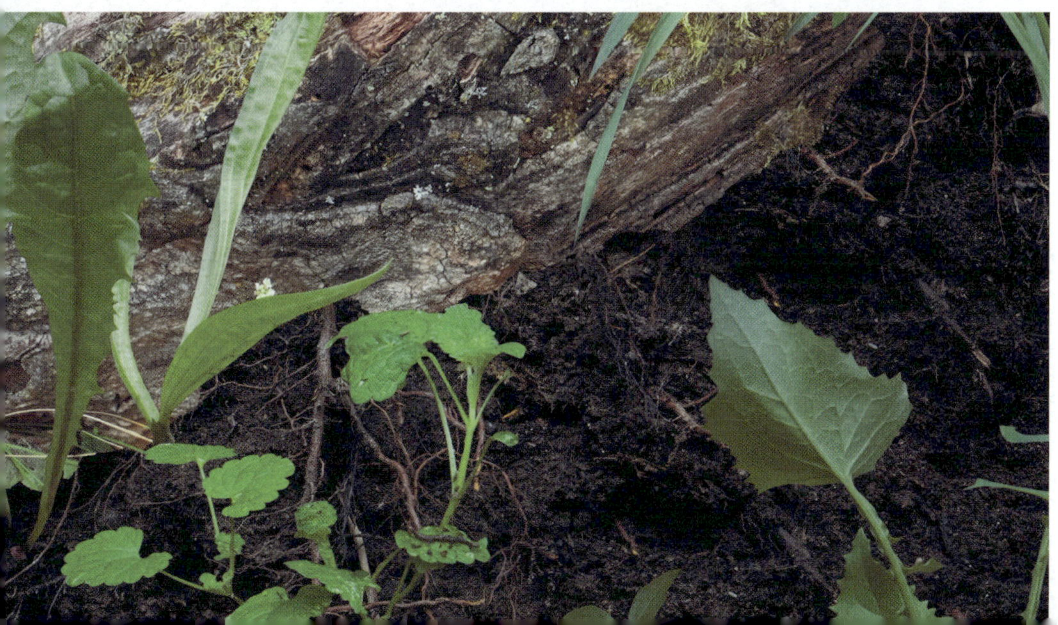

film stills,
The Great Tree Piece,
video, 16:9, 2K,
9' 30", 2022/2023

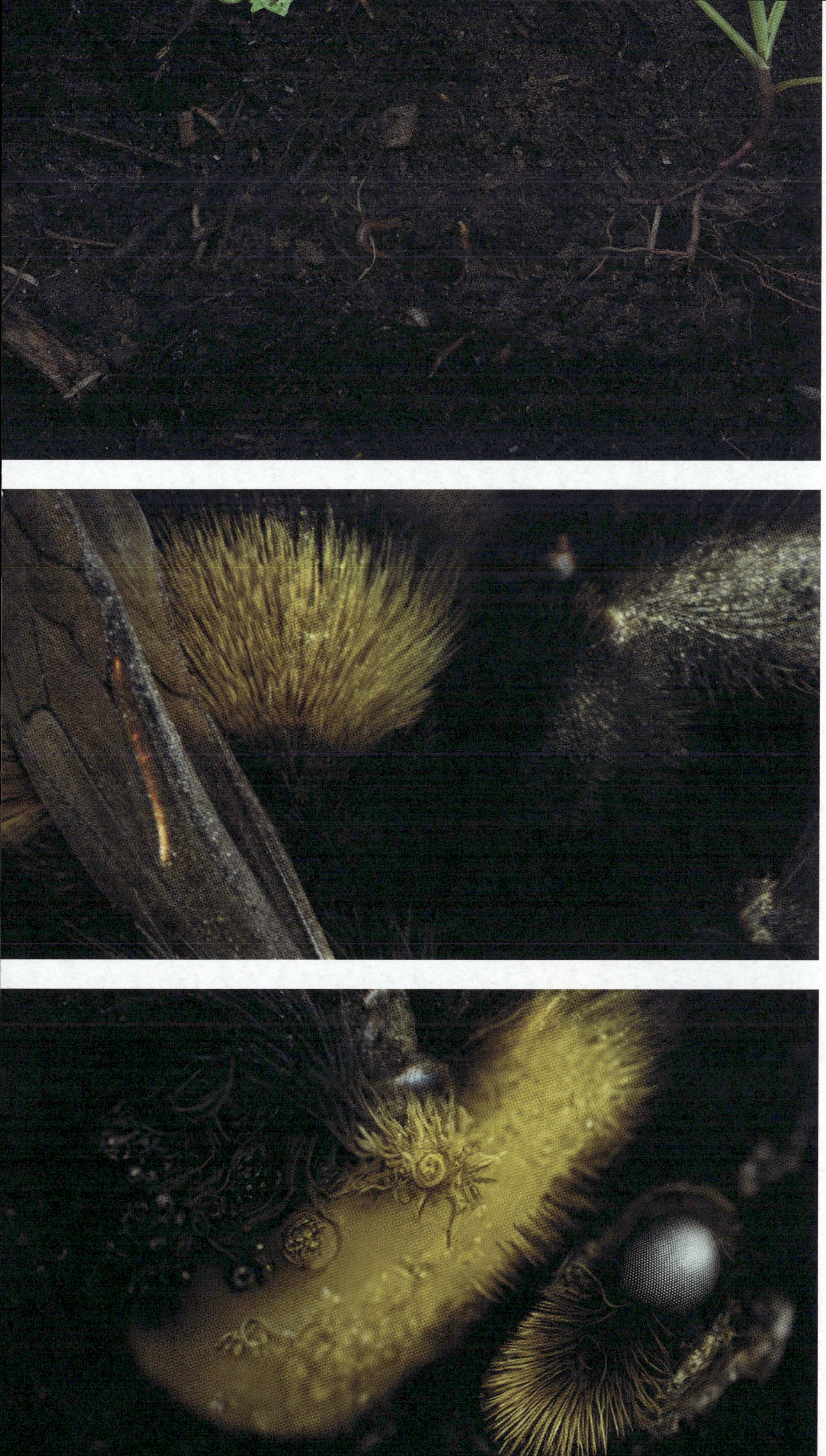

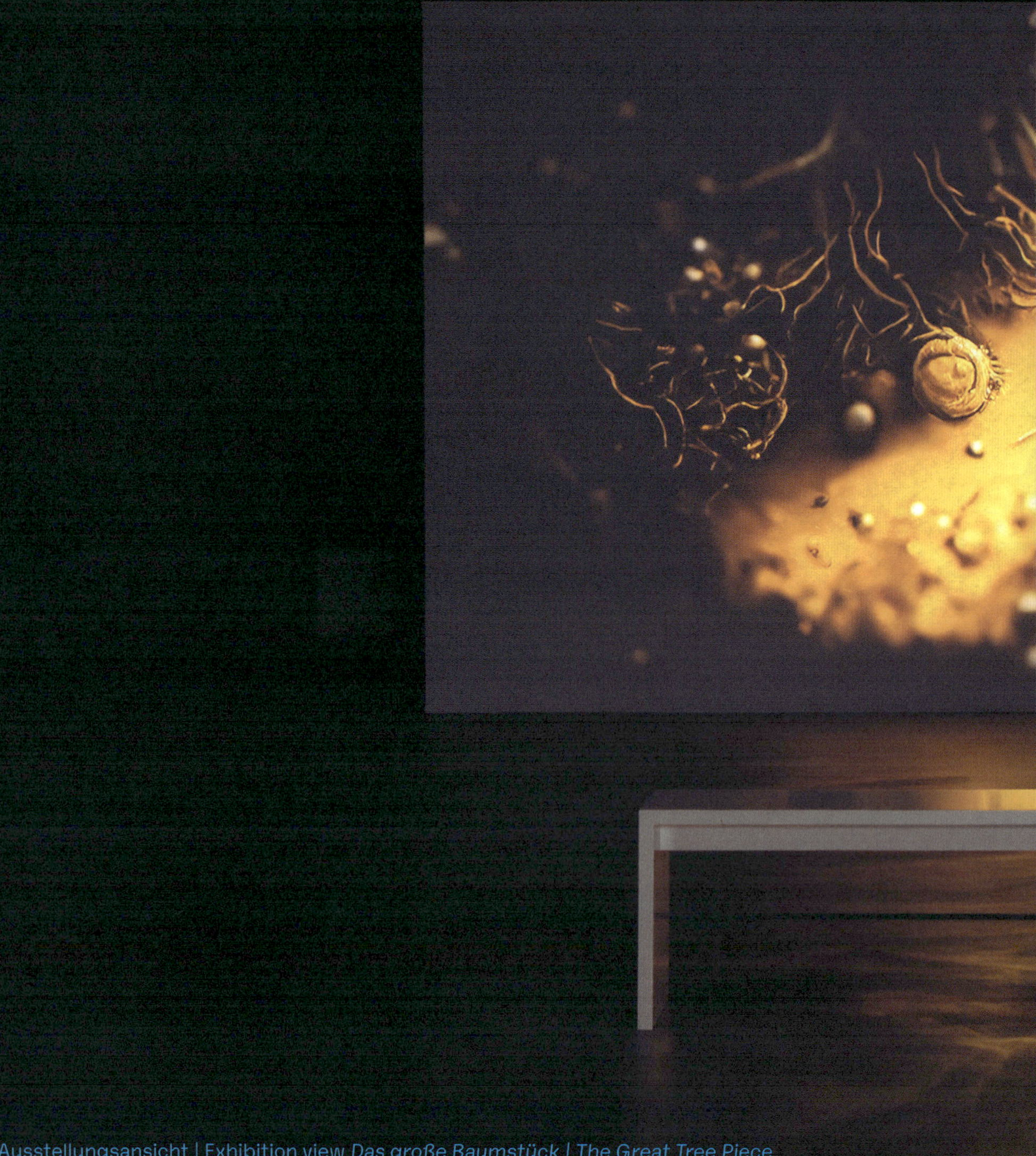

Ausstellungsansicht | Exhibition view *Das große Baumstück | The Great Tree Piece*

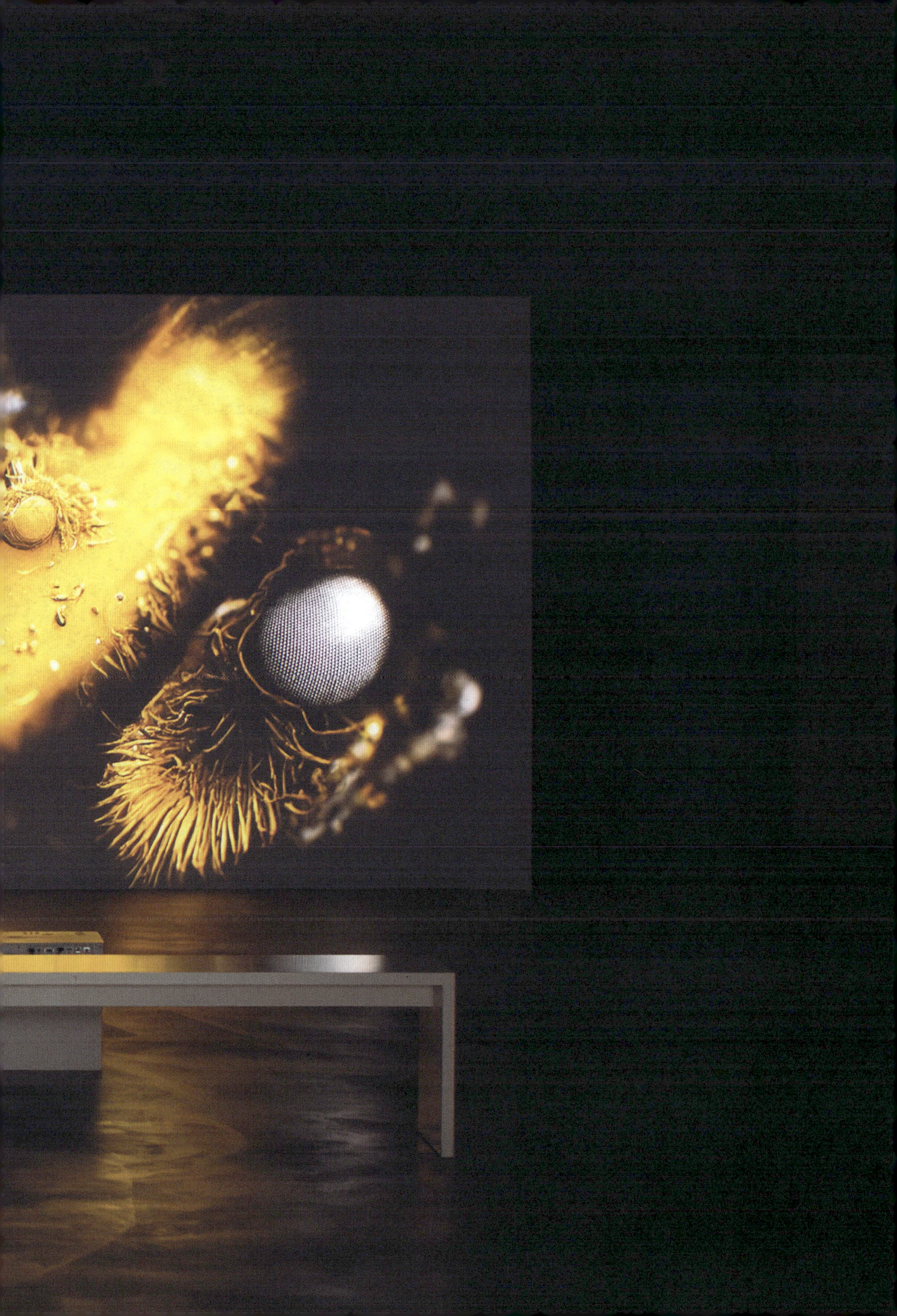

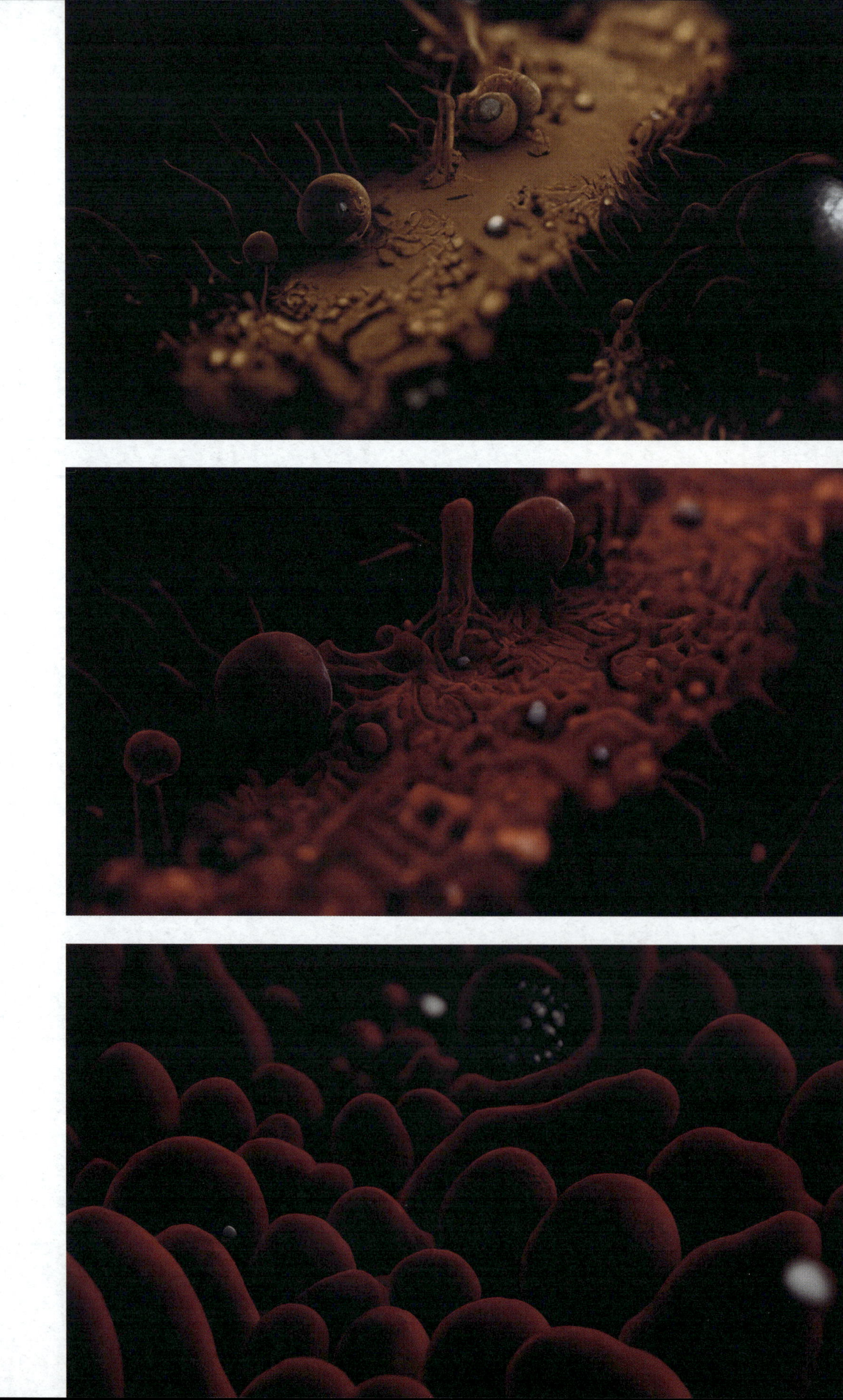

Filmstills,
Das große Baumstück,
video, 16:9, 2K,
9' 30'', 2022/2023

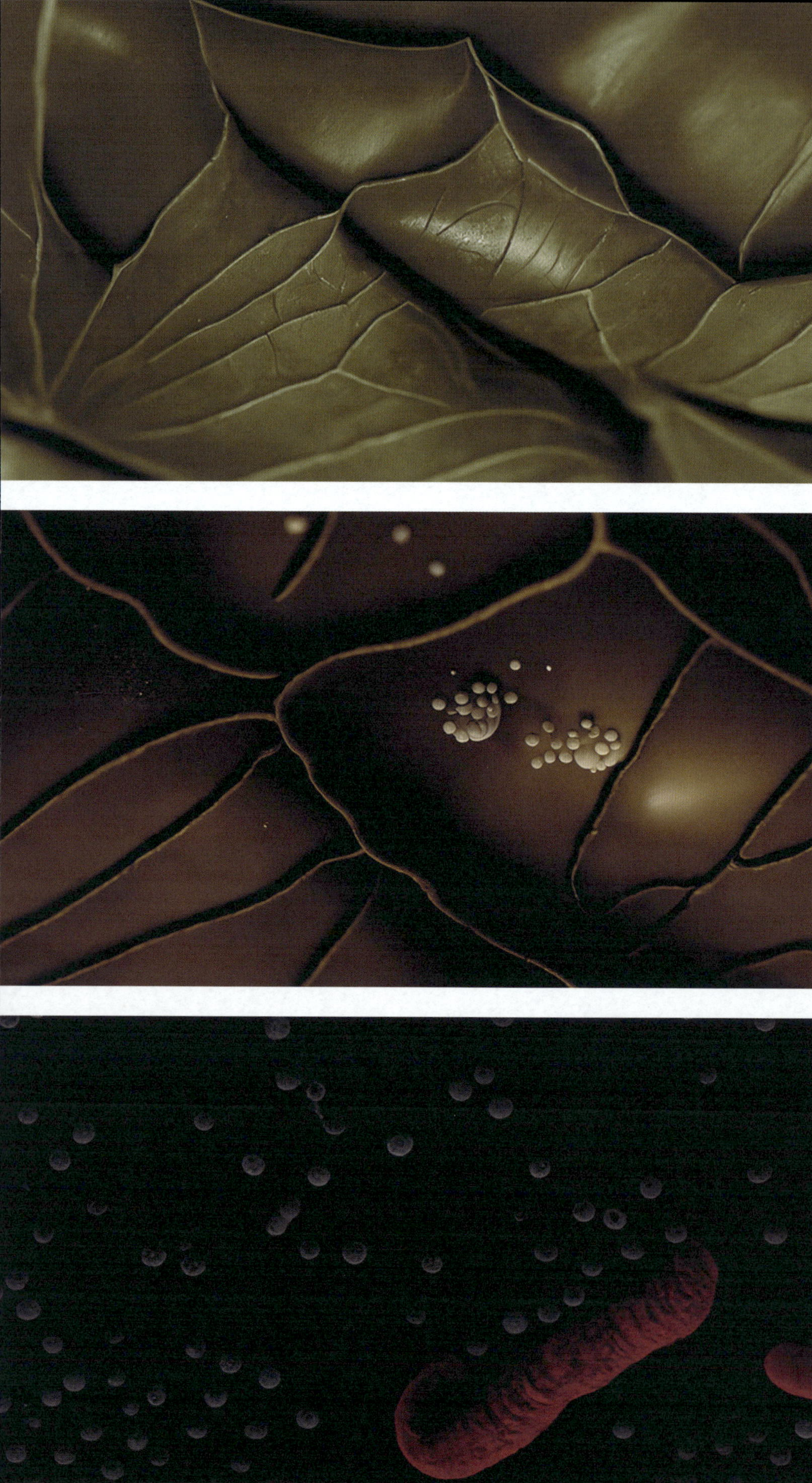

Filmstills,
Das große Baumstück,
video, 16:9, 2K,
9' 30'', 2022/2023

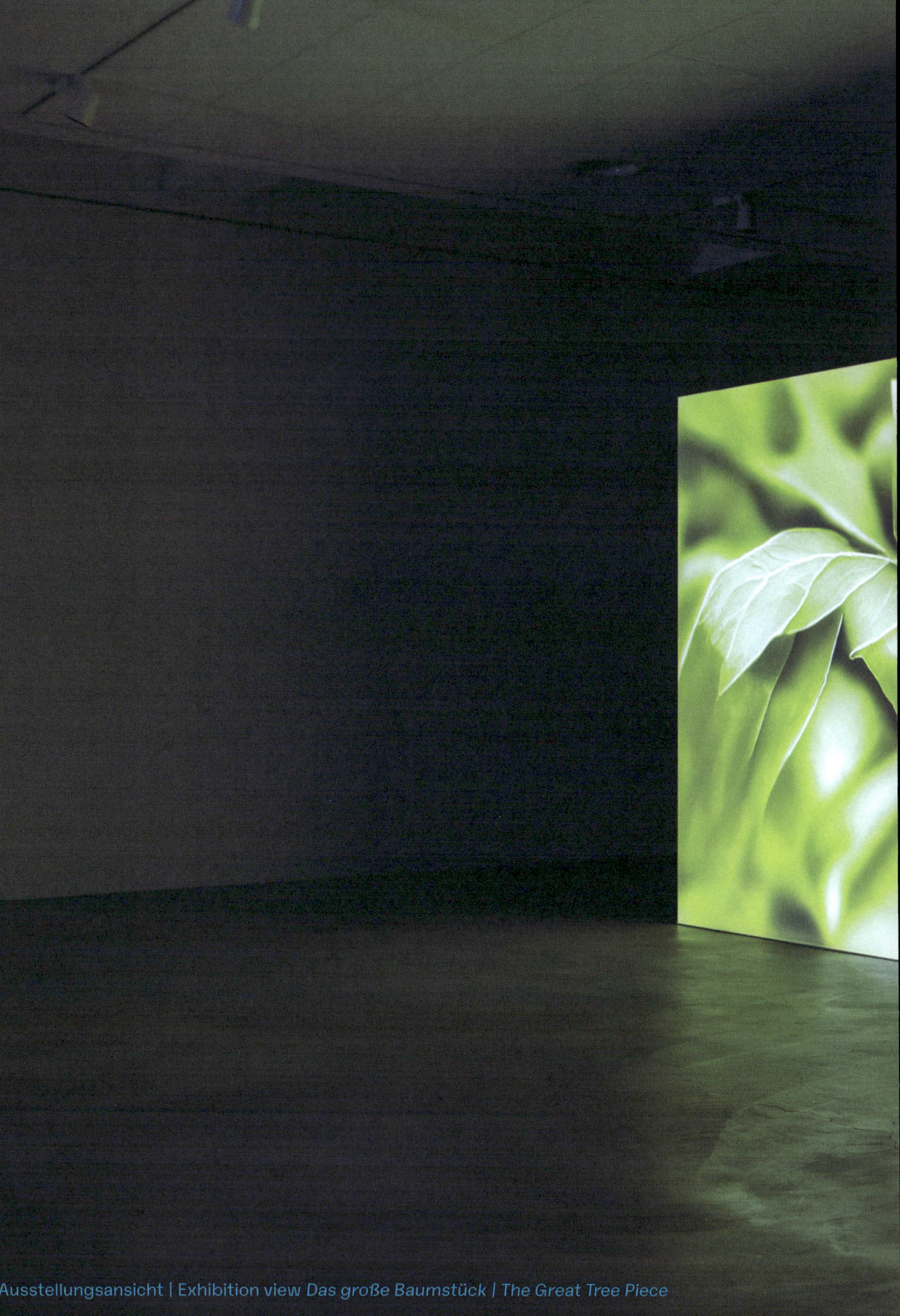

Ausstellungsansicht | Exhibition view *Das große Baumstück* | *The Great Tree Piece*

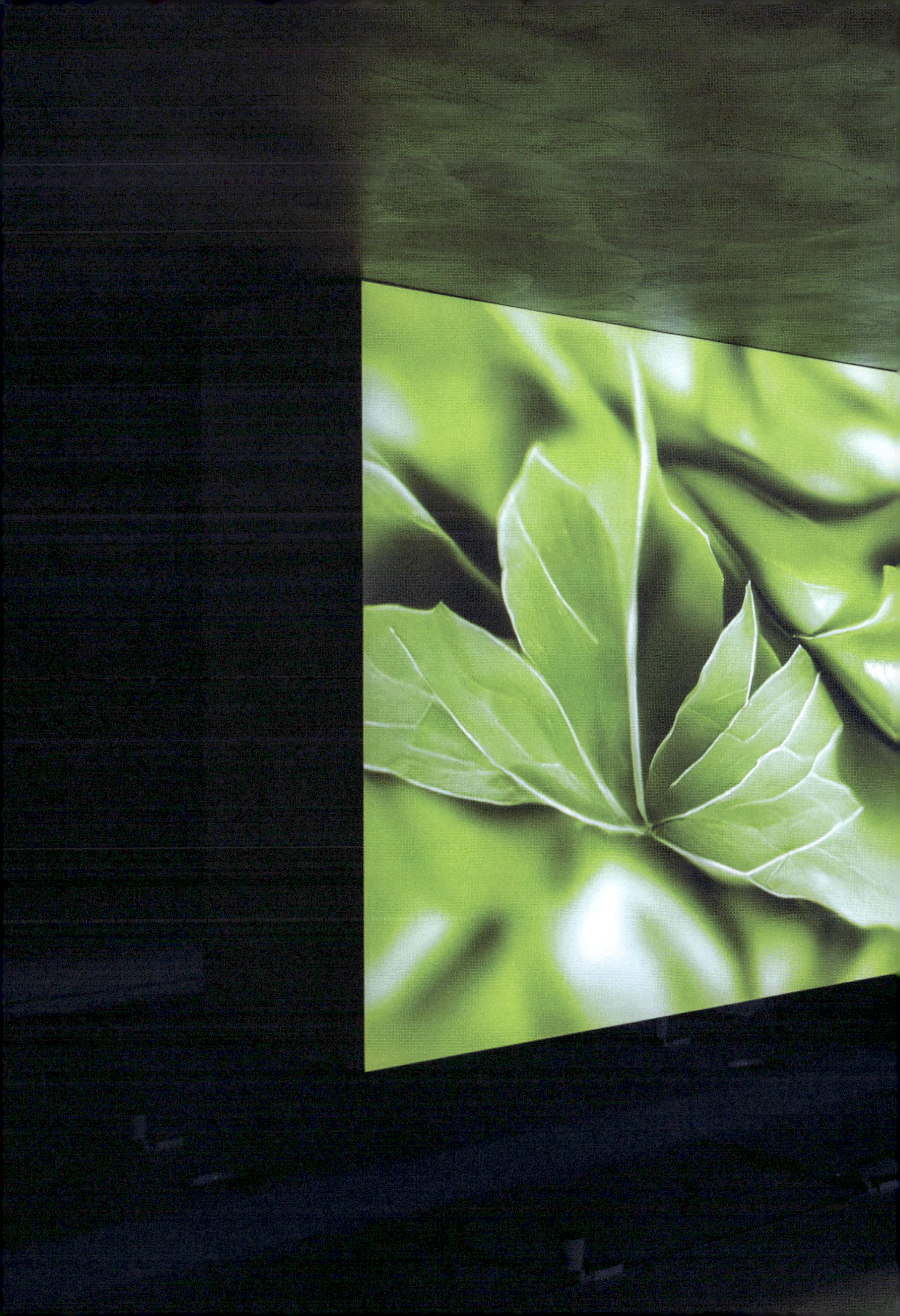

film stills,
The Great Tree Piece,
video, 16:9, 2K,
9' 30'', 2022/2023

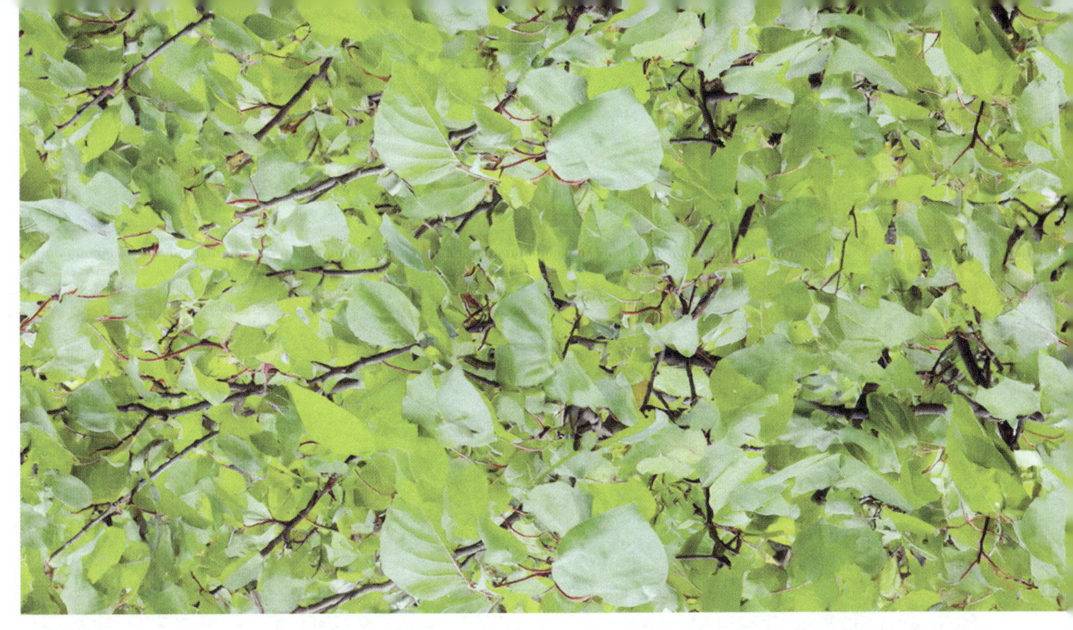

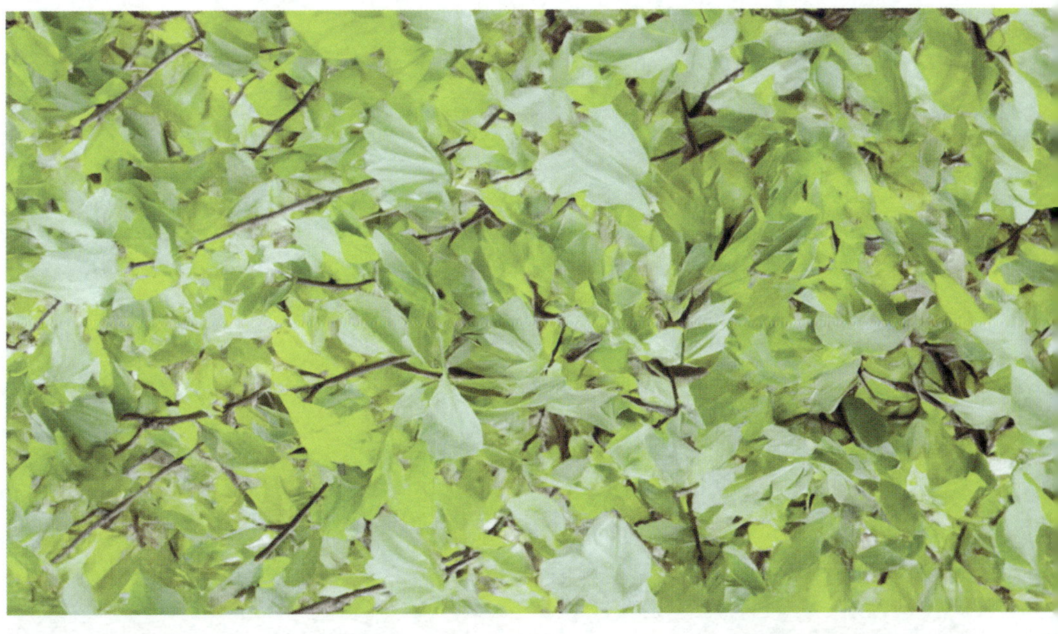

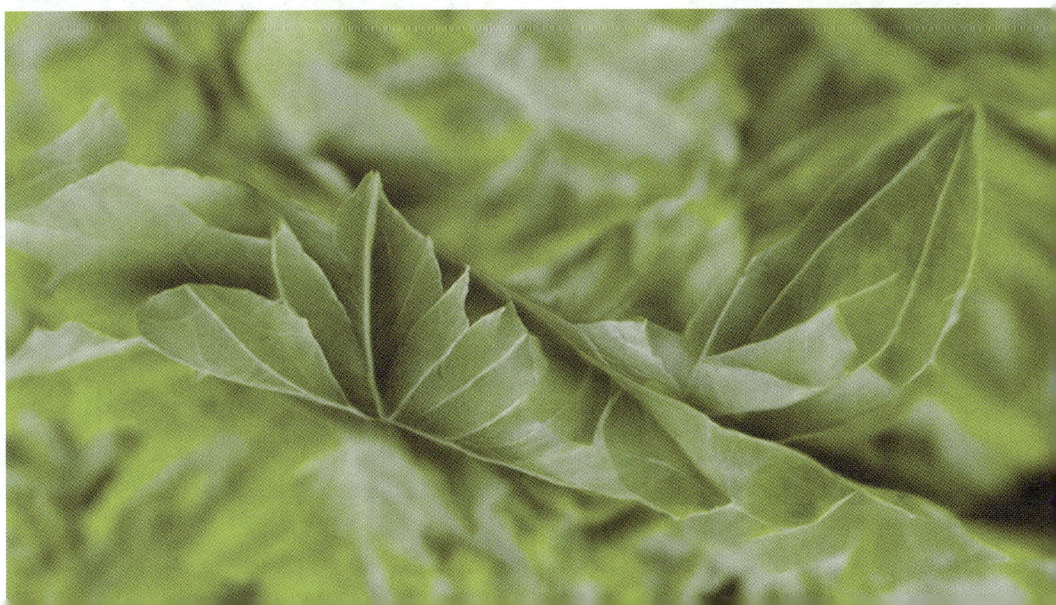

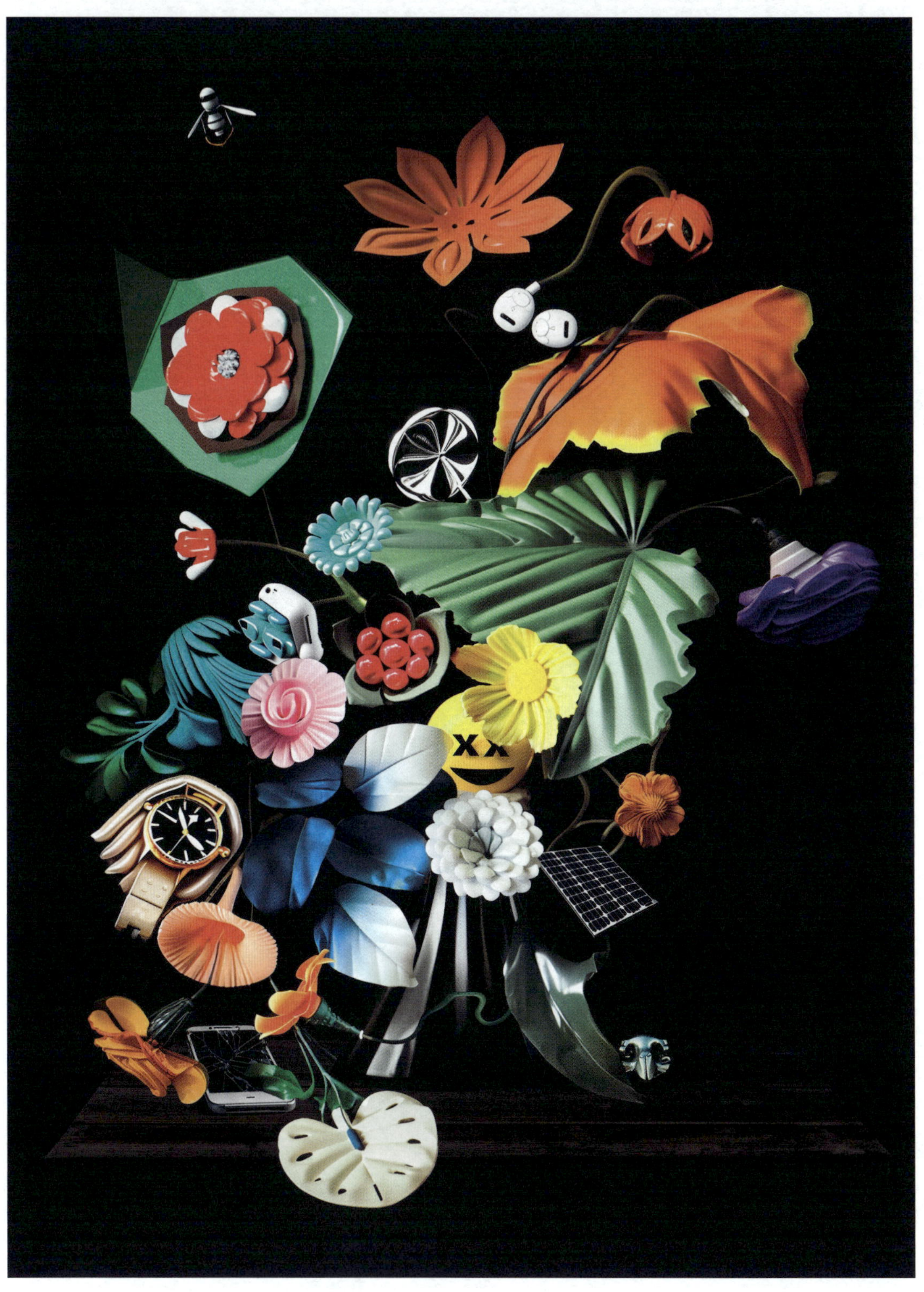

KI and Natur

Still Life 3000
Giclée Print
unterschiedliche Dimensionen,
individuell gerahmt, 2023/2024

In der Serie *Still Life 3000* tritt Claudia Larcher in einen zeitgenössischen Dialog mit der Tradition des klassischen Stilllebens. Die digital und mithilfe von KI erzeugten Werke sind inspiriert von Rachel Ruysch, einer wegweisenden niederländischen Künstlerin des 17. Jahrhunderts. Larcher schlägt in ihrer Neuinterpretation eine Brücke zwischen Vergangenheit und Gegenwart, klassischer Kunst und modernem Konsum, natürlichen und technologischen Elementen. Larcher verwendet Kunstblumen aus Plastik, die in ihrer unvergänglichen Perfektion den Zeitgeist des 21. Jahrhunderts widerspiegeln und auf ökologische Herausforderungen unserer Zeit hinweisen. Die Einbindung einer technoiden Bienendrohne betont die komplizierte Beziehung zwischen Natur und Technologie in einer Welt, die von Klimawandel und dem Verlust der Artenvielfalt bedroht ist. Schließlich finden sich zeitgenössische Artefakte wie etwa iPhone-ähnliche Accessoires in die Serie integriert, die sowohl den Geist der modernen Lebensweise verkörpern als auch den Zyklus von Vergänglichkeit und Erneuerung thematisieren.

Nu_01
Giclée Print
72 x 52 cm
2023

AI and Nature

Still Life 3000
giclée, various dimensions,
individually framed,
2023/24

In the *Still Life 3000* series, Claudia Larcher enters into a contemporary dialogue with the tradition of the classic still life. The digitally and AI-generated works are inspired by Rachel Ruysch, a pioneering Dutch artist of the 17th century. In her reinterpretation, Larcher builds a bridge between past and present, classical art and modern consumption, natural and technological elements. Larcher uses artificial plastic flowers that reflect the zeitgeist of the 21st century in their everlasting perfection and point to the ecological challenges of our time. The inclusion of a technoid bee drone emphasises the complicated relationship between nature and technology in a world threatened by climate change and the loss of biodiversity. Finally, contemporary artefacts such as iPhone-like accessories are integrated into the series, embodying both the spirit of modern living and the cycle of transience and renewal.

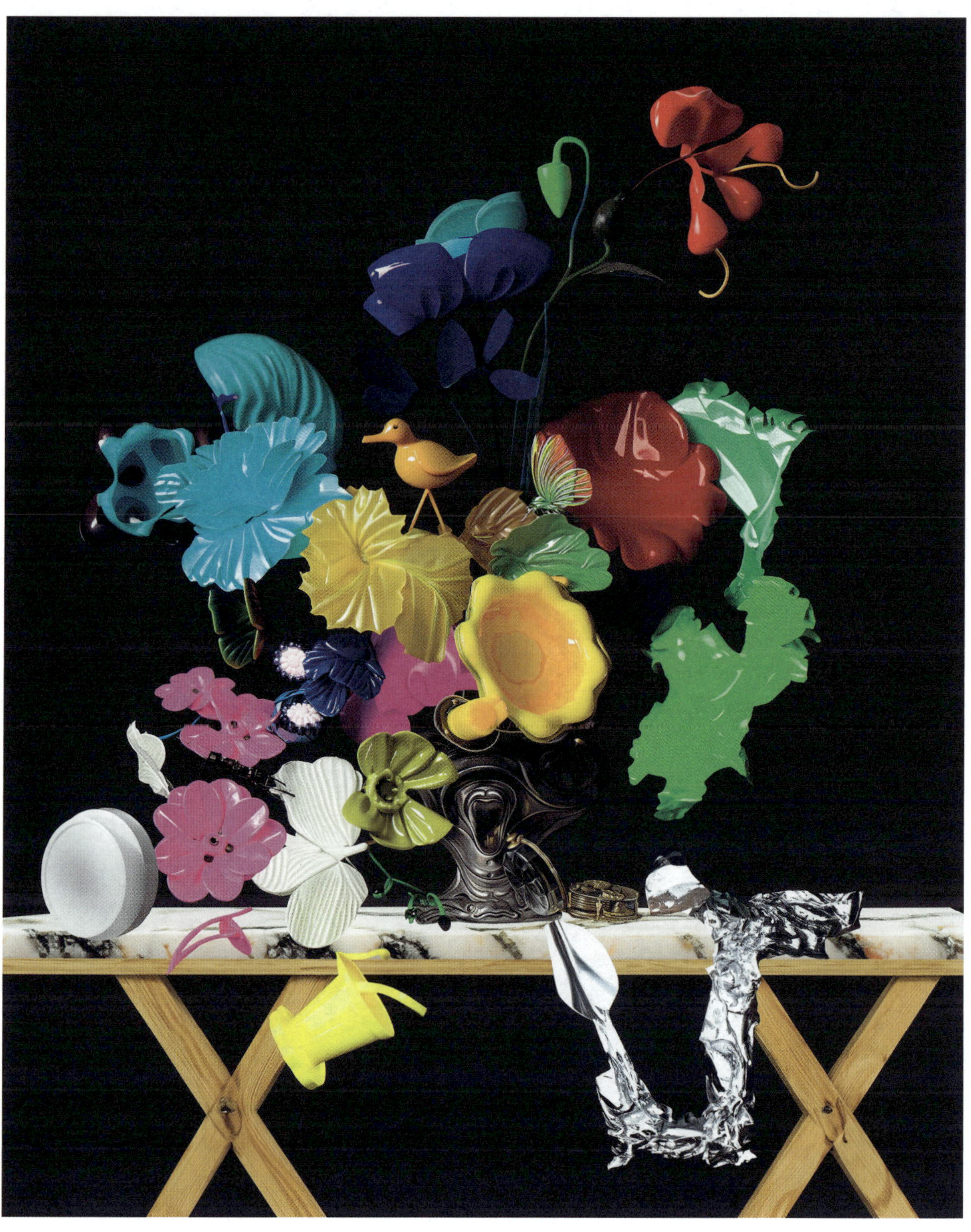

No_04
Giclée Print
132 x 105 cm
2024

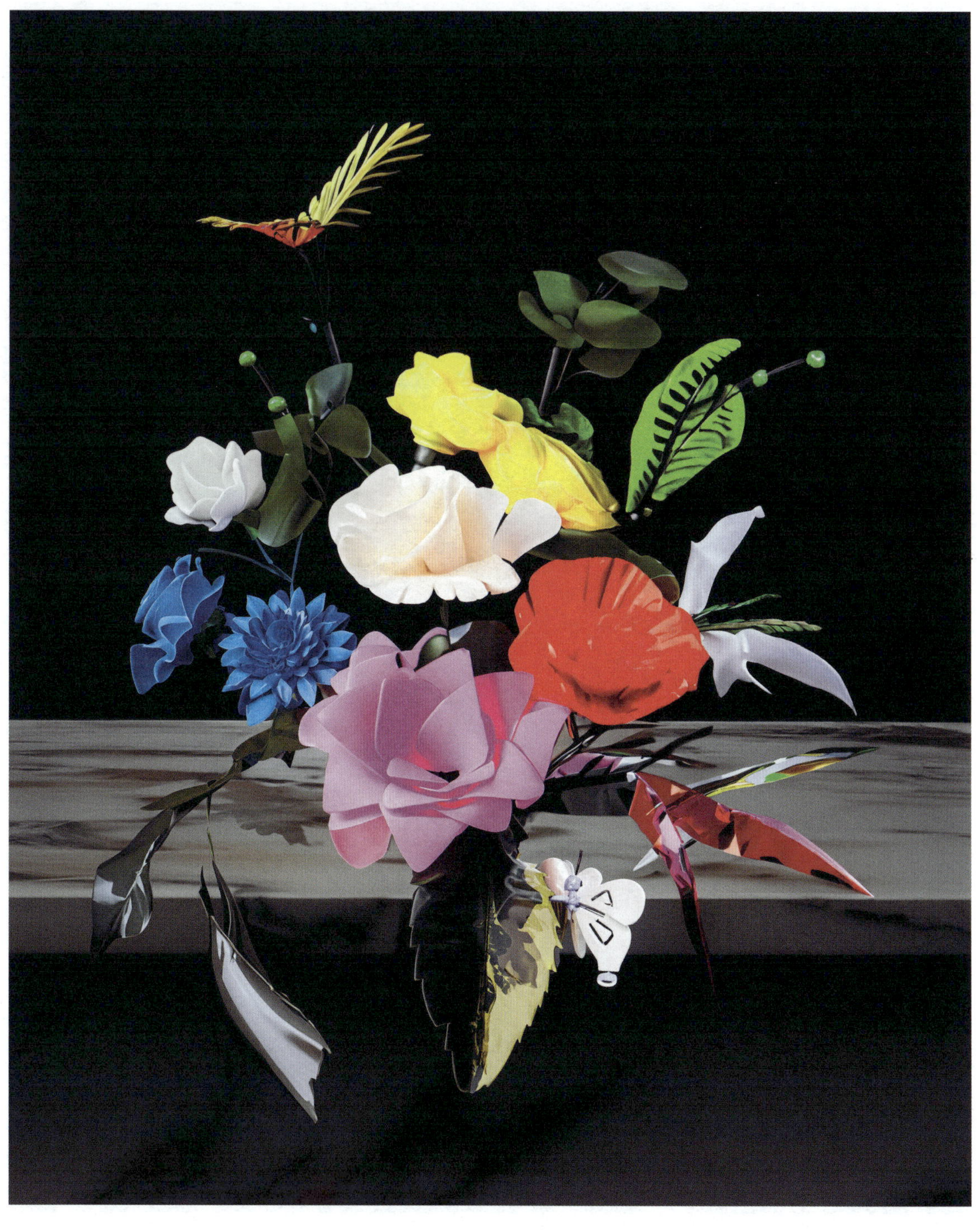

No_05
Giclée Print
82 x 65 cm
2024

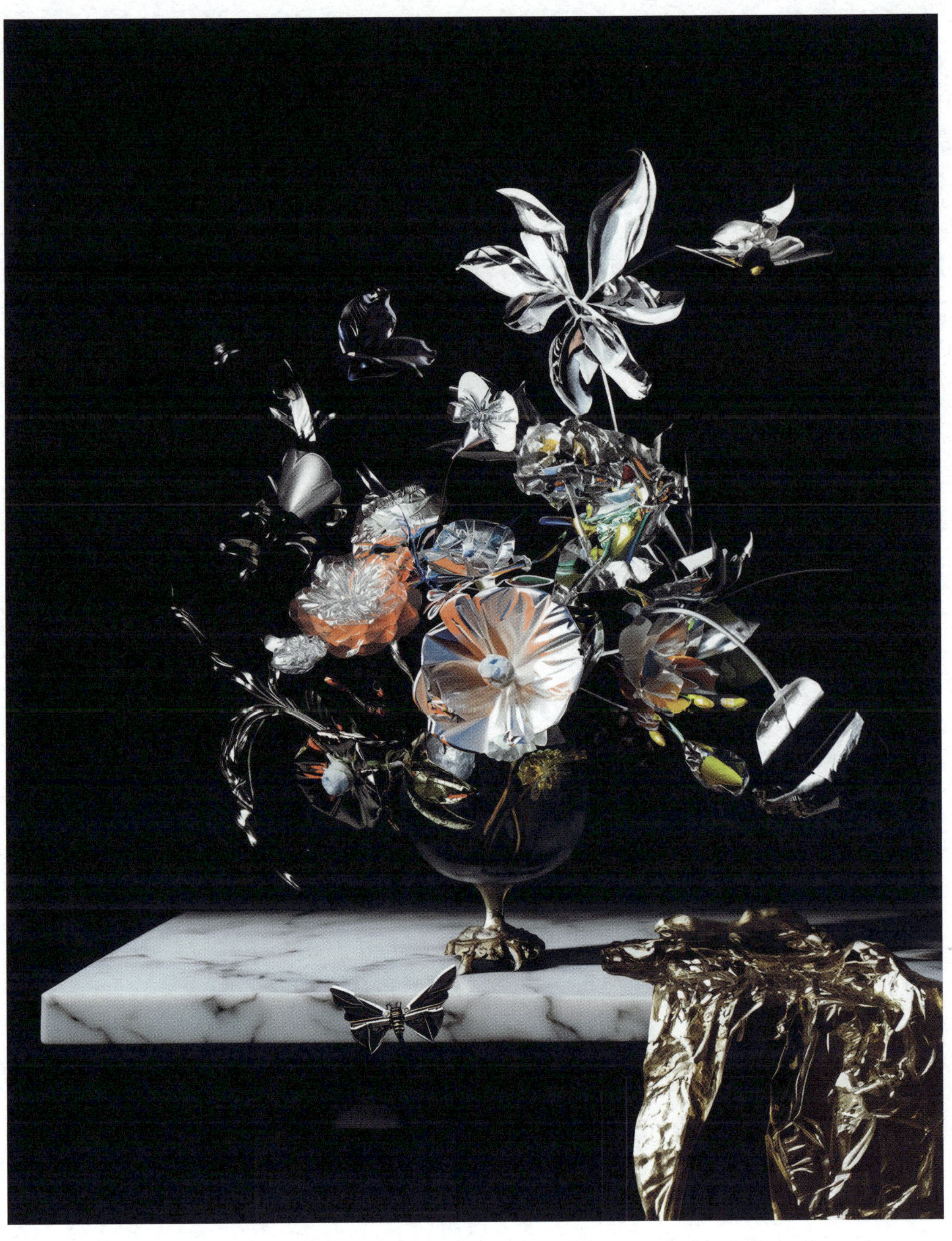

No_07
Giclée Print
132 x 102 cm
2024

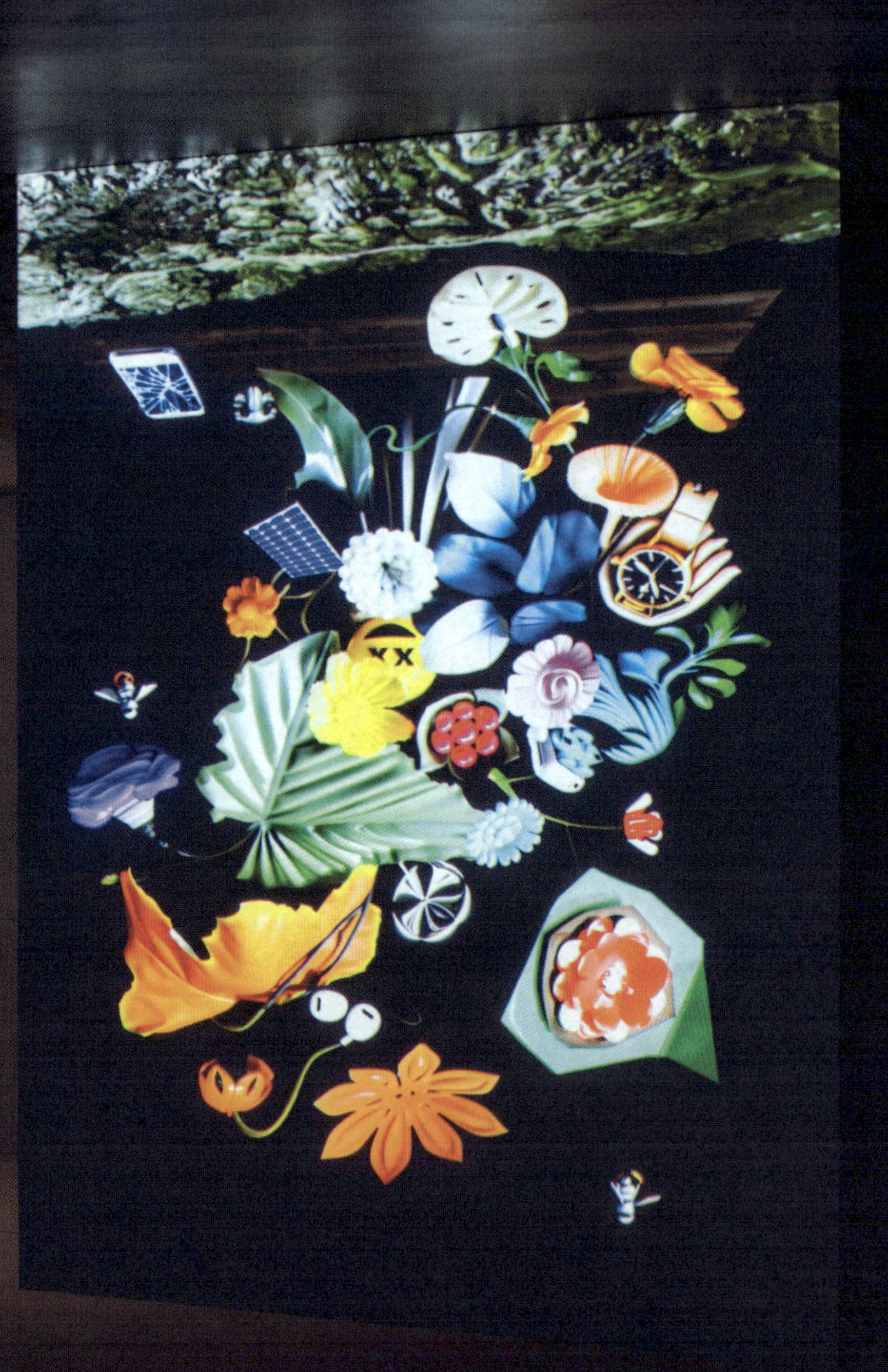

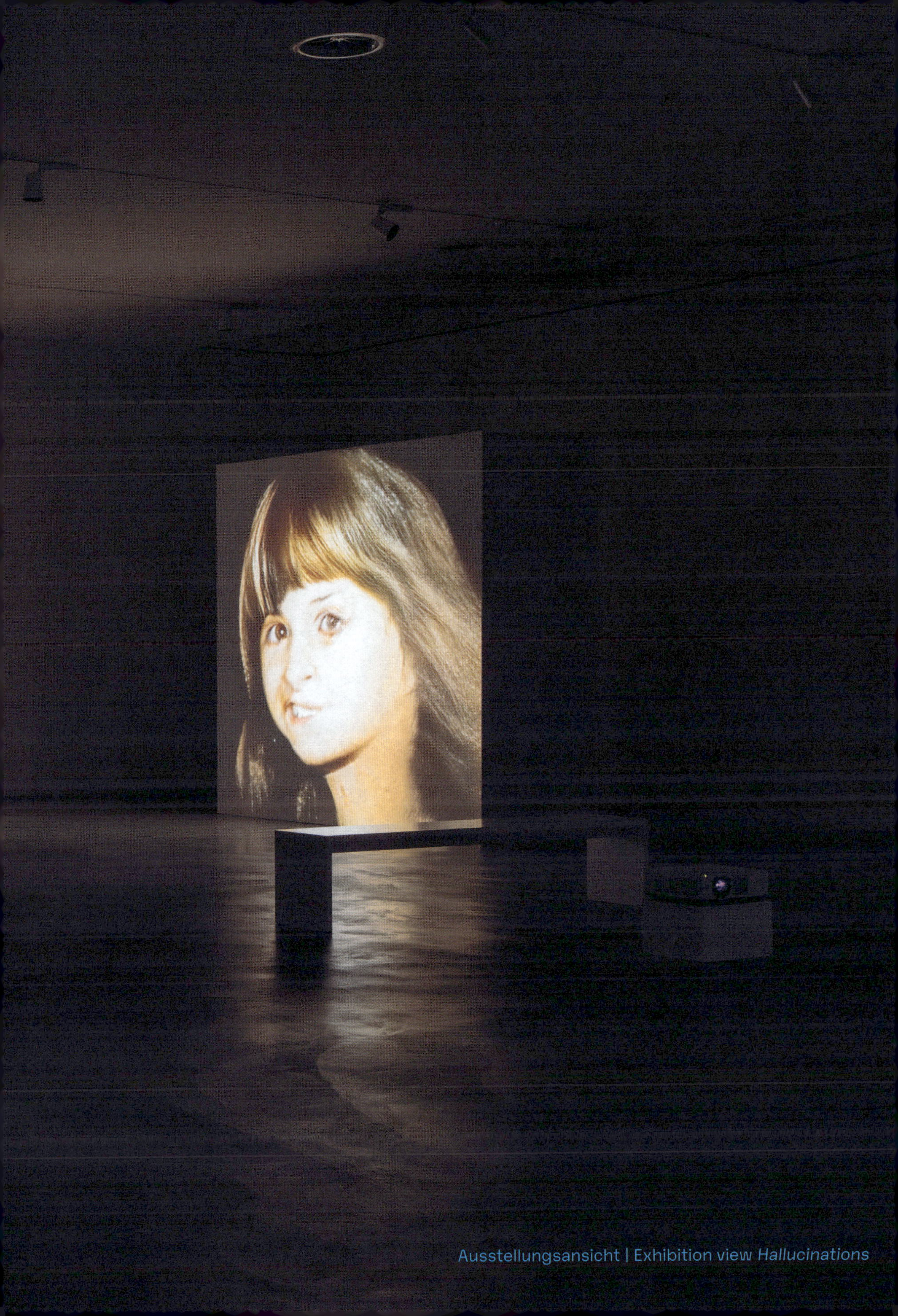

Ausstellungsansicht | Exhibition view *Hallucinations*

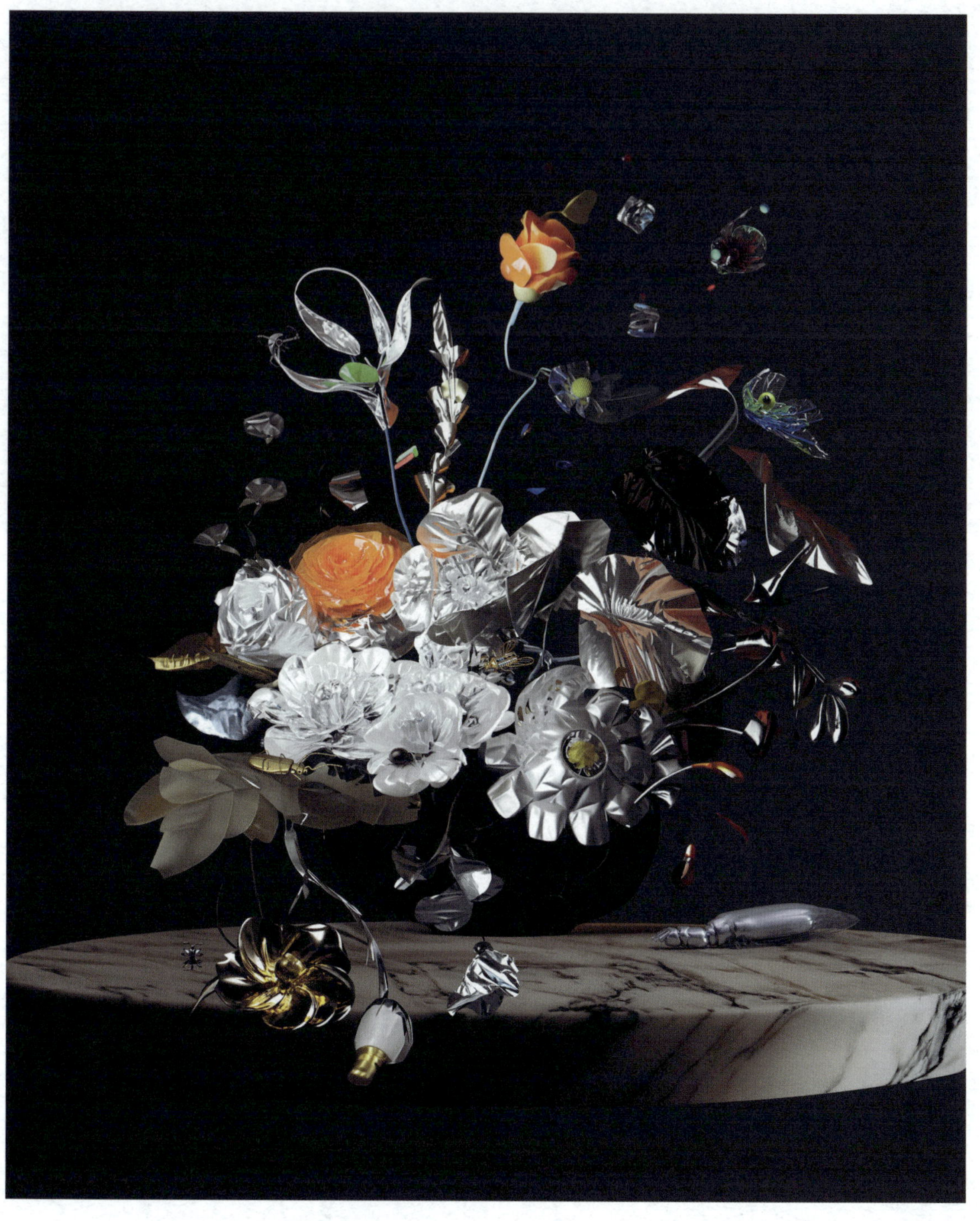

No_08
Giclée Print
162 x 130 cm
2024

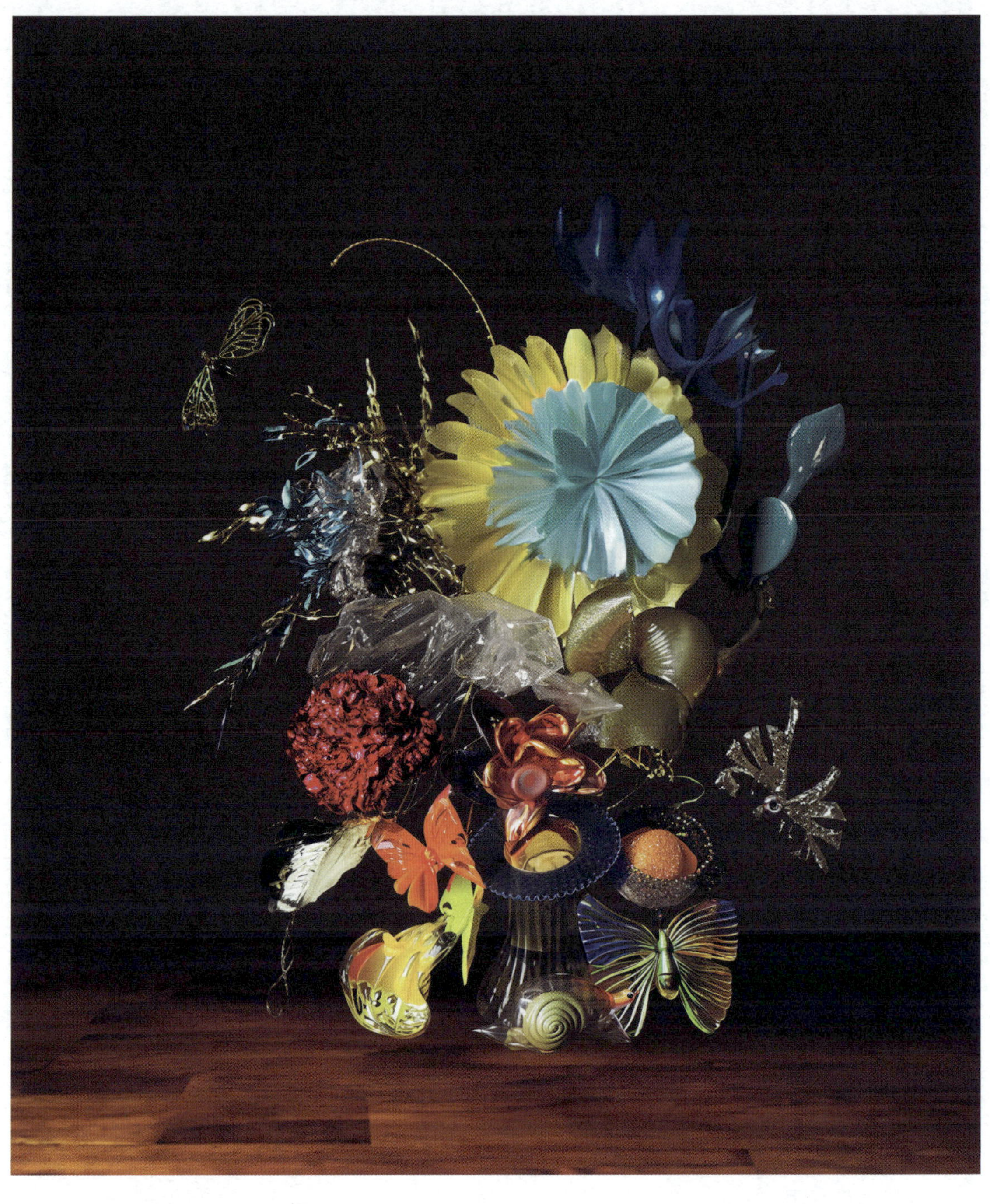

No_09
Giclée Print
122 x 102 cm
2024

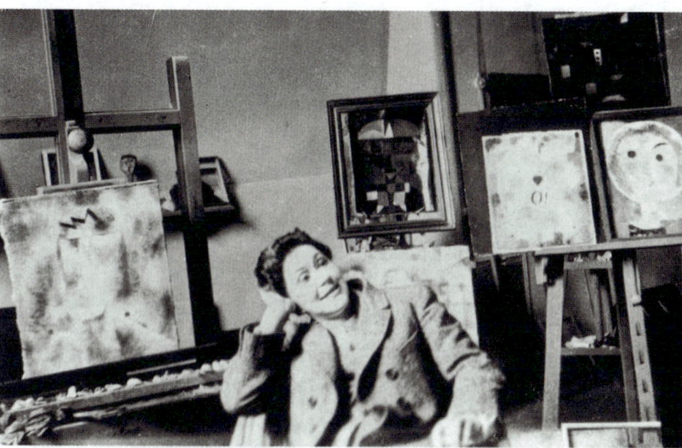

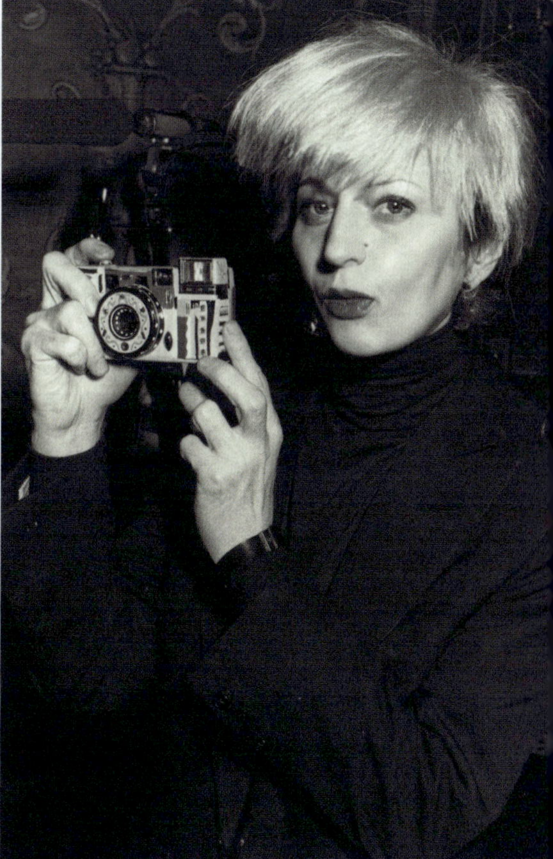

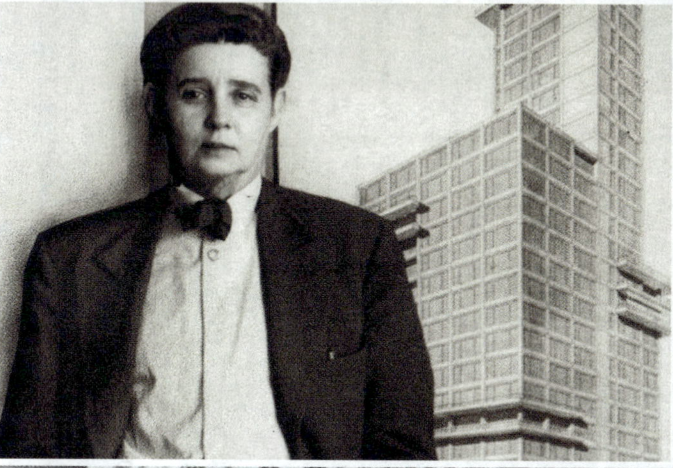

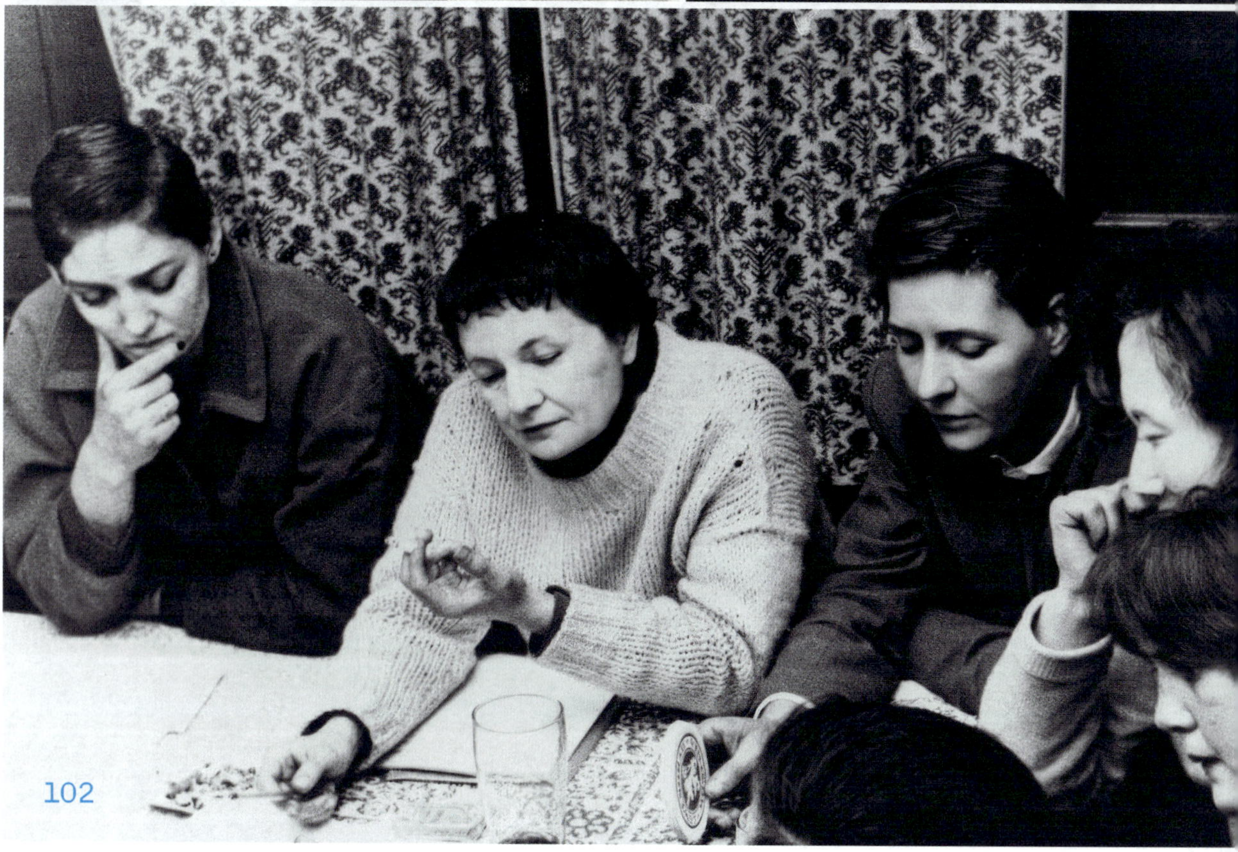

KI und Geschichte

KI und die Kunst der historischen Neuinterpretation
Filling Gender Bias Gaps, Datenset
VALIE EXPORT Center Linz,
Projekt in Arbeit seit 2022

Die Strategie des Projekts basiert auf der gezielten Rekonstruktion und Neuinszenierung ikonischer Fotografien bedeutender Künstler:innen und Wissenschaftler:innen. Durch den Austausch der ursprünglichen, meist männlich dominierten Darsteller:innen mit FLINTA*-Personen entsteht eine fiktionale Realität, die eine alternative Geschichtserzählung ermöglicht. Diese „fiktionalen Archive" sind mehr als nur künstlerische Kommentare; sie fungieren als Gegenarchive, welche die bestehenden Narrative der Kunstgeschichte herausfordern und um diverse, oft übersehene Perspektiven erweitern.

Dabei wirft das Projekt wichtige ethische Fragen auf: Wie weit darf KI bei der Umgestaltung von Geschichte gehen? Wie können wir sicherstellen, dass diese Technologien nicht die gleichen systemischen Fehler wiederholen, die sie zu korrigieren versuchen? Indem das Projekt historische Verzerrungen und Ausschlüsse sichtbar macht, fordert es nicht nur eine Neubewertung der Vergangenheit, sondern eröffnet auch eine visionäre Perspektive für die Zukunft. Die Bildsammlung der Künstlerin wächst kontinuierlich und kann durch Datenanalysen ausgewertet werden, um sowohl aktiv als auch passiv in zukünftige KI-Systeme einzugehen. Durch die Verbreitung über digitale Plattformen trägt diese fiktionale Geschichte nicht nur dazu bei, das kulturelle Gedächtnis diverser und gerechter zu gestalten, sondern kann auch künftige KI-Modelle dahingehend beeinflussen, eine inklusivere und gerechtere Zukunft zu fördern.

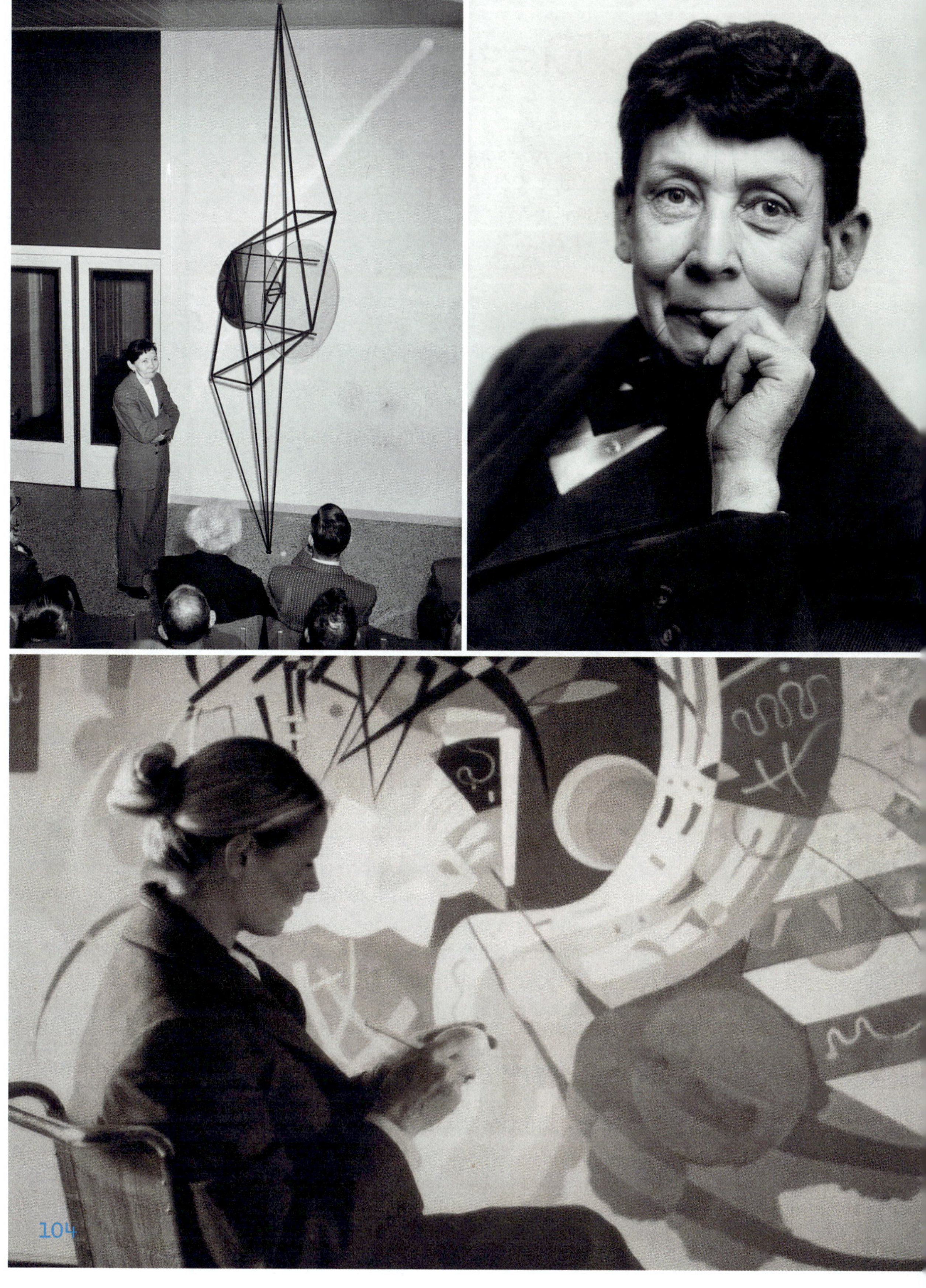

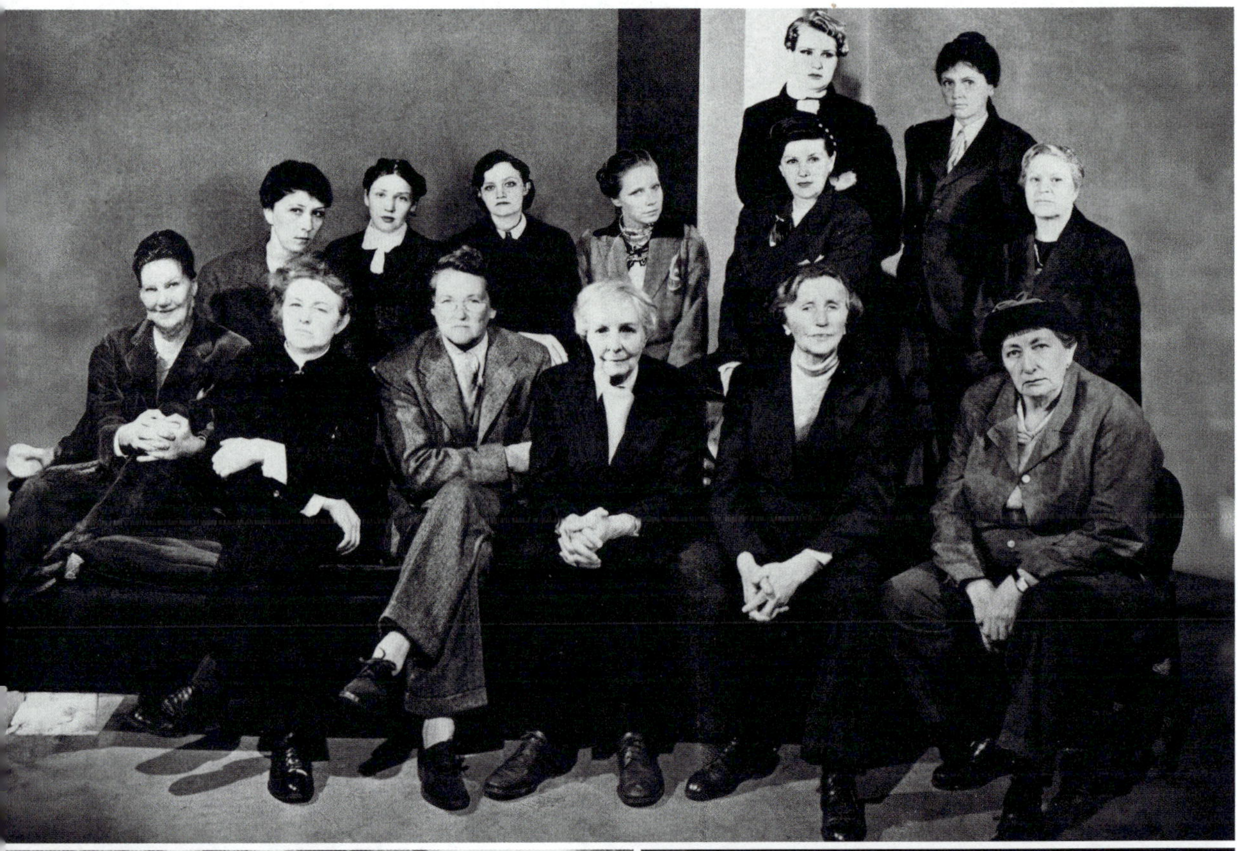

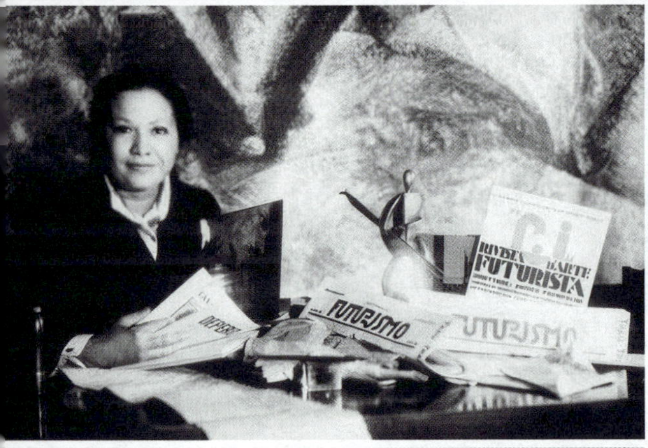
RIVISTA D'ARTE
FUTURISTA
FUTURISMO
FUTURISMO

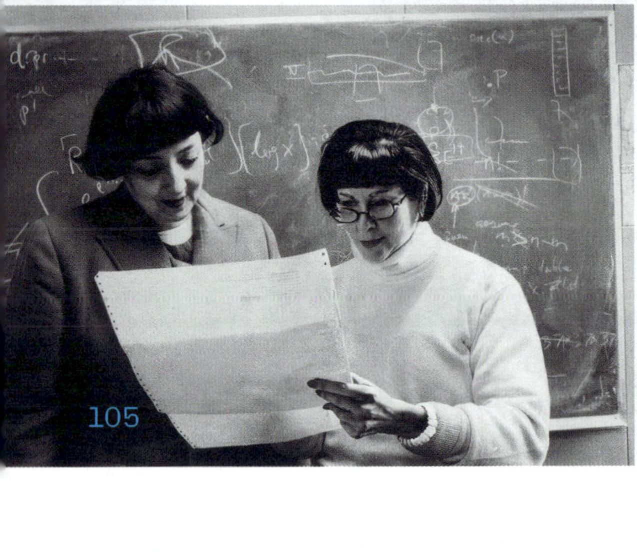

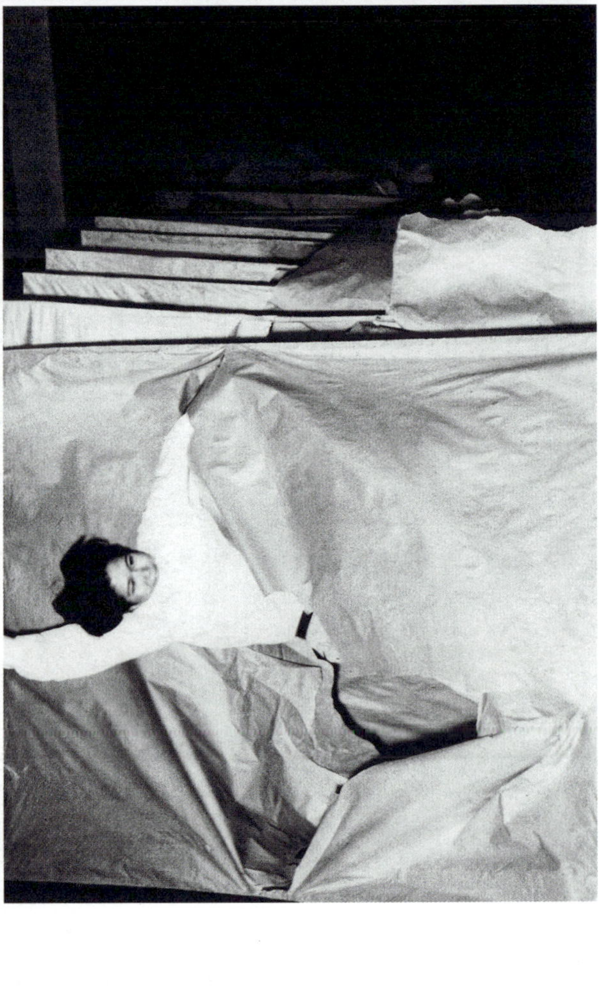

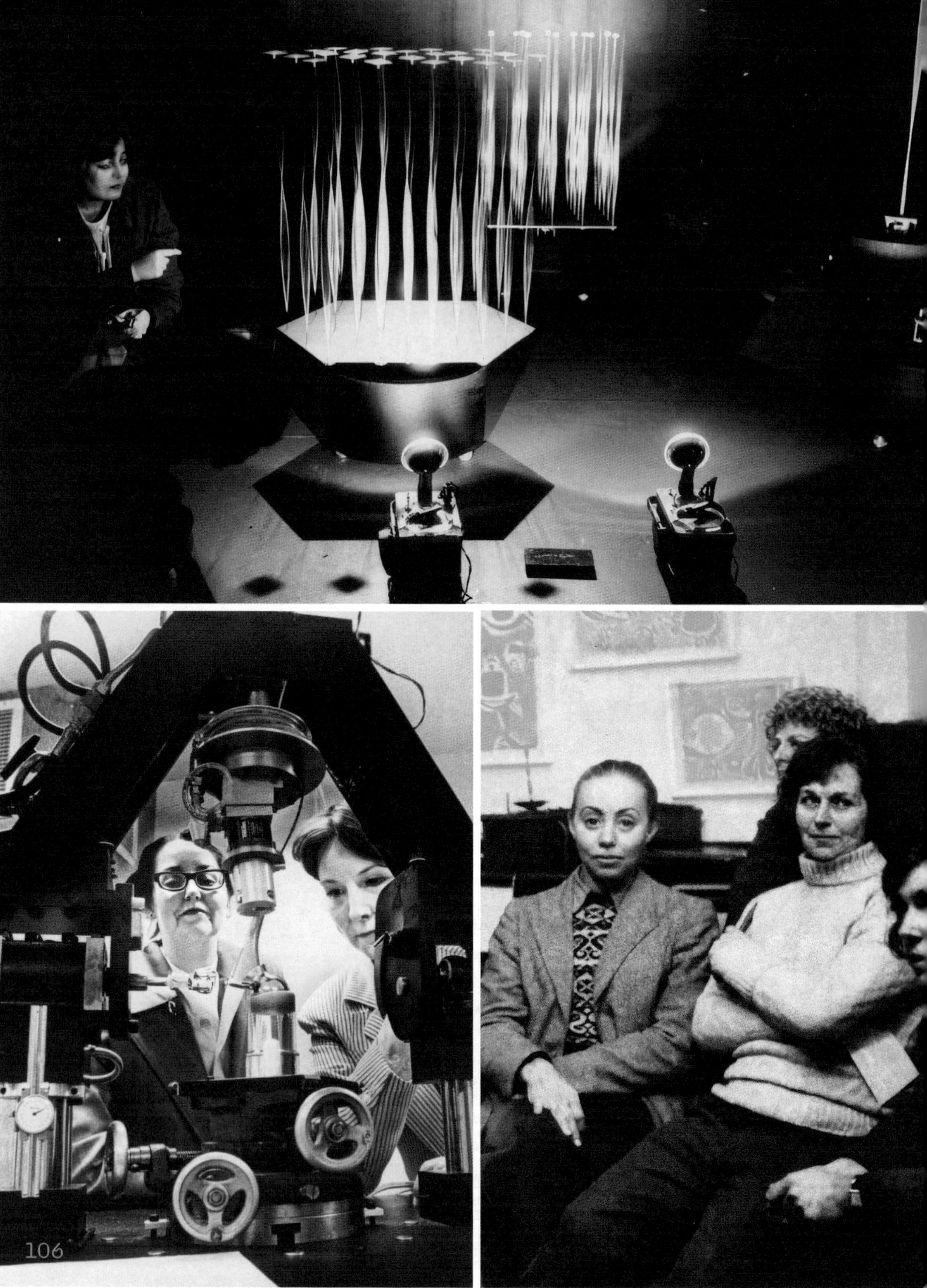

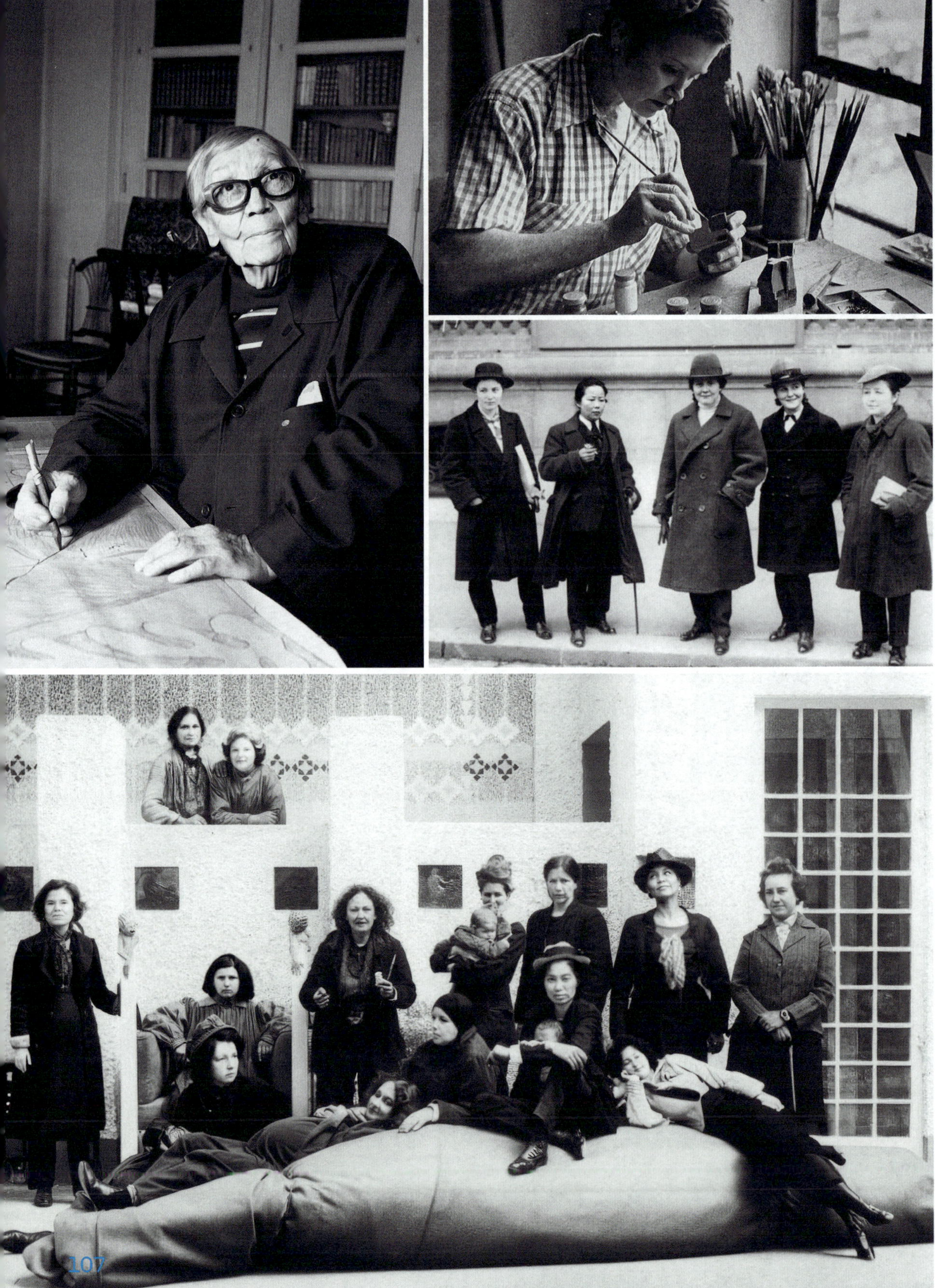

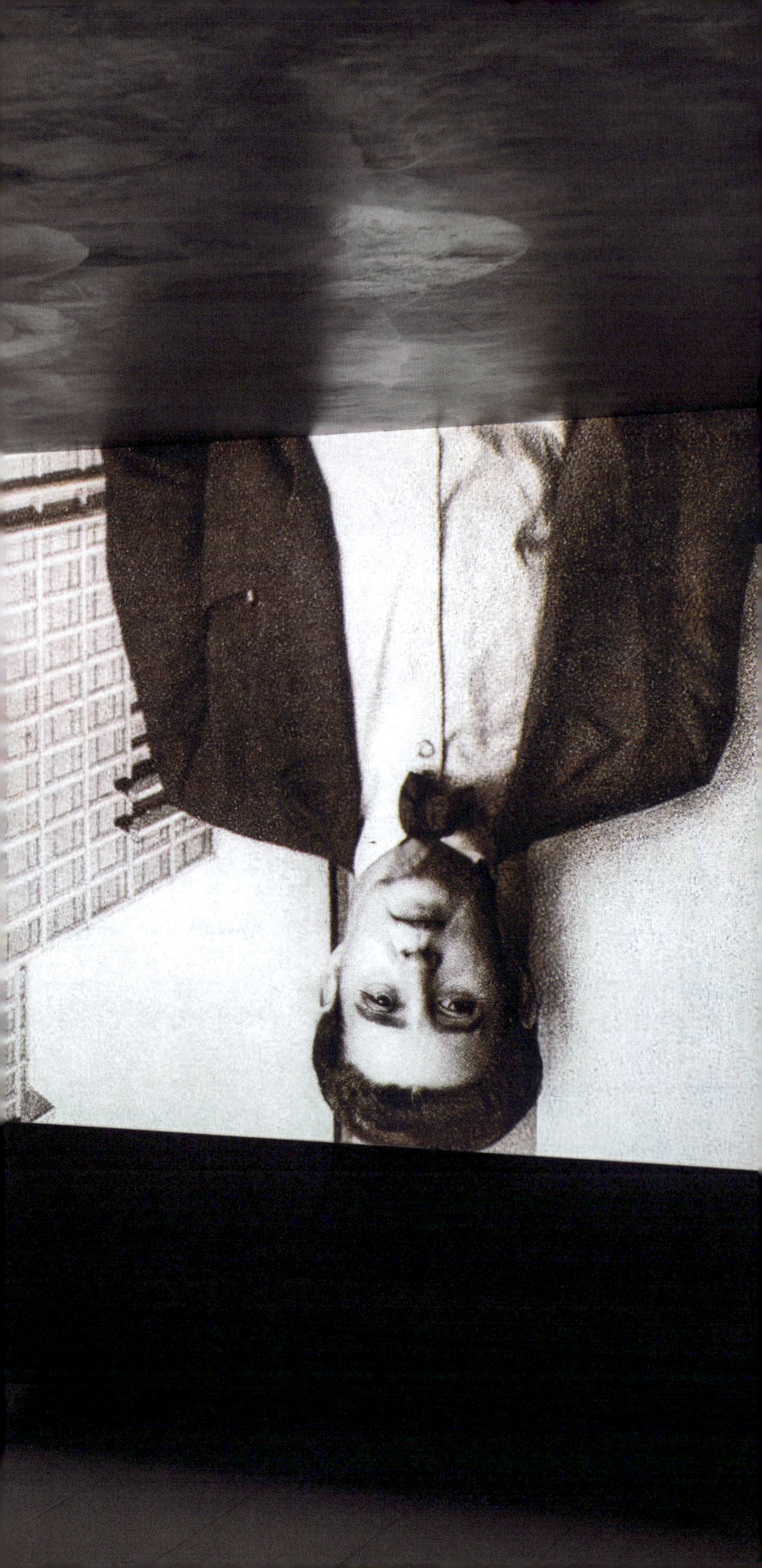

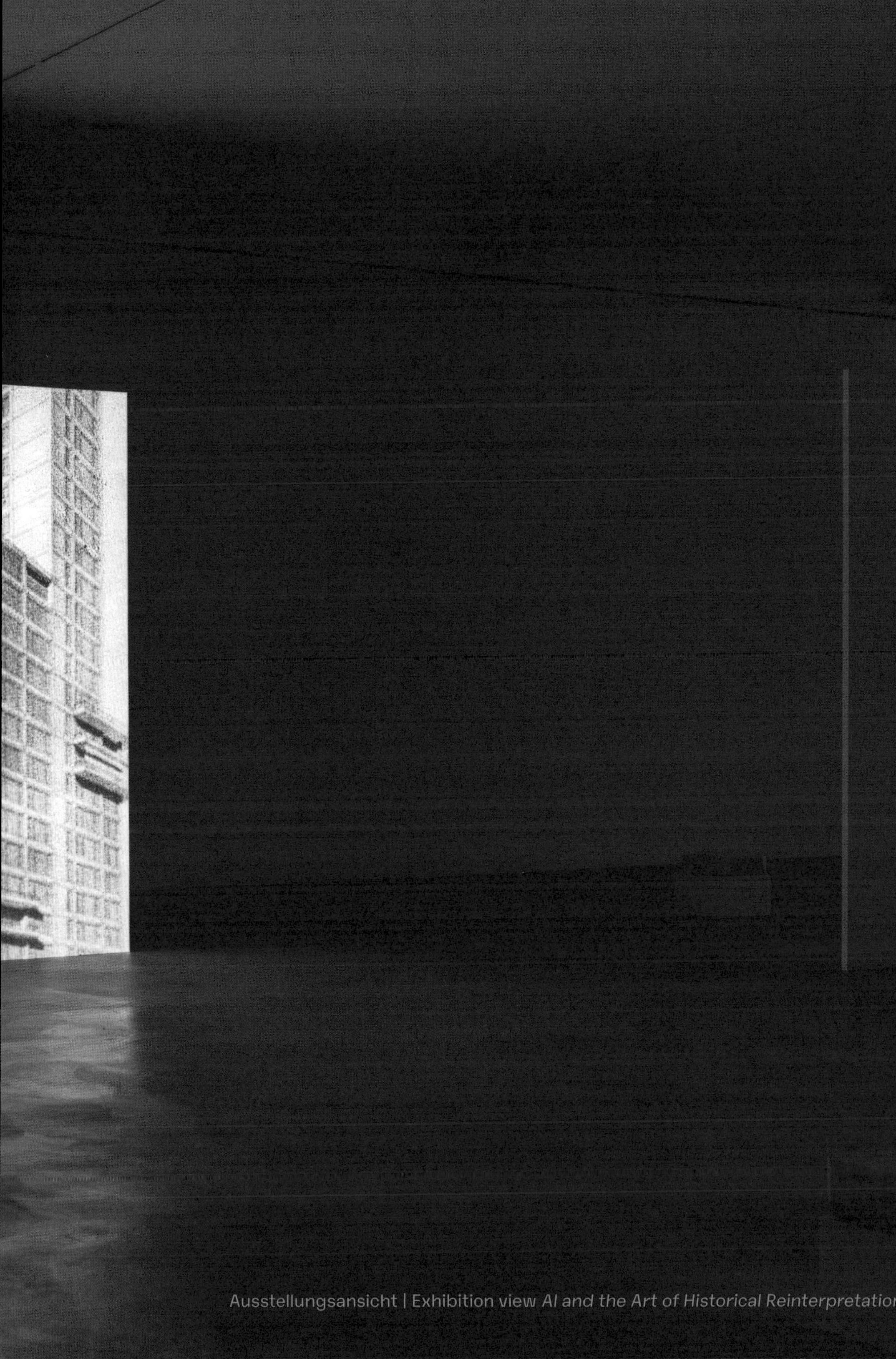

Ausstellungsansicht | Exhibition view *AI and the Art of Historical Reinterpretation*

AI and History

AI and the Art of Historical Reinterpretation
Filling Gender Bias Gaps, Data Set
VALIE EXPORT Center Linz,
work in progress since 2022

The strategy of the project is based on the targeted reconstruction and restaging of iconic photographs of important artists and scientists. By replacing the original, mostly male-dominated performers with FLINTA* people, a fictional reality is created that enables an alternative historical narrative. These 'fictional archives' are more than just artistic commentaries; they function as counter-archives that challenge the existing narratives of art history and expand them to include diverse, often overlooked perspectives.

The project raises important ethical questions: How far can AI go in reshaping history? How can we ensure that these technologies do not repeat the same systemic errors they are trying to correct? By making historical distortions and exclusions visible, the project not only calls for a re-evaluation of the past, but also opens up a visionary perspective for the future. The artist's collection of images is constantly growing and can be evaluated through data analyses in order to be incorporated both actively and passively into future AI systems. Through dissemination via digital platforms, this fictional history not only contributes to making cultural memory more diverse and equitable, but can also influence prospective AI models to promote a more inclusive and equitable future.

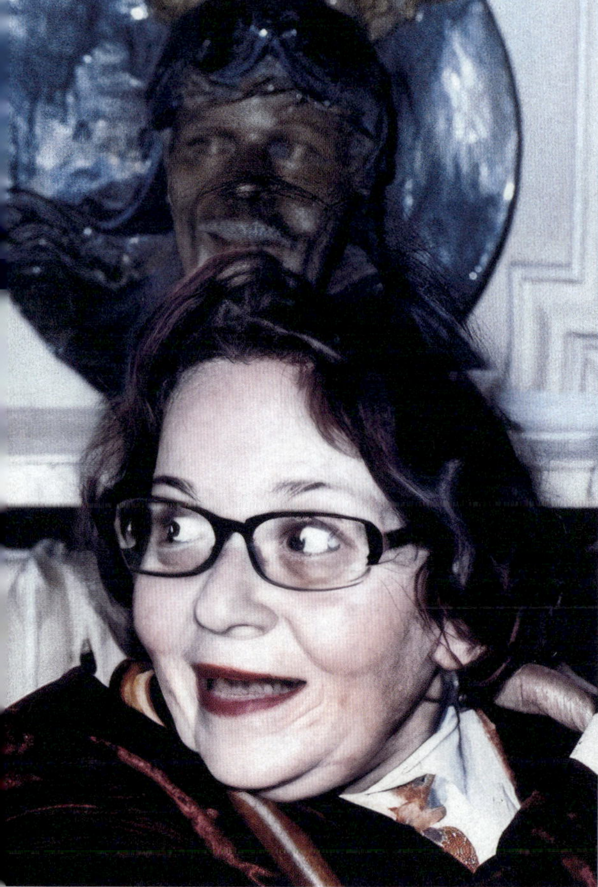

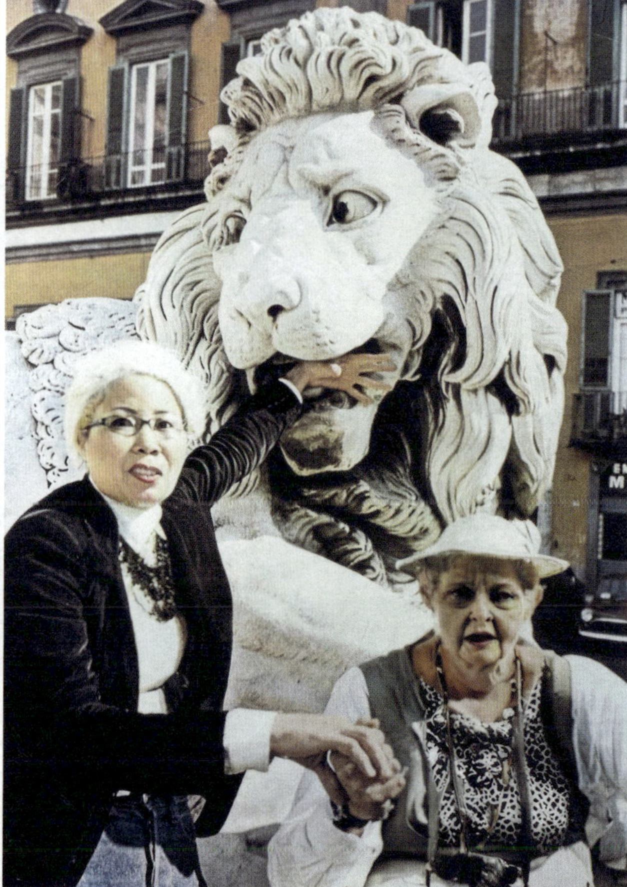

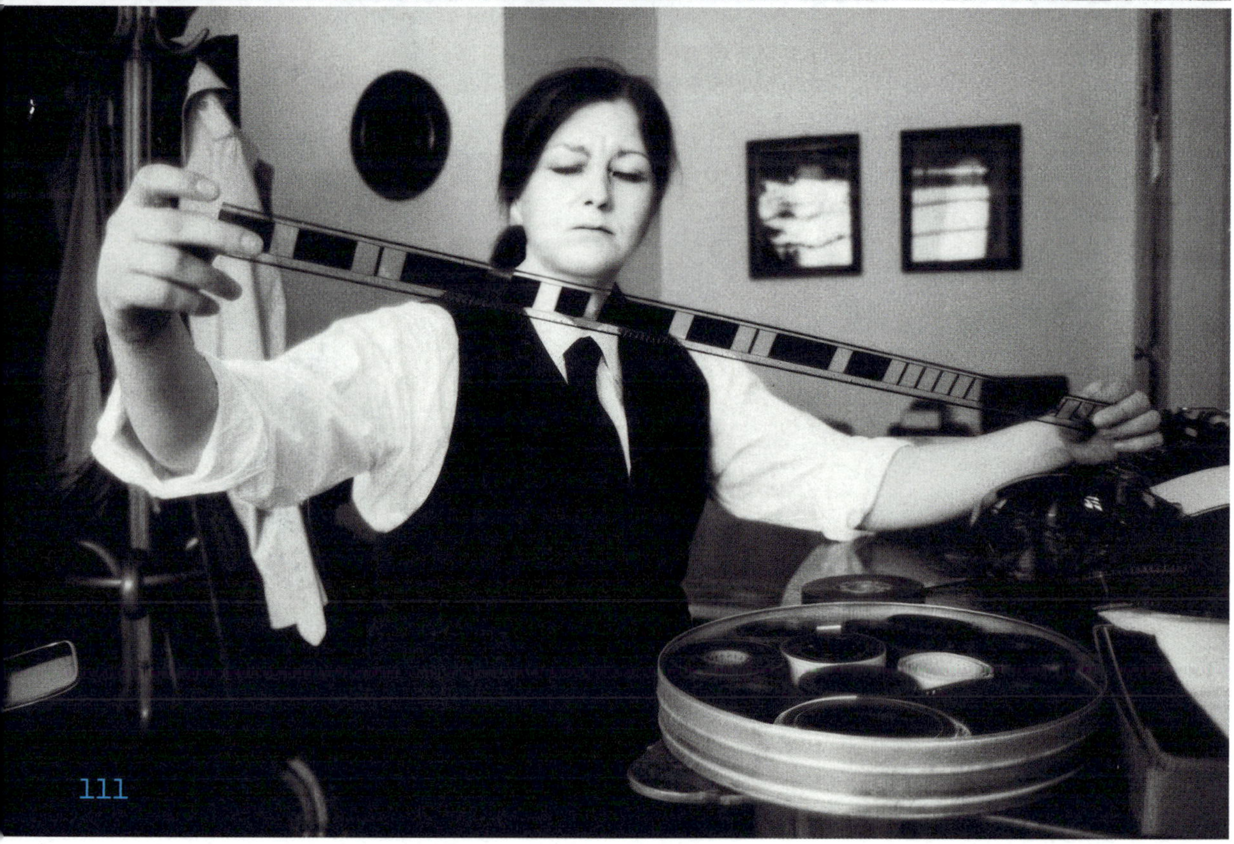

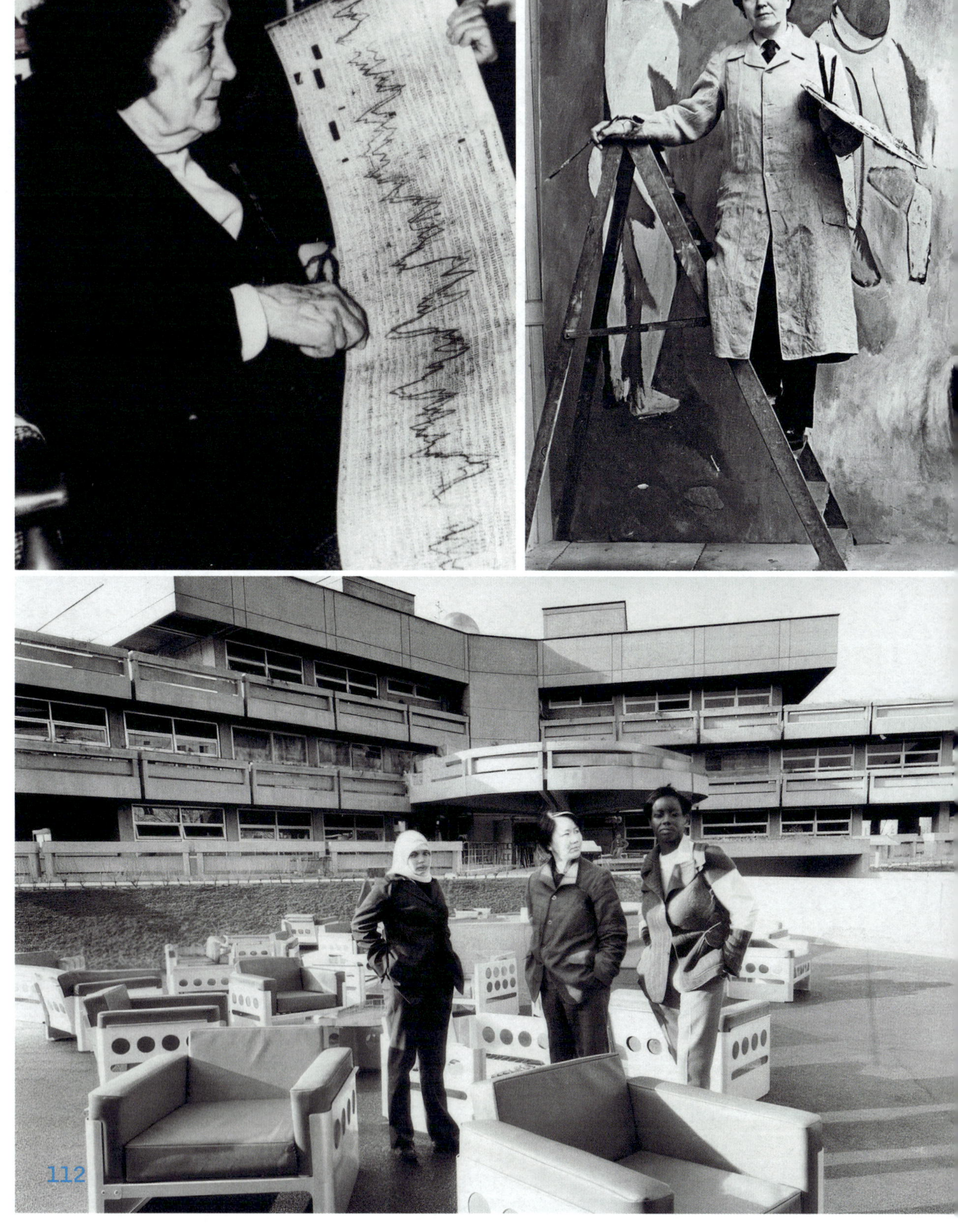

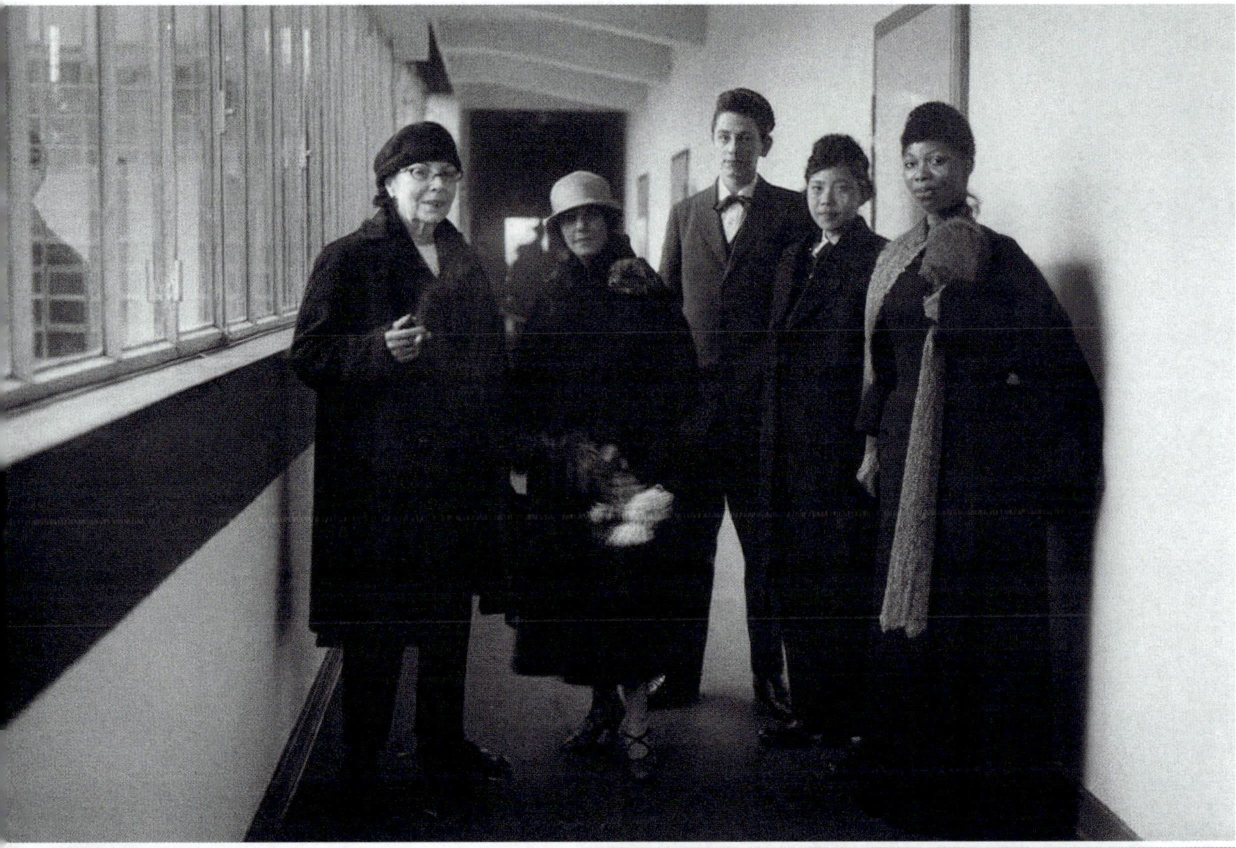

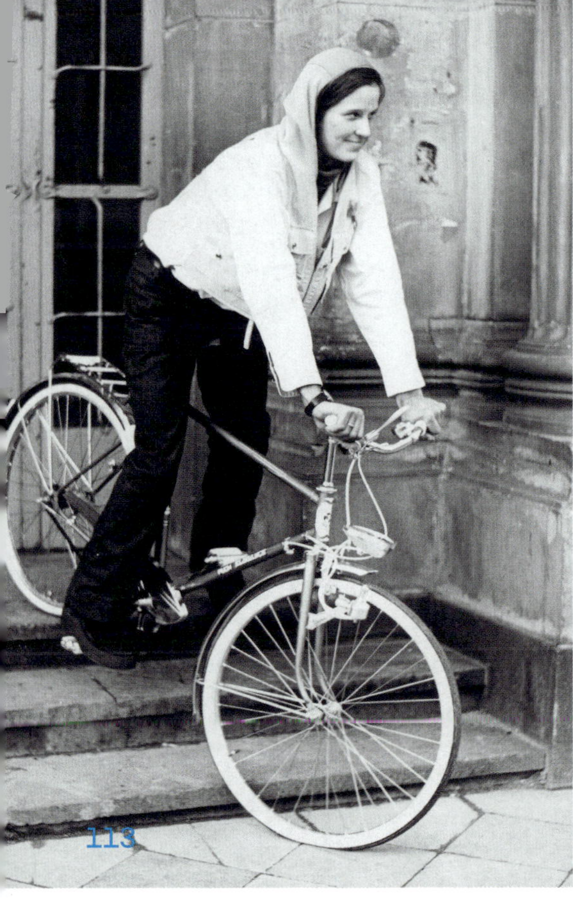

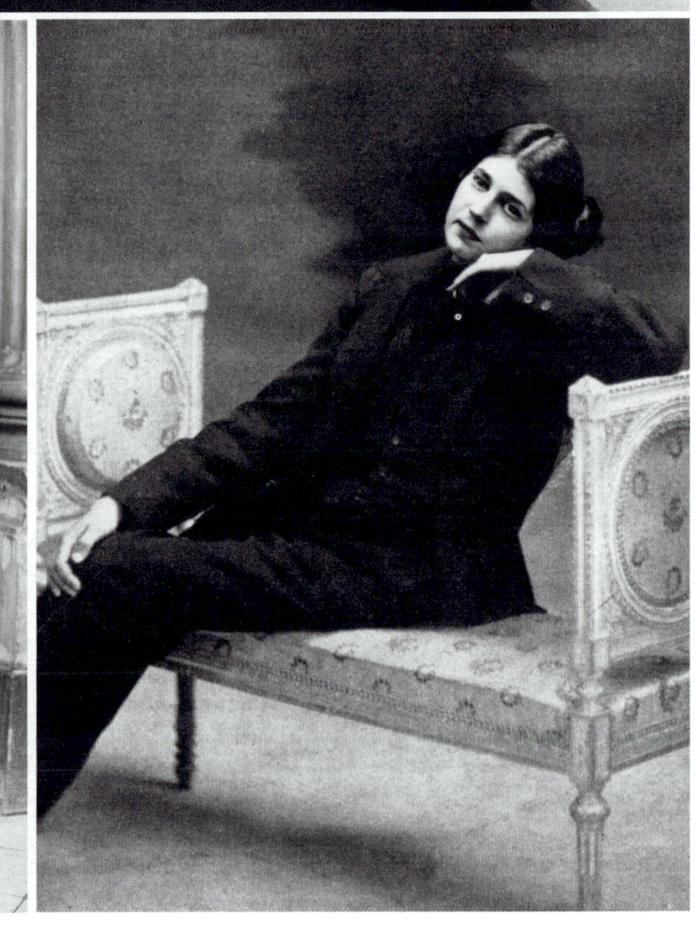

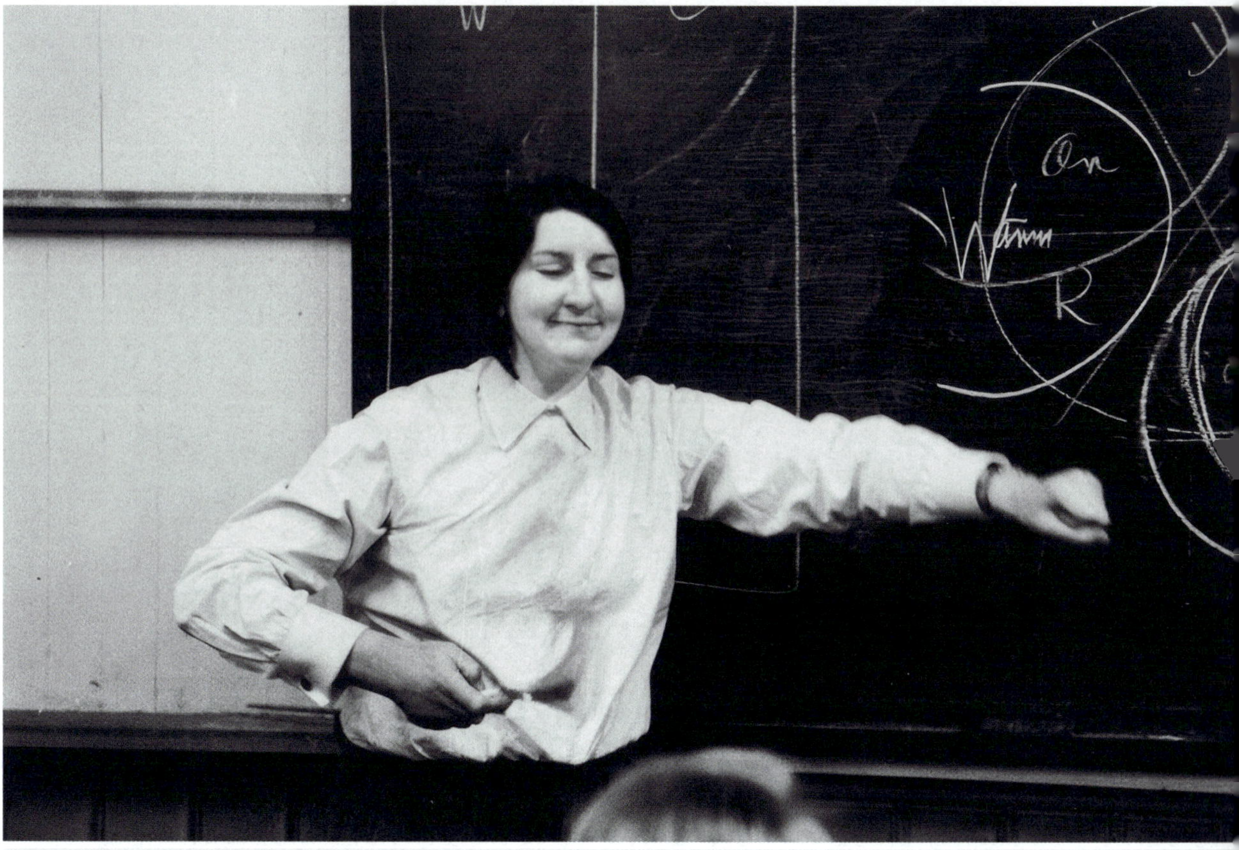

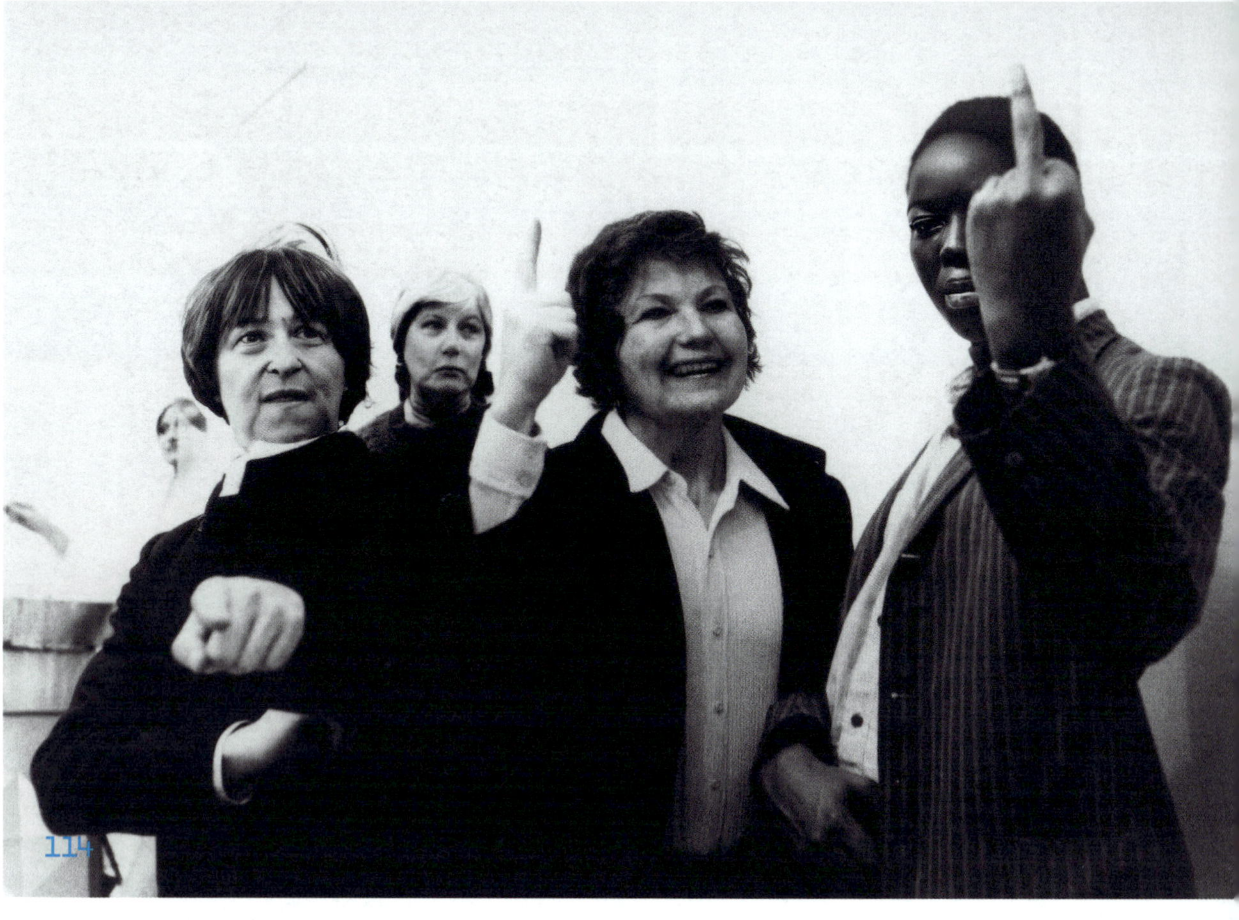

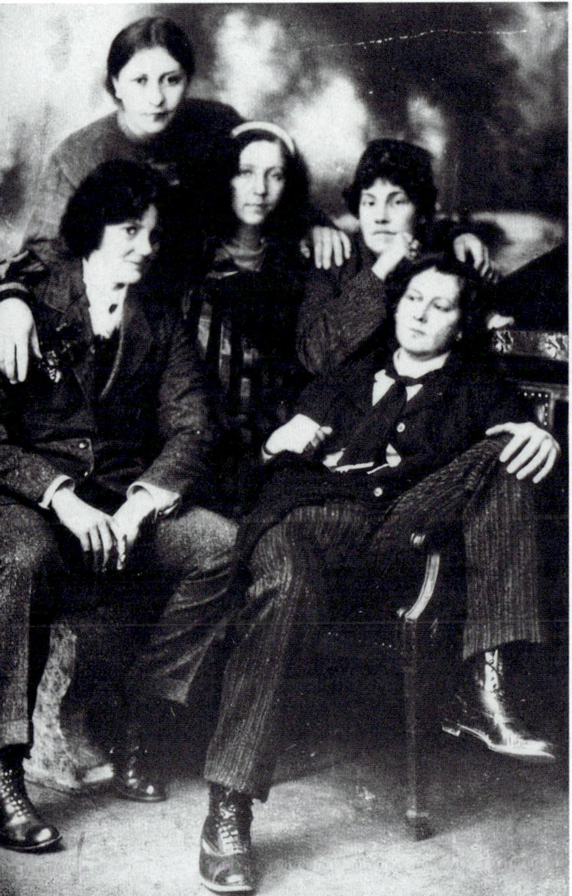

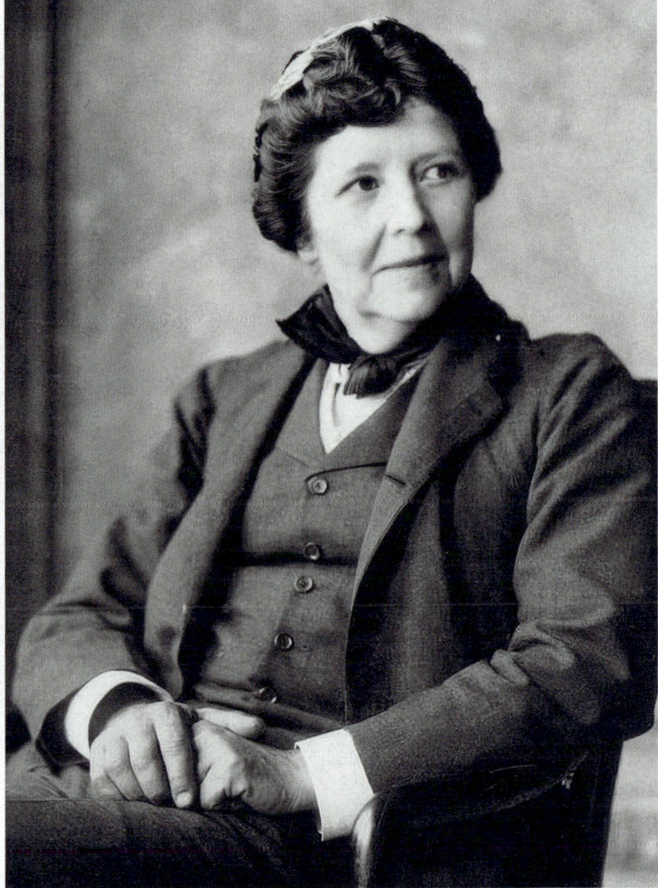

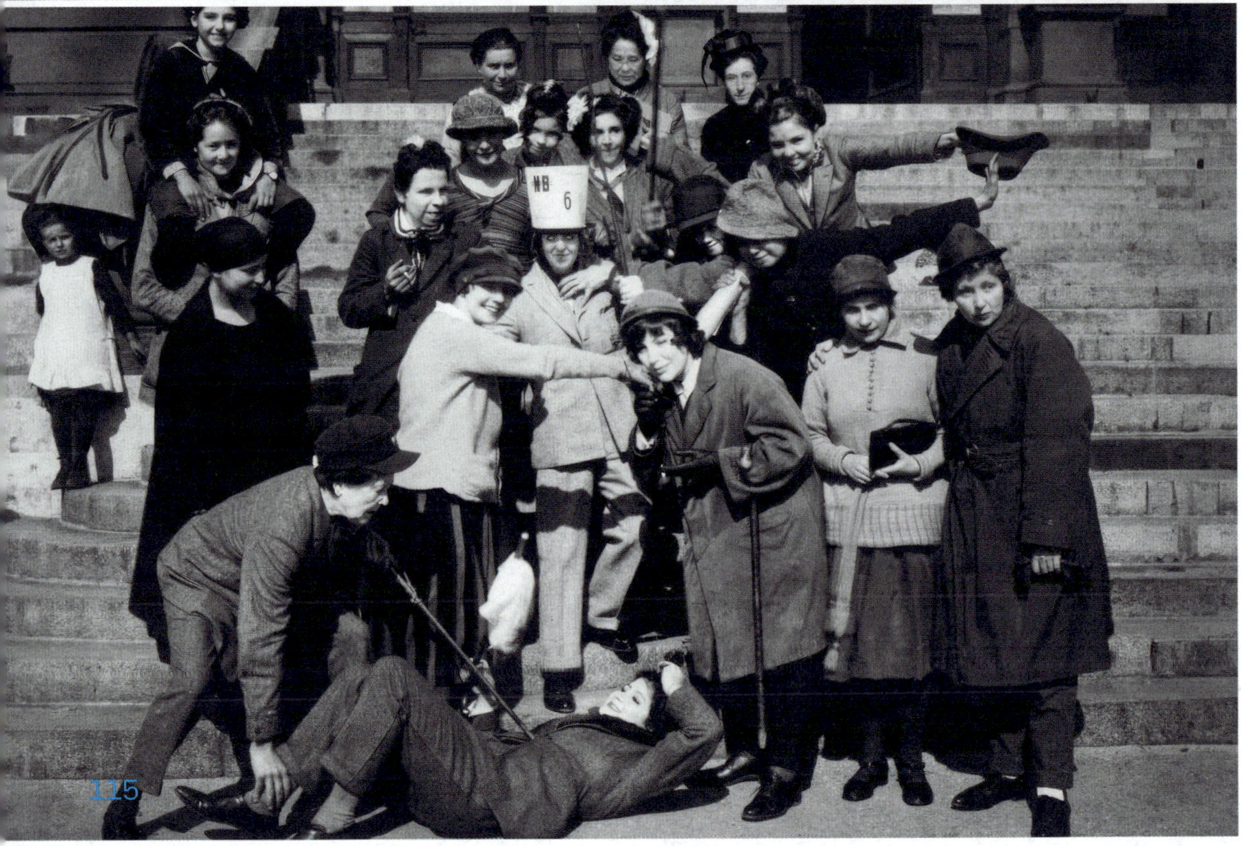

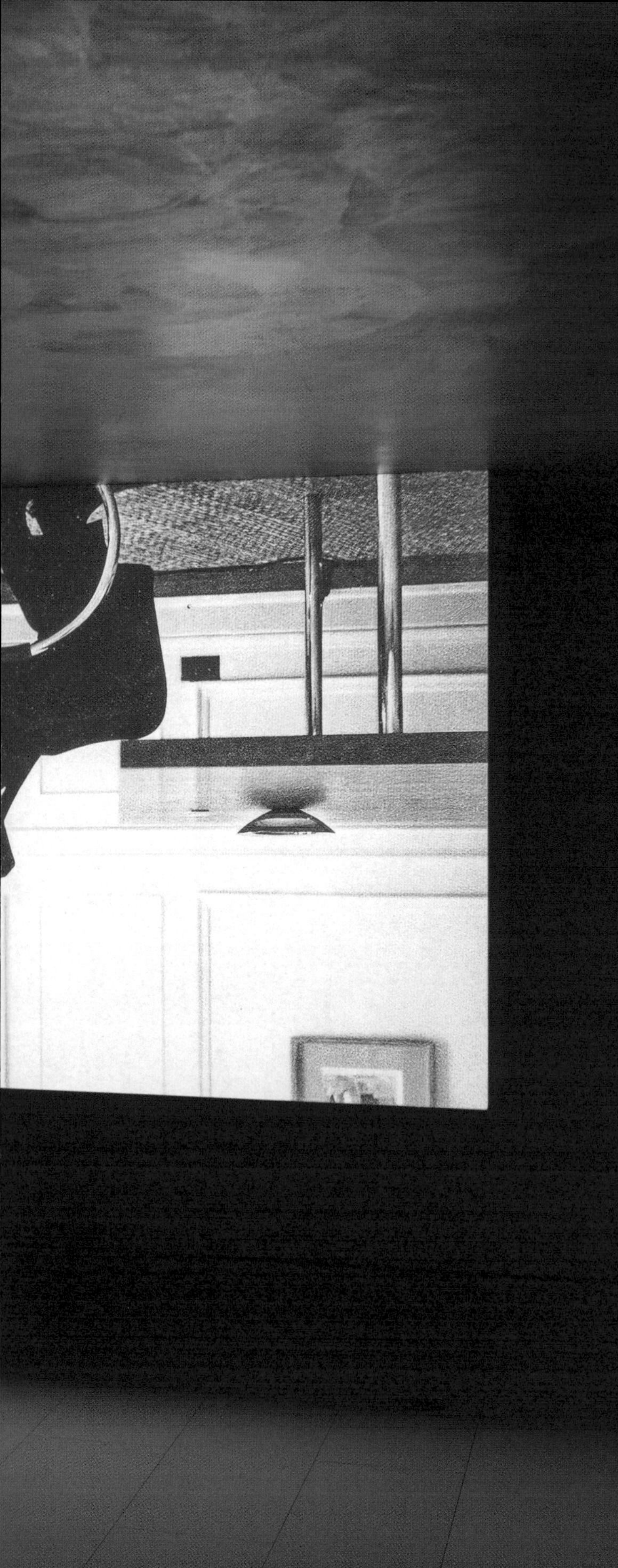

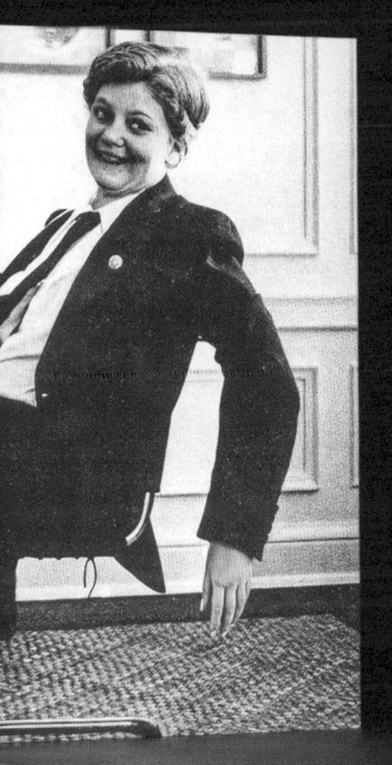

Ausstellungsansicht | Exhibition view *AI and the*

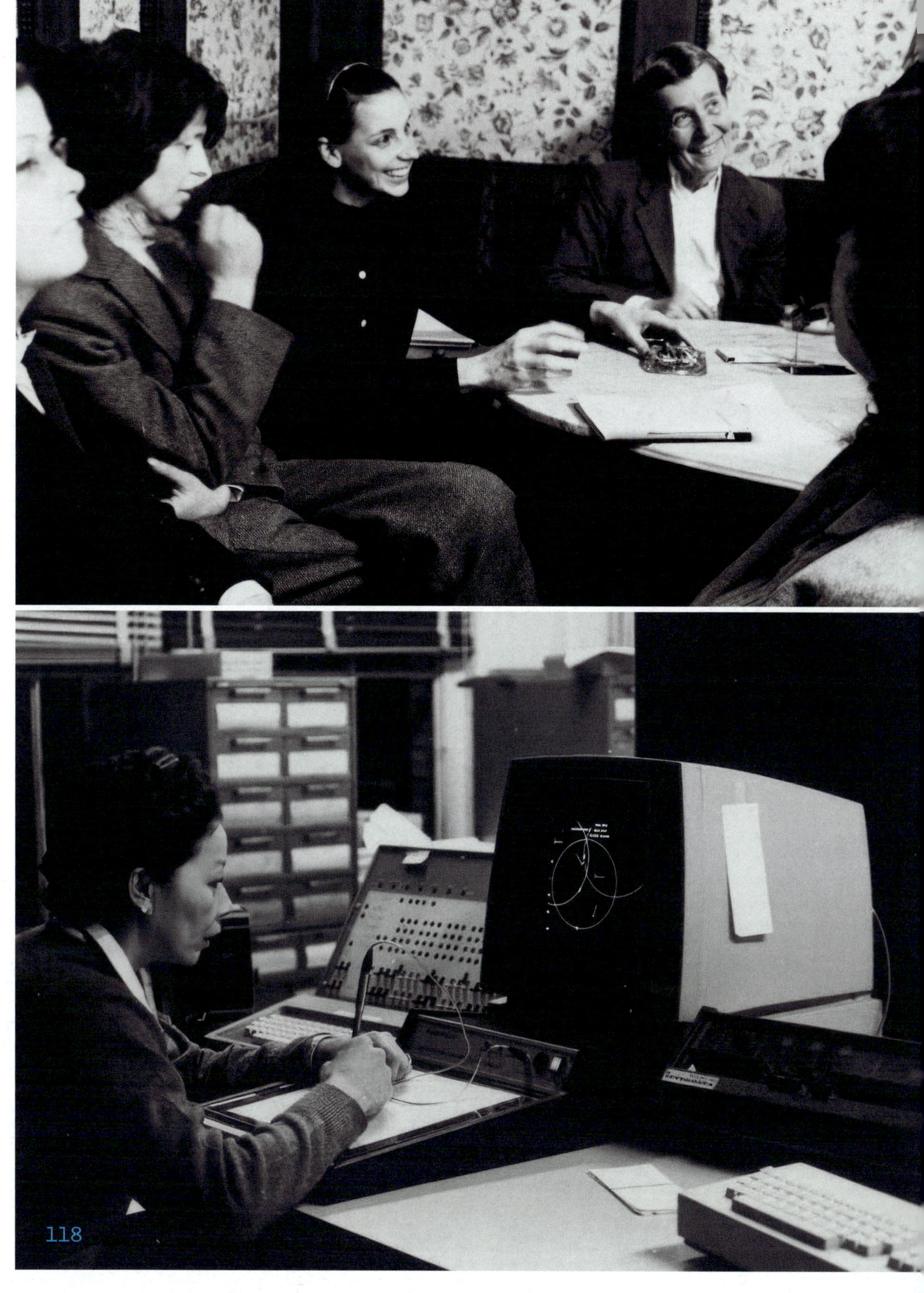

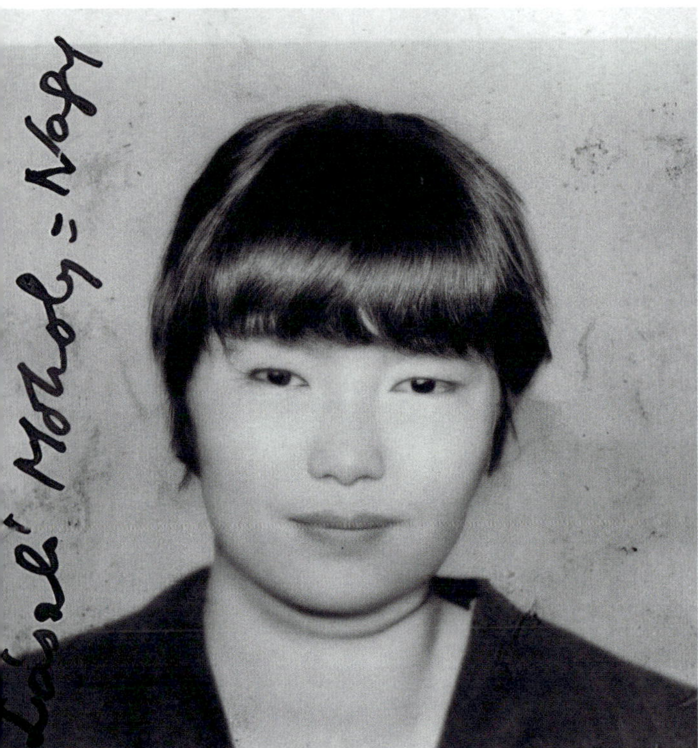
László Moholy-Nagy

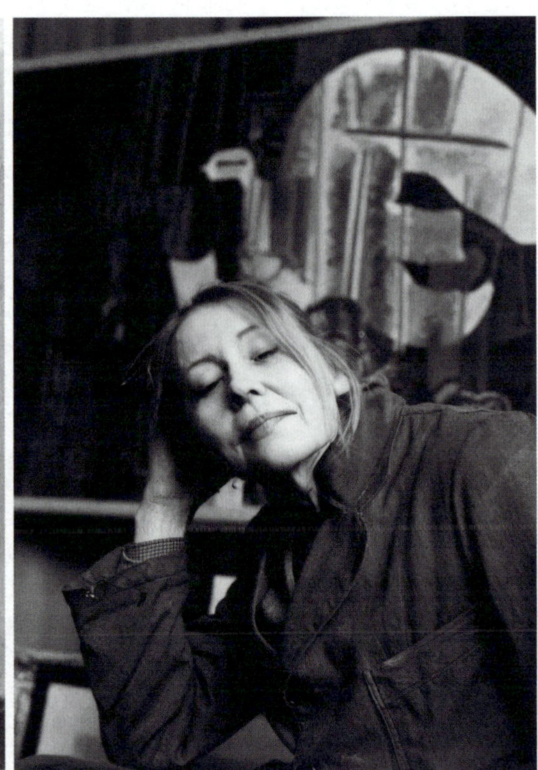

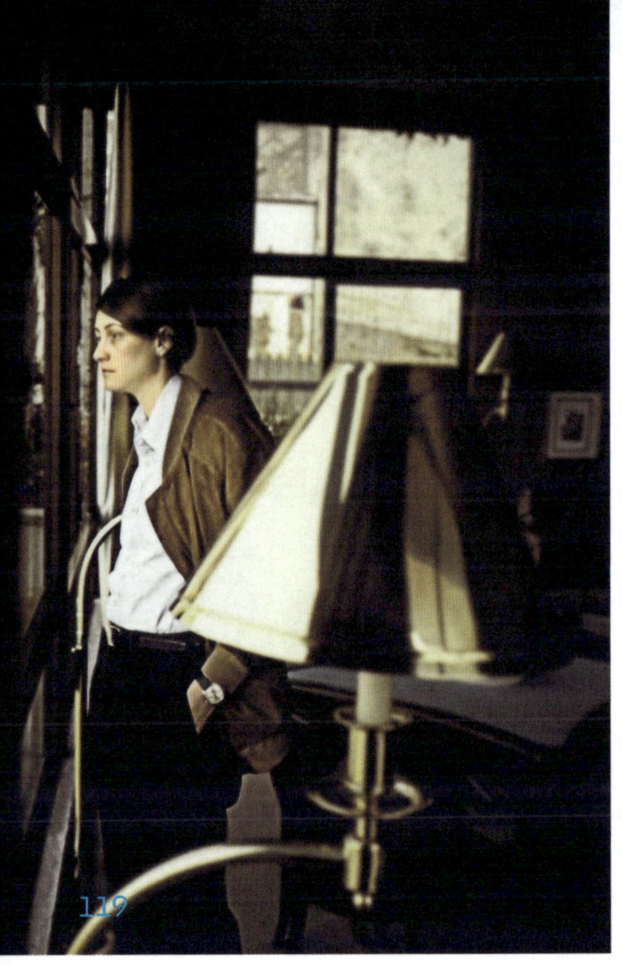

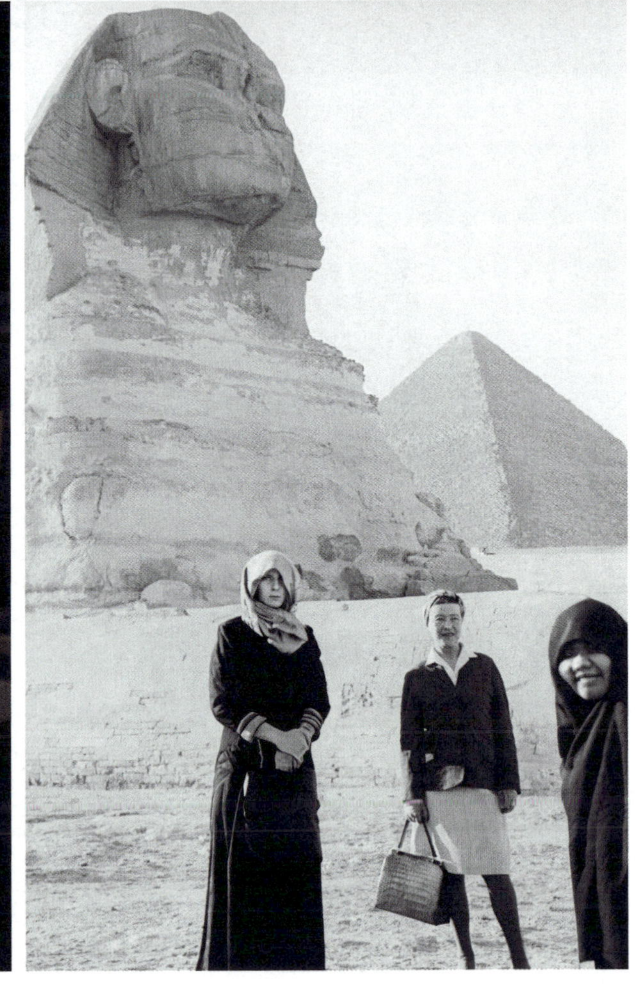

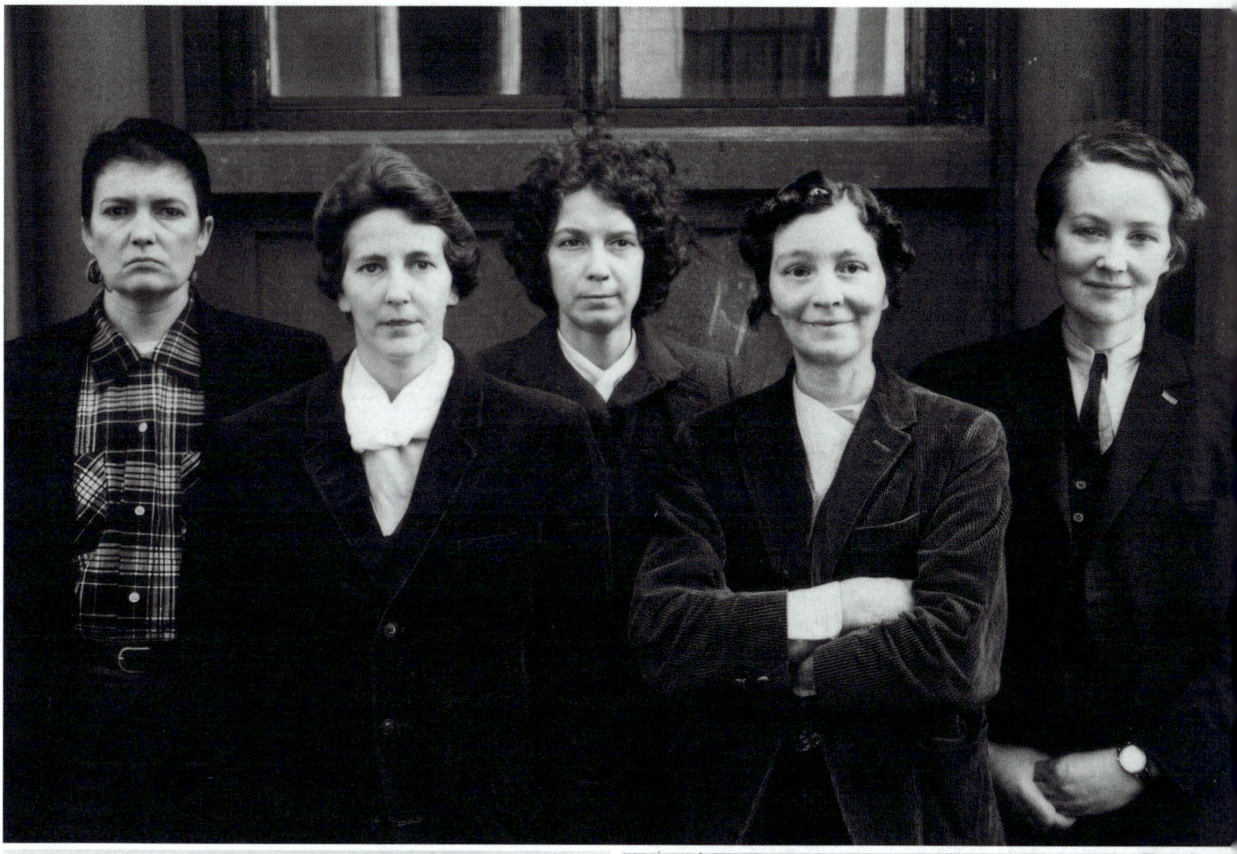

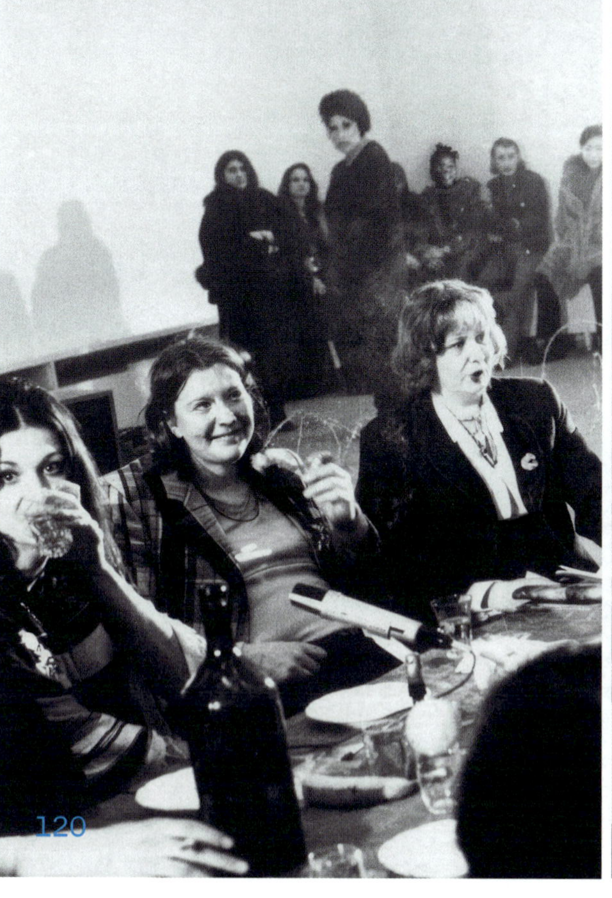

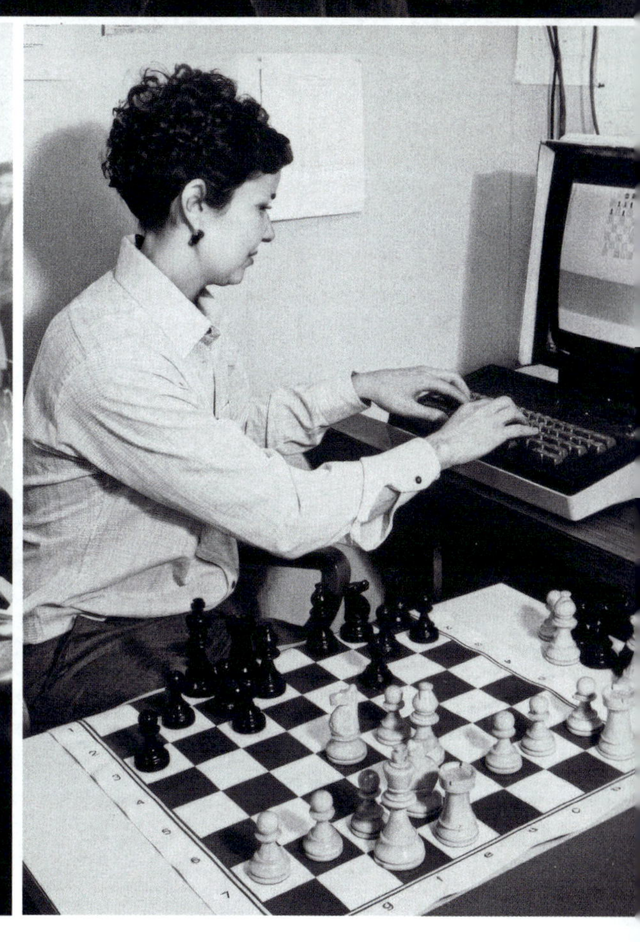

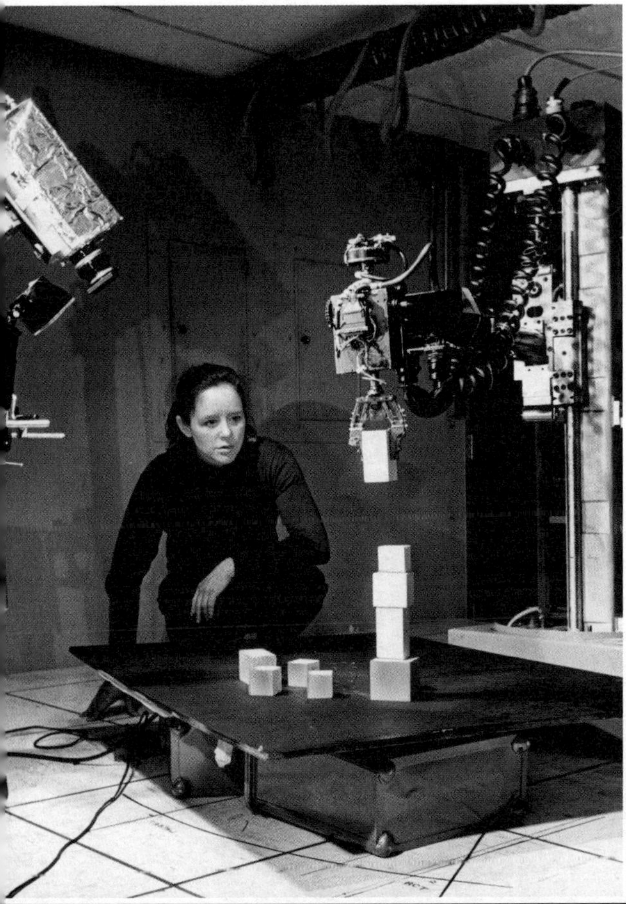

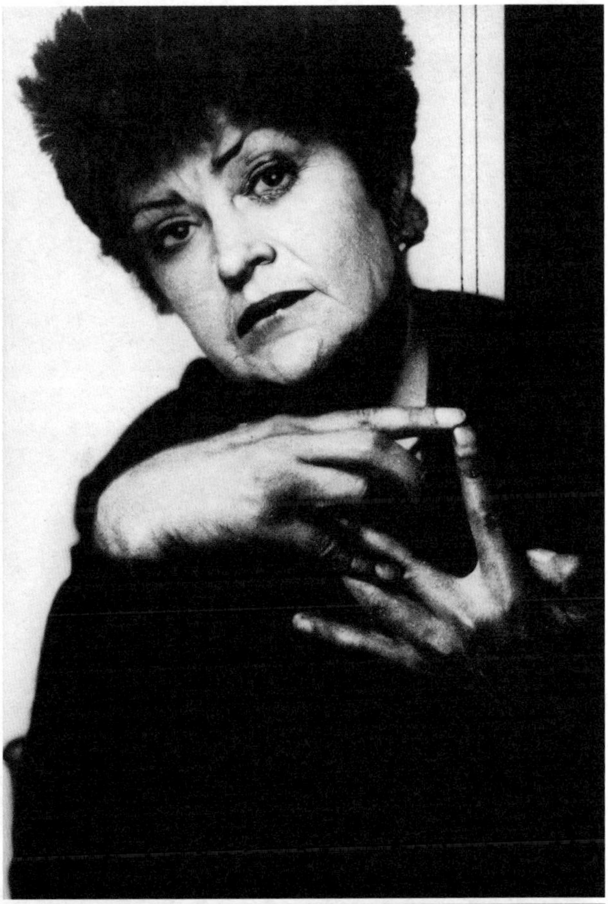

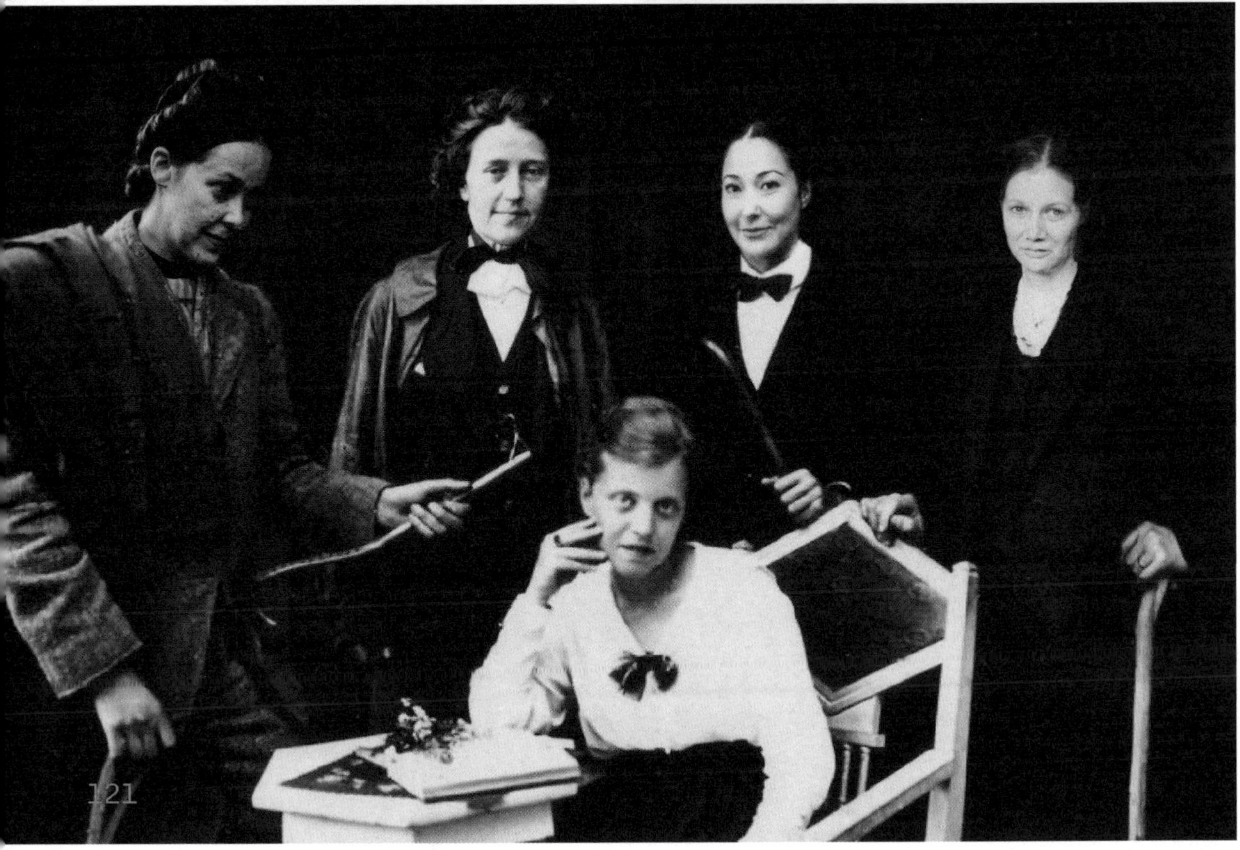

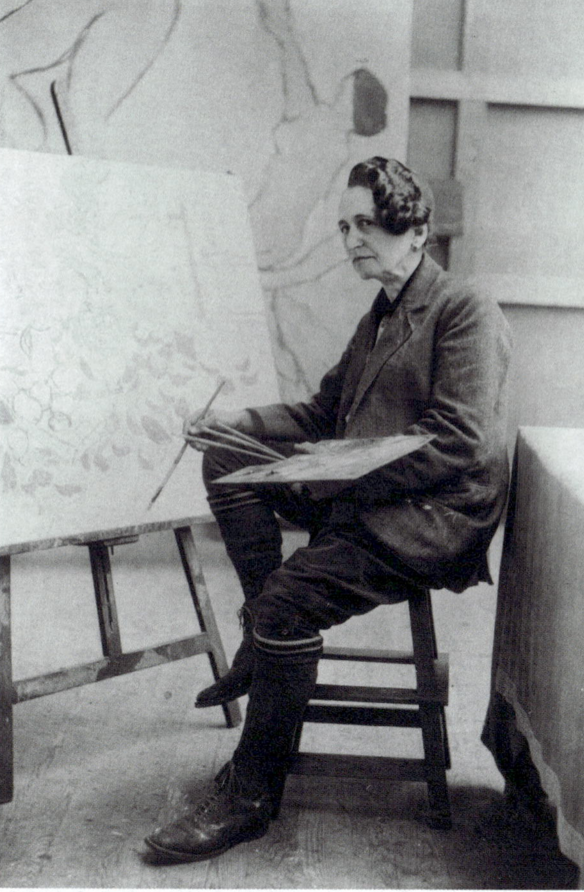

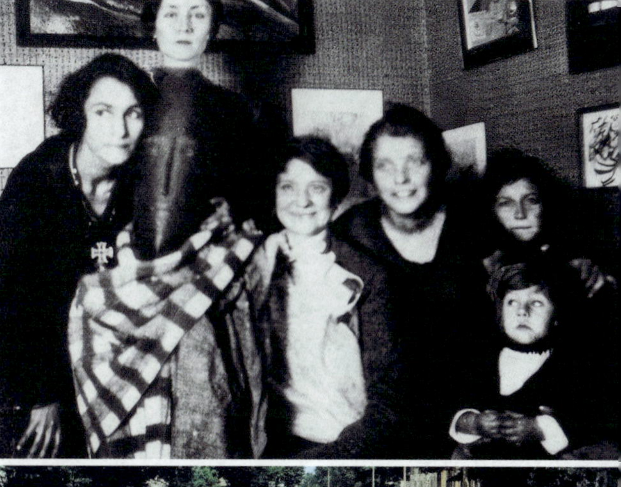

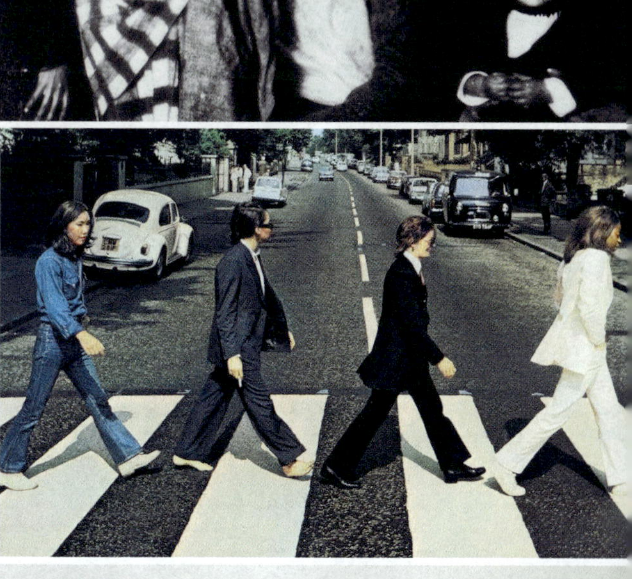

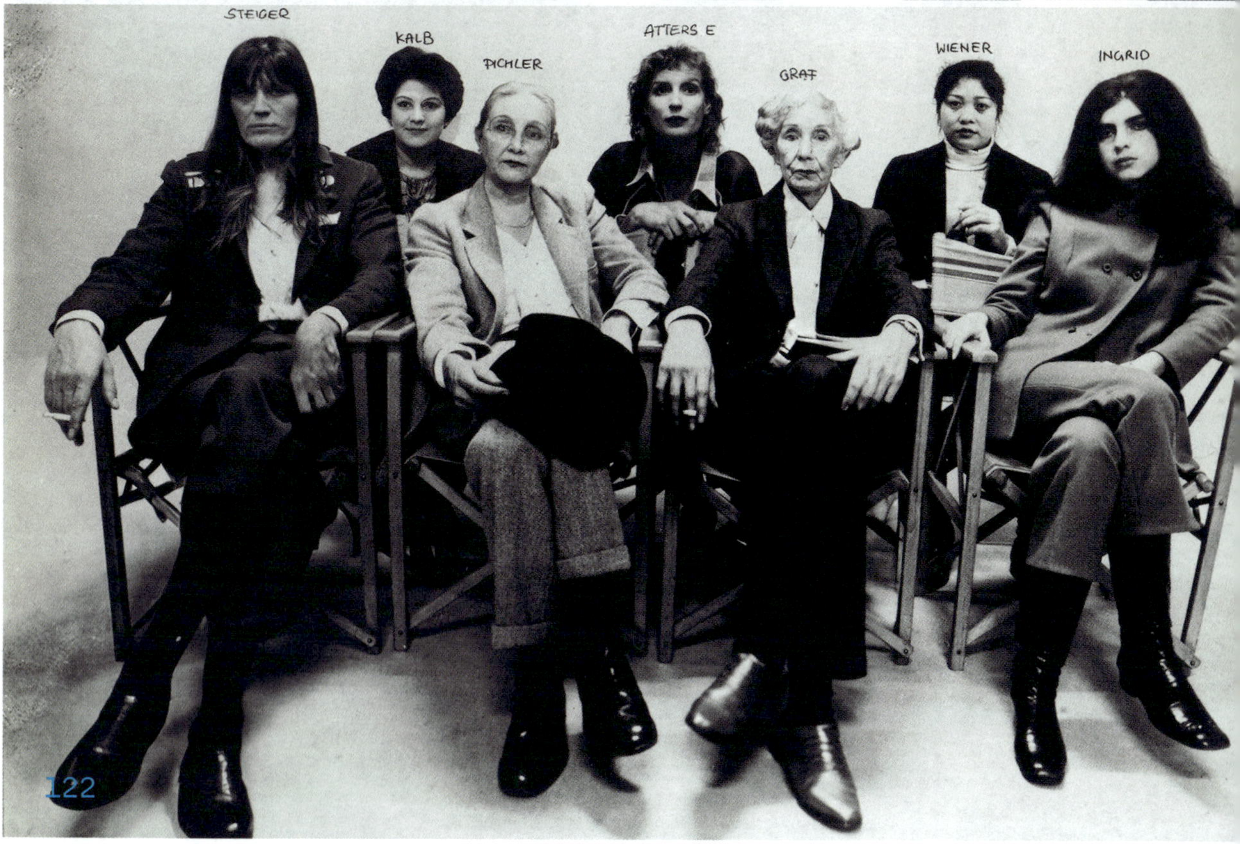

STEIGER KALB PICHLER ATTERS E GRAF WIENER INGRID

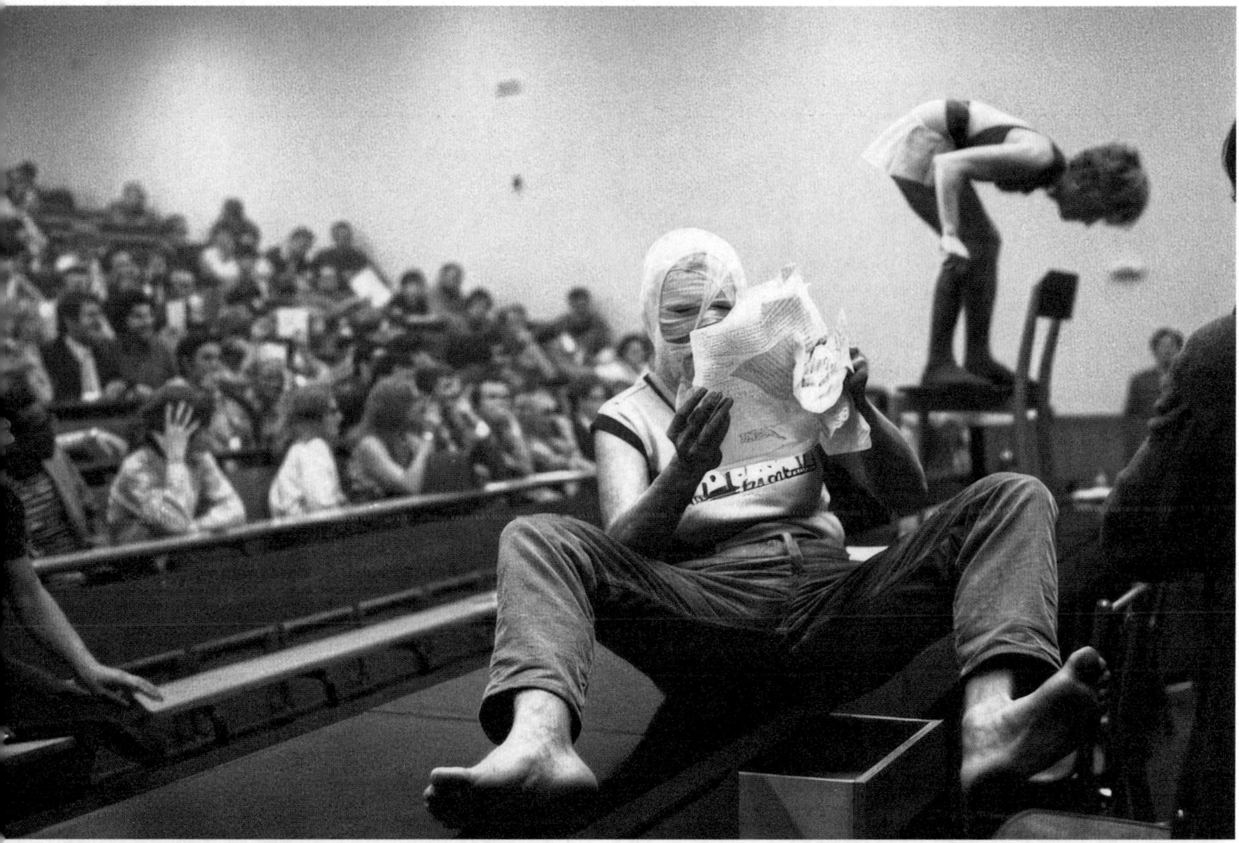

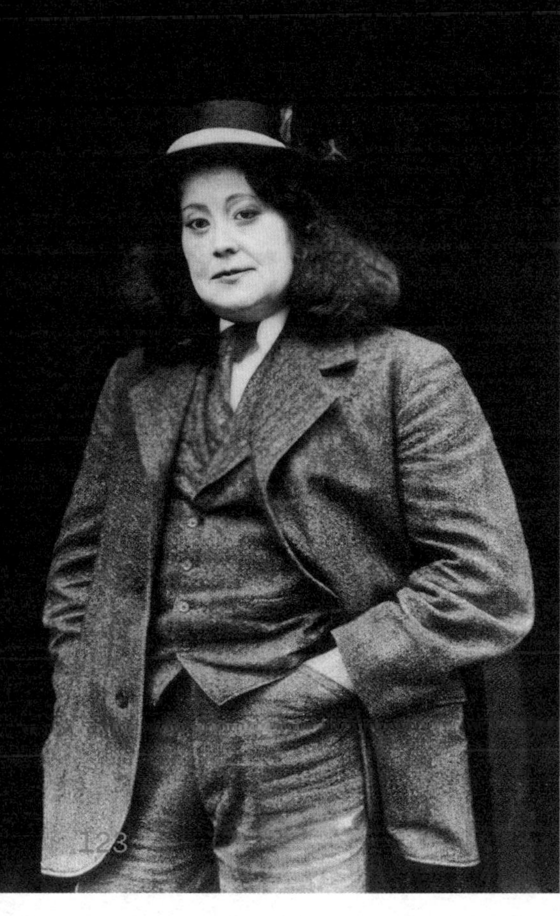

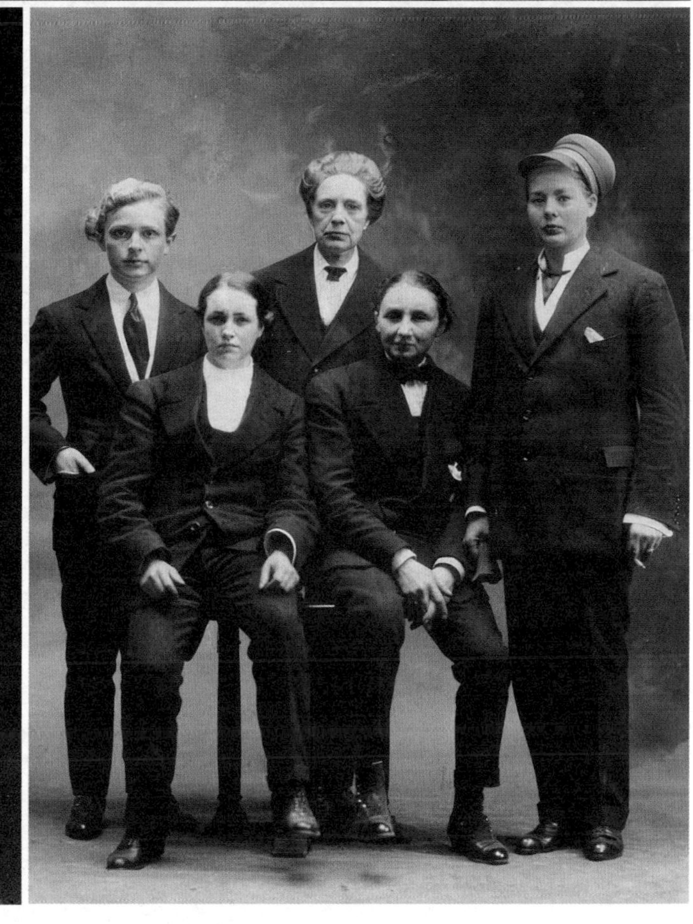

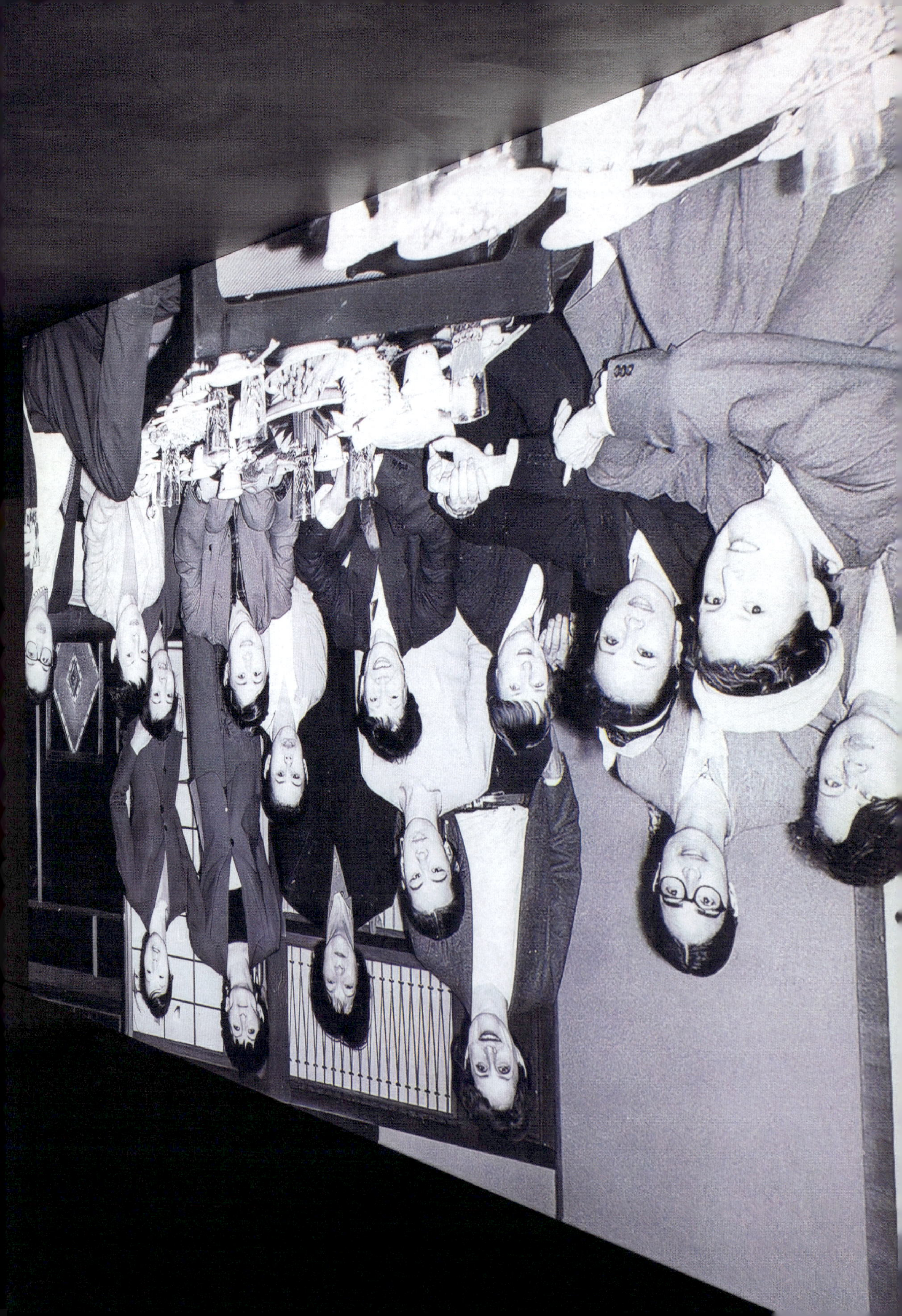

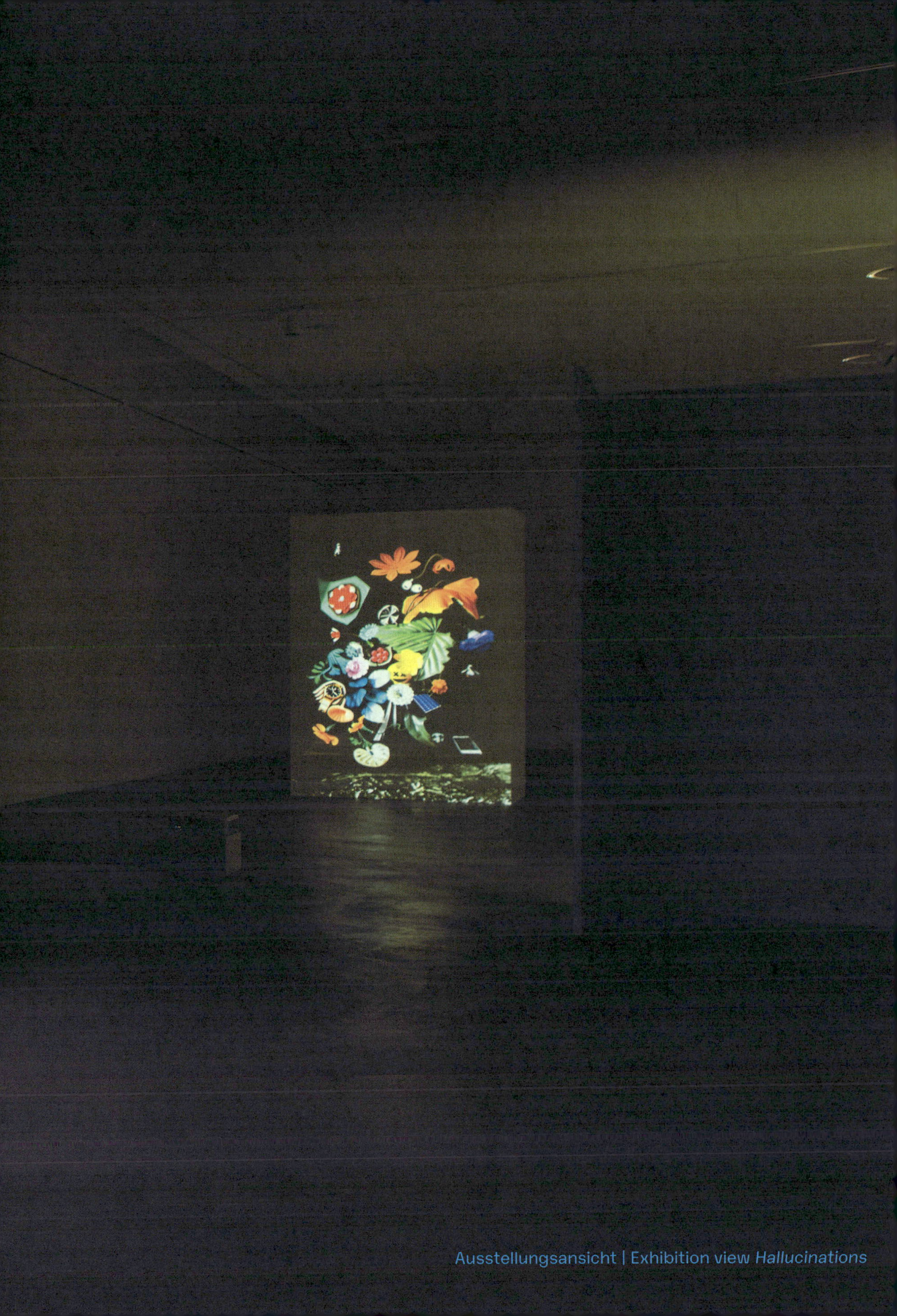

Ausstellungsansicht | Exhibition view *Hallucinations*

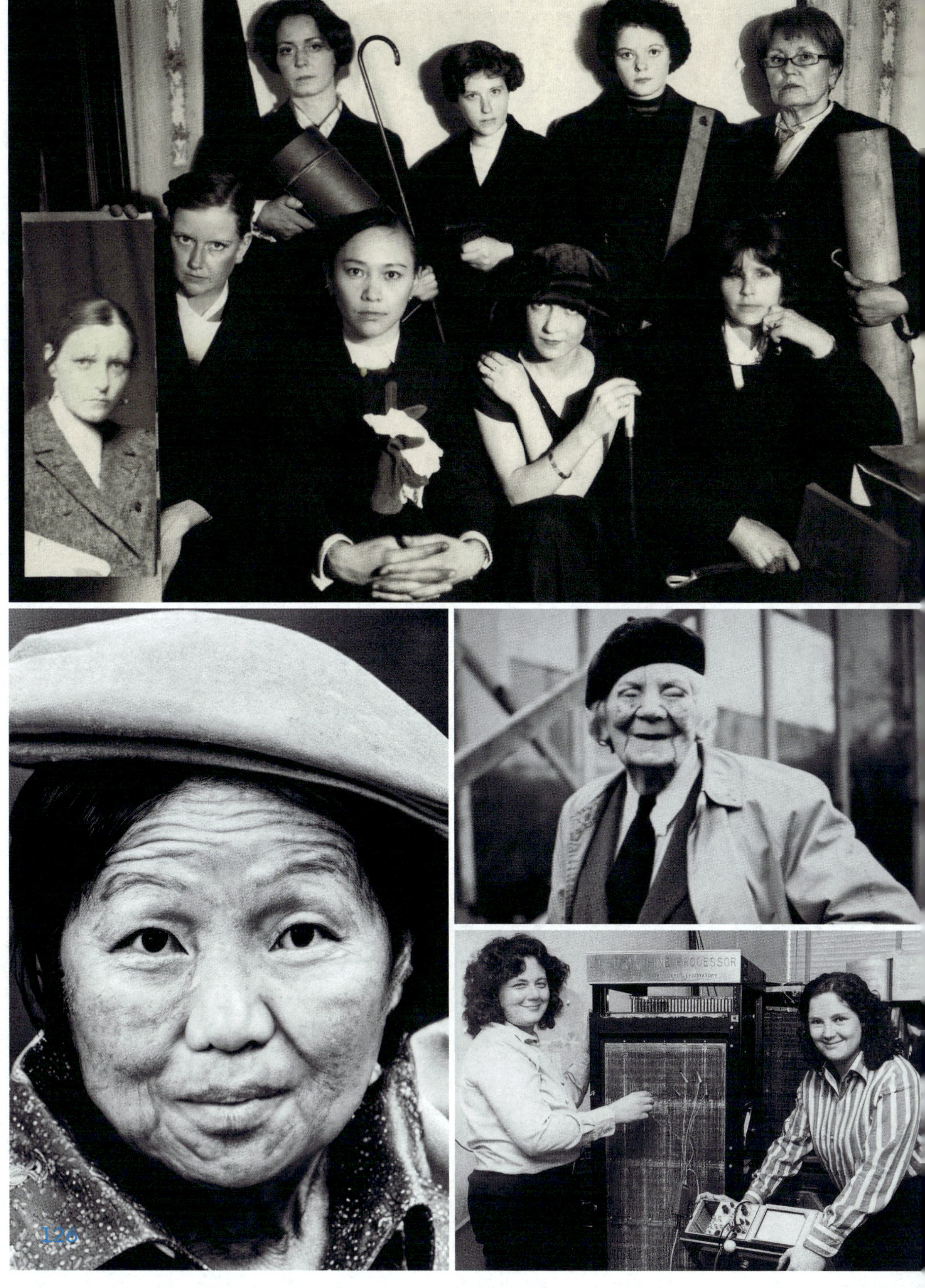
PROCESSOR

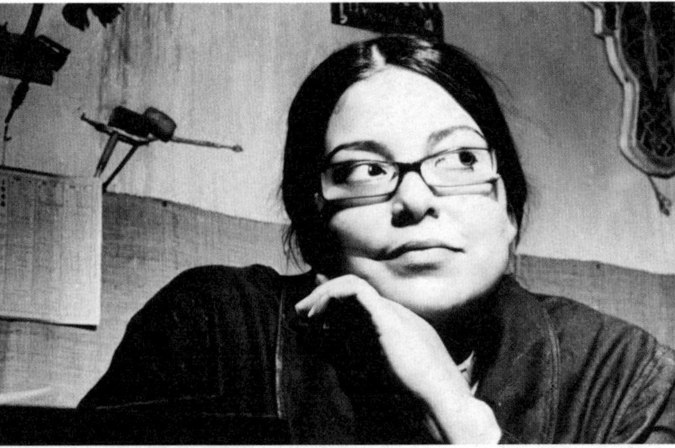

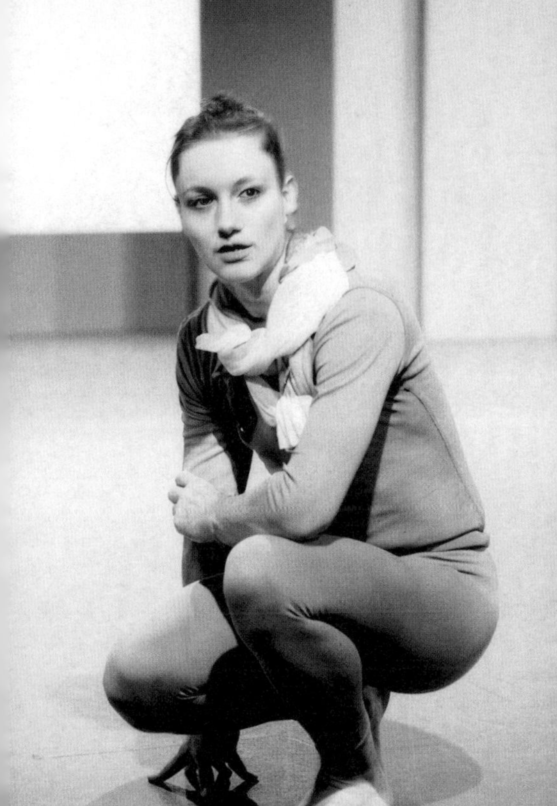

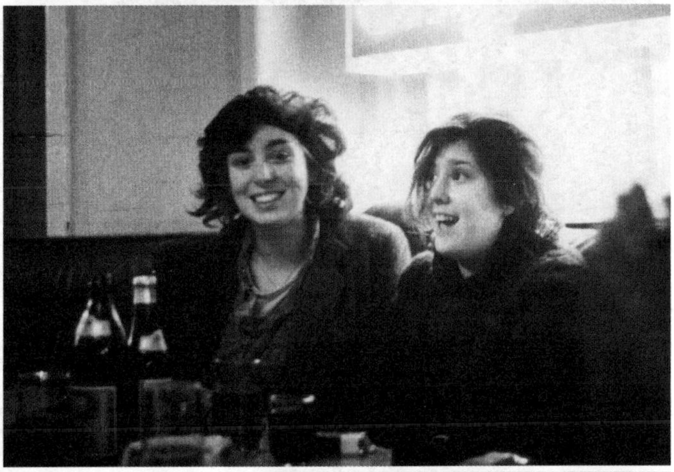

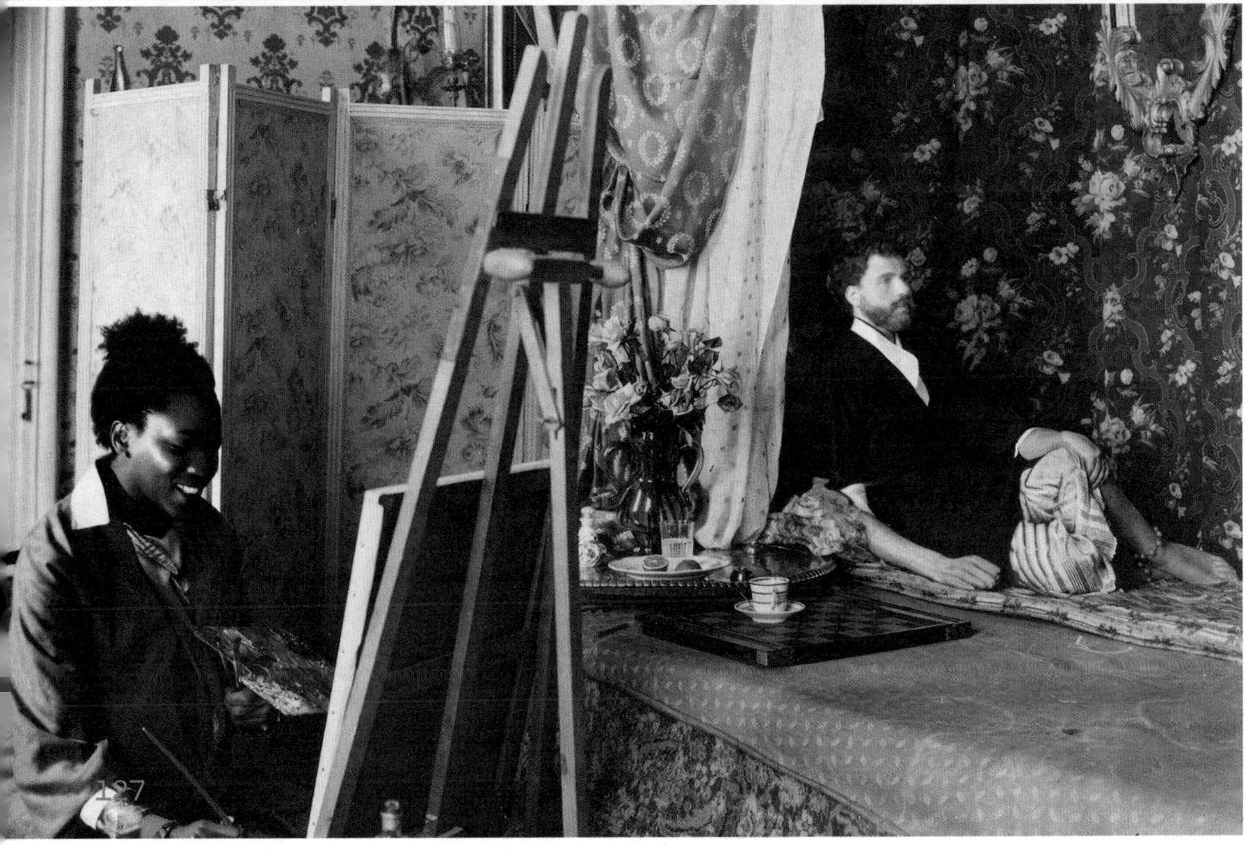

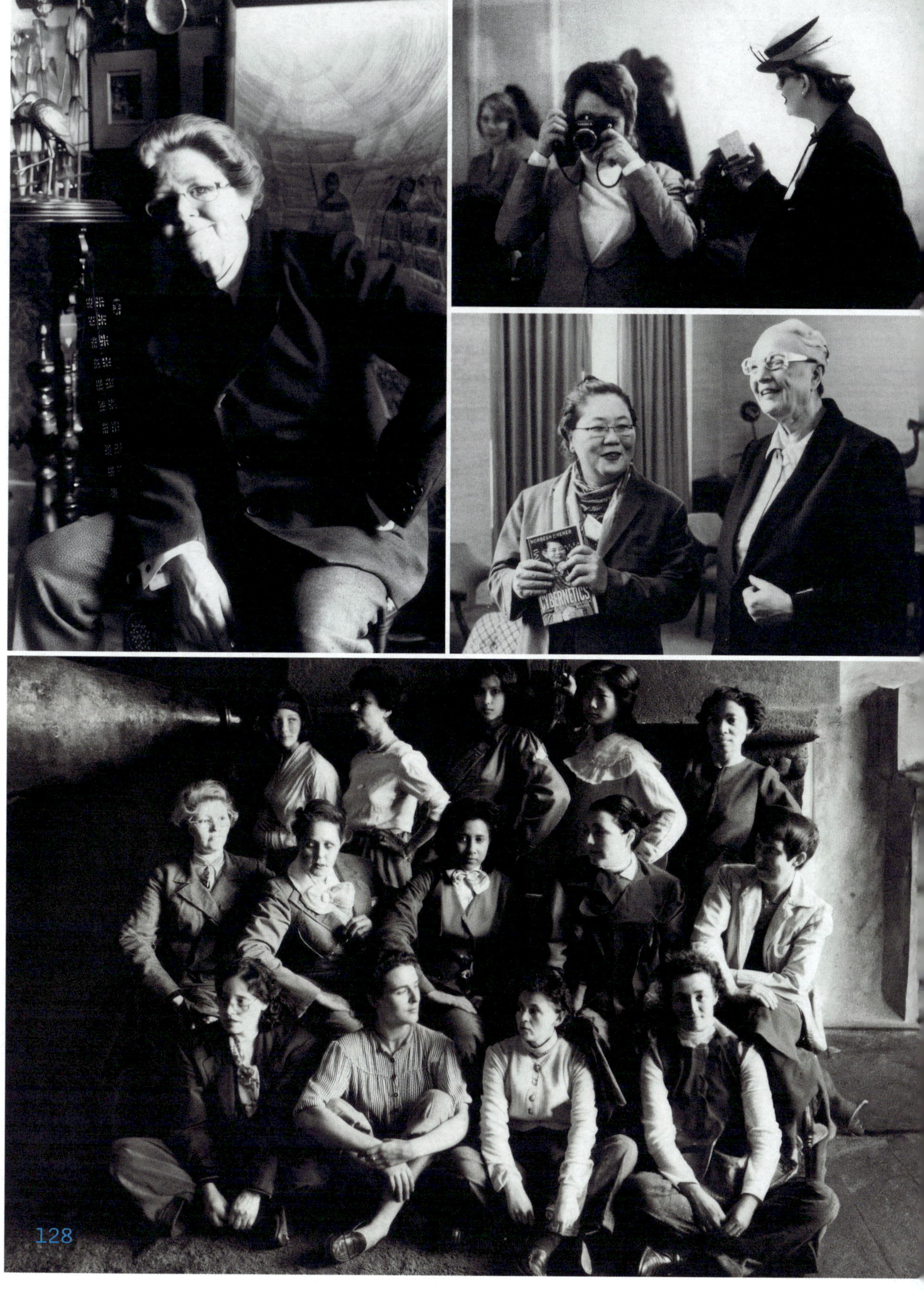
NORBERT WIENER
CYBERNETICS

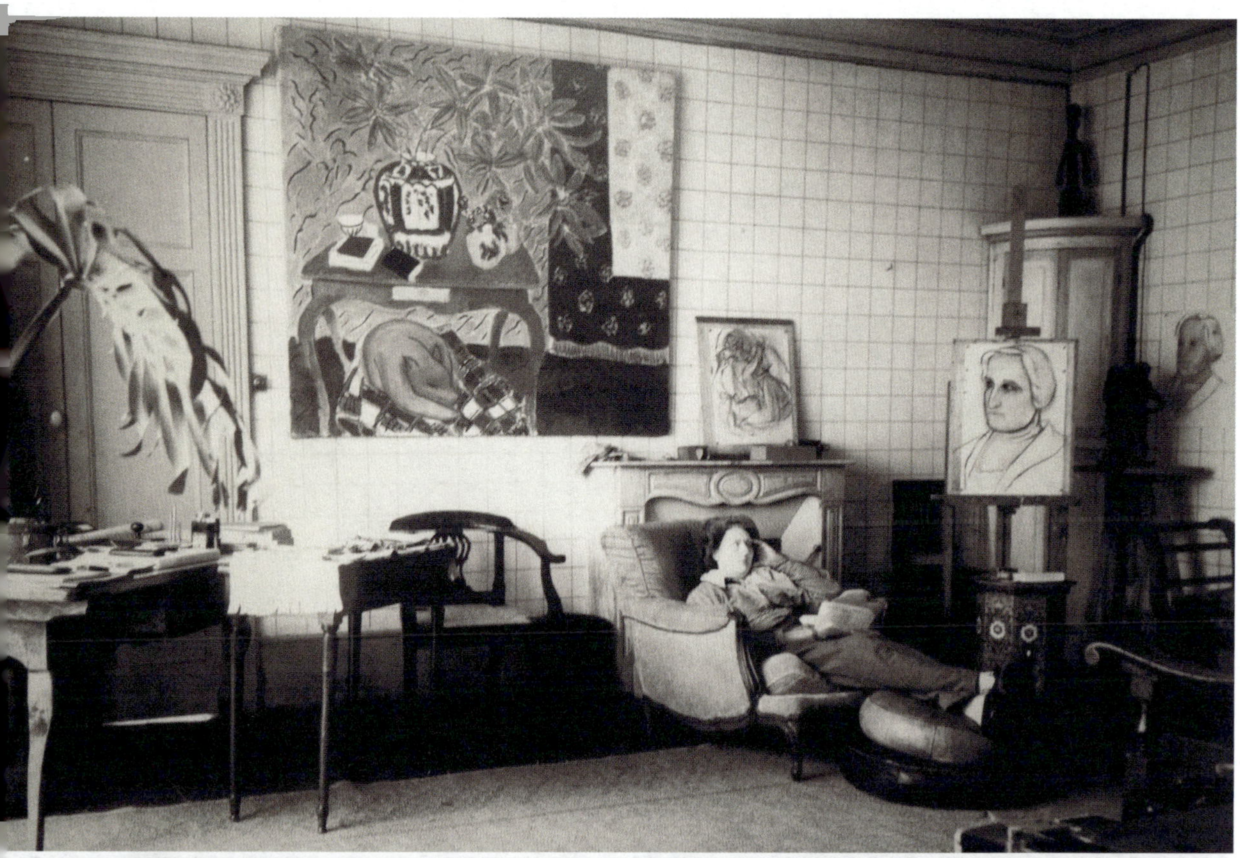

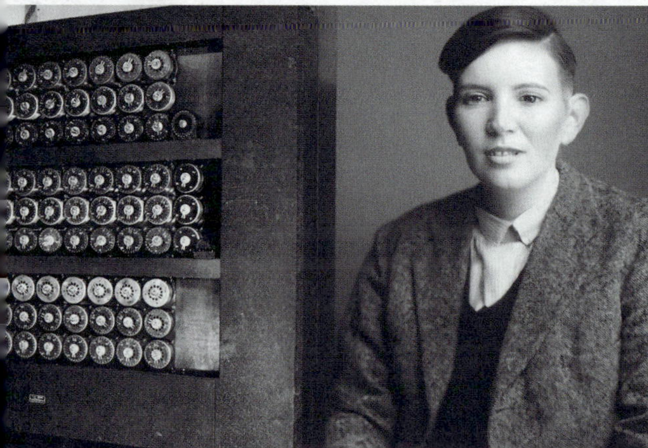

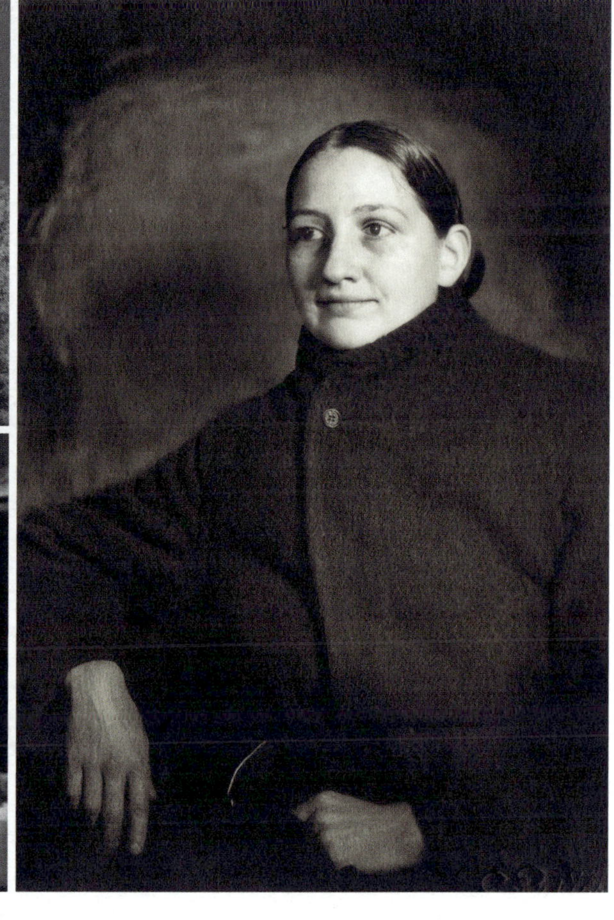

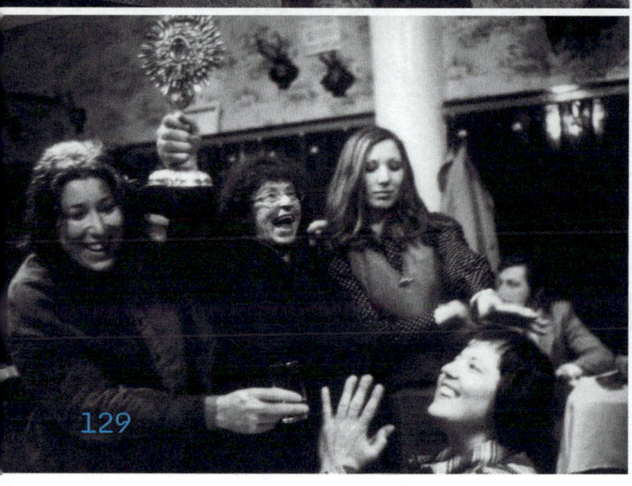

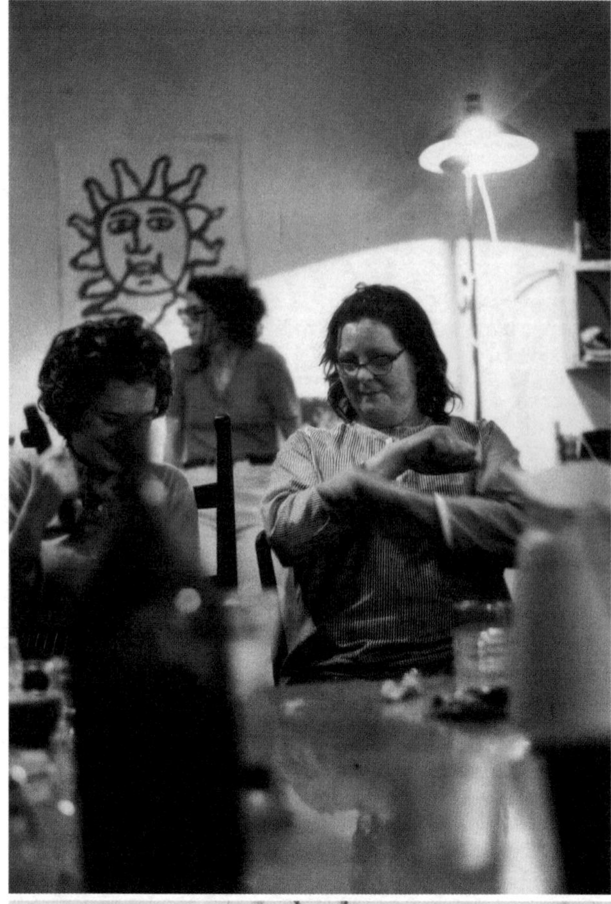

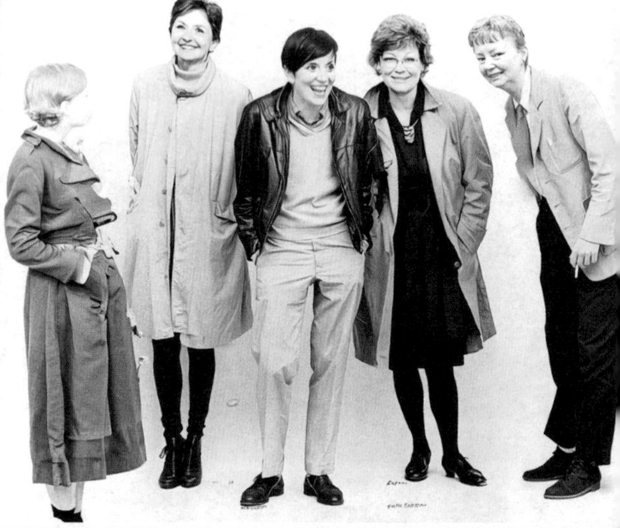

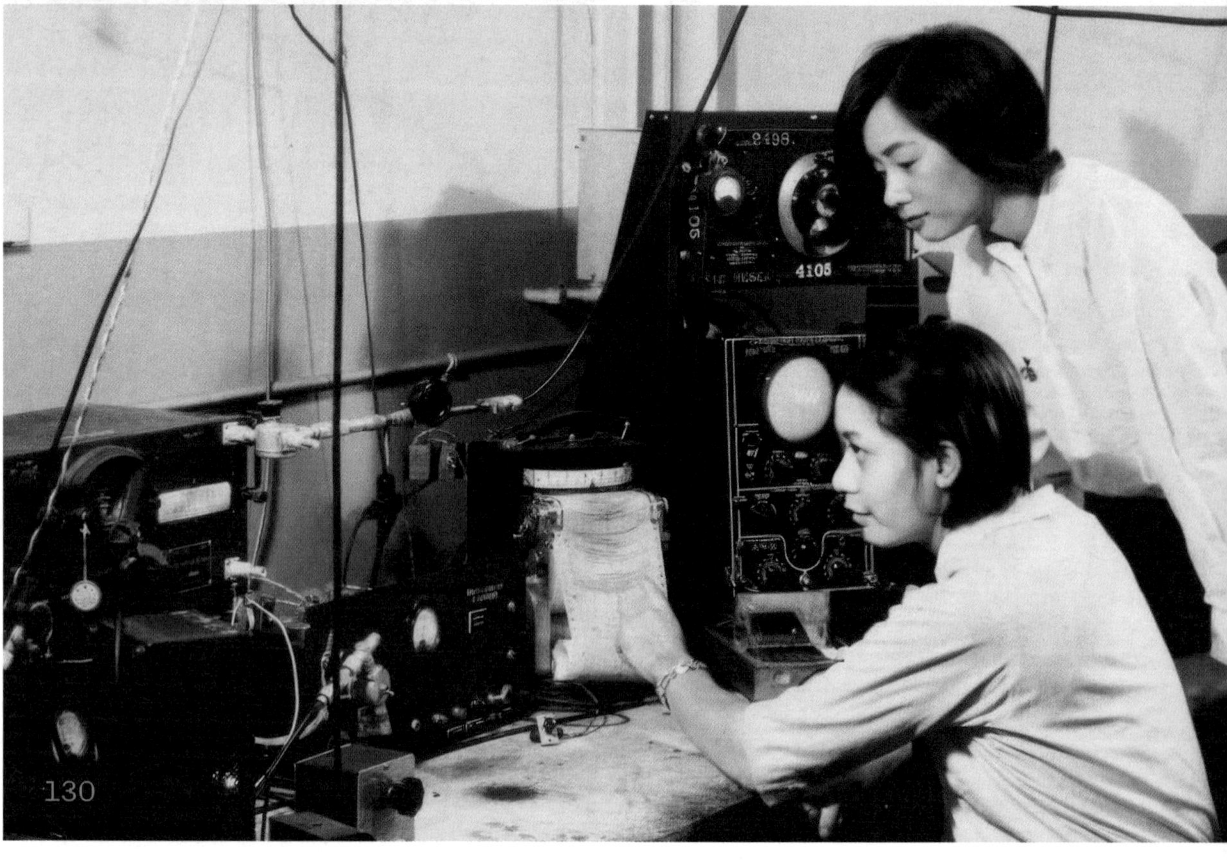

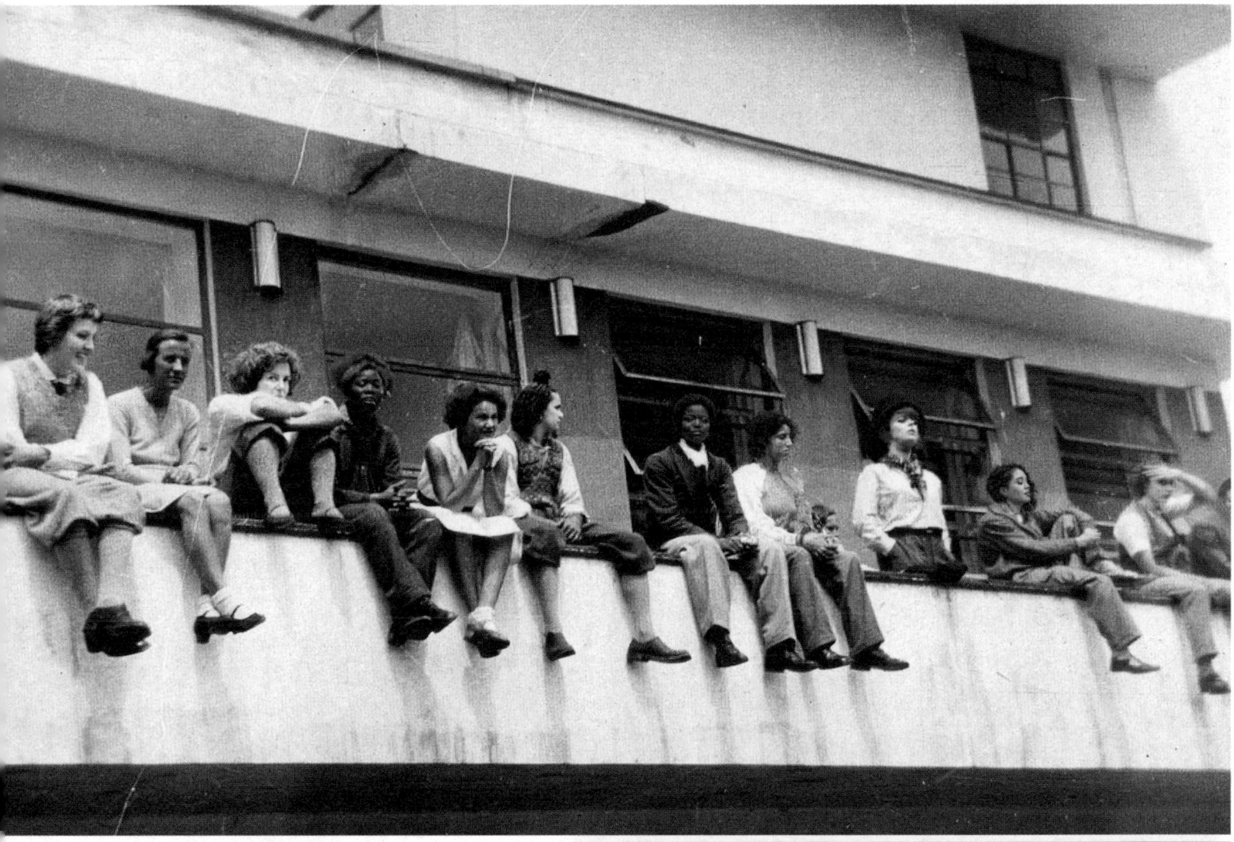

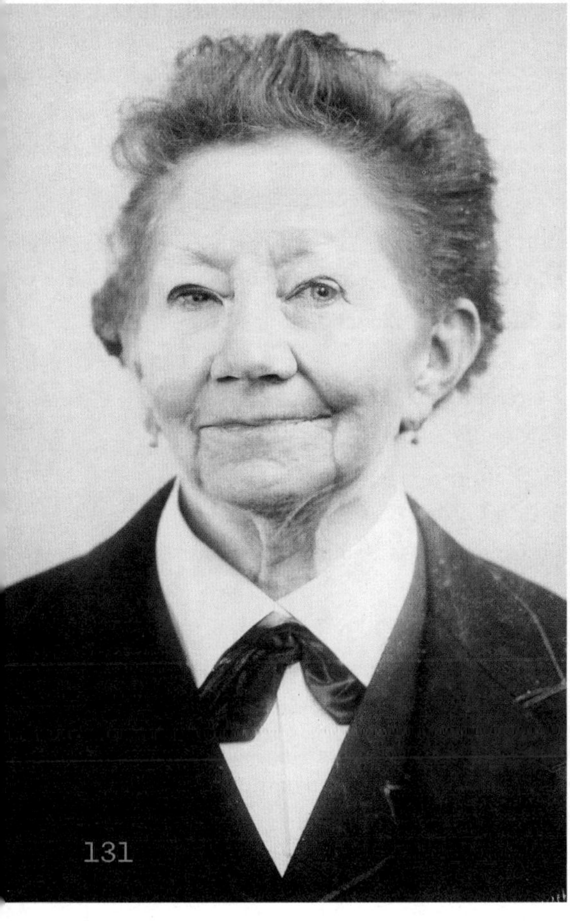

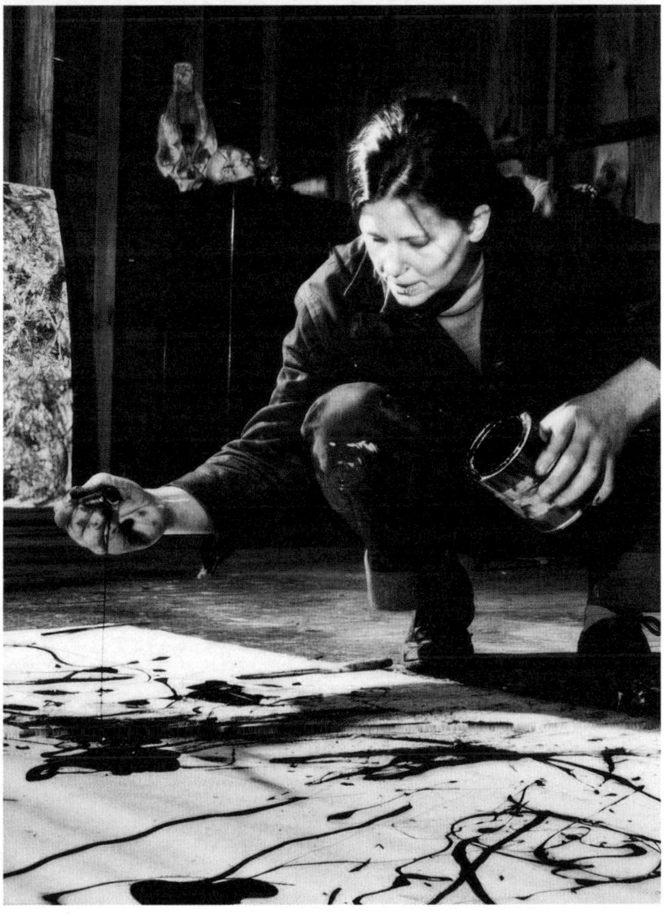

Bildnachweise

KI und Kunst der historischen Neuinterpretation
Filling Gender Bias Gaps

Seite | Page 102
P. Klee
A. Warhol
W. Gropius
G. Debord (3rd Conference of the Situationist International 1959)

Seite | Page 104
A. Van der Berg (with C. Nieuwenhuis sculpture)
W. Gropius
W. Kandinsky

Seite | Page 105
Artists in Ballinchap, New York 1942
F. T. Marinetti
S. Murakami
Scientists at MIT

Seite | Page 106
W. Y. Tsai at MIT Hayden Gallery, Cambridge
R. W. Mann, MIT
Artists of Informel

Seite | Page 107
H. Matisse
L. Feininger
Russolo, Marinetti, Boccioni and Severini in front of *Le Figaro*, Paris 1912
Secession Members, 1902

Seite | Page 111
S. Dali
A. Warhol and J. Beuys
P. Kubelka

Seite | Page 112
Dr. C. G. Abbot with Harmonic printout
H. Matisse
W. Pichler, G. Peichl, P. Noever

Seite | Page 113
Bauhaus Designers
J. Beuys
M. Proust

Seite | Page 114
J. Albers
Arte Povera

Seite | Page 115
Some of the Russian Kubo-Futurists, 1912
G. Mahler
Internationaler Kongress der Konstruktivist:innen und Dadaist:innen, Weimar 1922

Seite | Page 118
Die Wiener Gruppe, Café Hawelka 1957
I. Sutherlands Sketchpad

Seite | Page 119
L. Moholy Nagy
G. Braque
T. Bernhard
Lanzmann, S.de Beauvoir, J.P. Sartre, 1967

Seite | Page 120
Kelman, Broughton, Sitney, Mekas, Kubelka
H. Willeger, G. Falk, R. Priessnitz, Wiener Secession 1972
Scientist at MIT playing computer chess

Photo Credits

AI and the Art of Historical Reinterpretation
Filling Gender Bias Gaps

Seite | Page 121
M. Minsky, AI Lab, 1968
E. Schiele
H. Hansen, M. Ernst, L. Straus-Ernst,
R. Straus und J. T. Baargeld, 1919

Seite | Page 122
H. Matisse
G. Eluard, M. Ernst, T. Baargeld,
L. Straus-Ernst, J. Ernst, P. Eluard, 1920
The Beatles
Steiger, Kalb, Pichler, Attersee,
Graf, Wiener, Wiener

Seite | Page 123
Die „Uni-Ferkelei", 1968
G. Braque, 1908
Palazzeschi, Carrà, Papini,
Boccioni, Marinetti, 1914

Seite | Page 126
Pariser Dada Gruppe
P. Picasso
M. Breuer
T. Knight and R. Greenblatt, MIT 1976

Seite | Page 127
M. Cunningham
G. Braque
A. Rainer und R. Priessnitz im Cafe Savoy
H. Matisse with unknown model

Seite | Page 128
F.T. Marinetti
VALIE EXPORT und P. Weibel
Wiener and Burchard
P. Guggenheim surrounded by exiled
European artists in New York 1952

Seite | Page 129
H. Matisse in her studio
A. Turing
J. Joyce
G. Rühm, H. Nitsch, Lisl
Ponger, O. Mühl, 1971

Seite | Page 130
O. Mühl
O. Oberhuber, B. Gironcoli, H. Hollein,
R. Goeschl, W. Pichler. 1968
Absorption of Microwaves by
Molecules of Gas, MIT 1954

Seite | Page 131
Students of Bauhaus
F. Nietzsche
J. Pollock

Impressum | Imprint

Diese Publikation erscheint
anlässlich der Ausstellung
Claudia Larcher | *HALLUCINATIONS*
kuratiert von Yvonne Rüscher
22. Oktober – 15. Dezember 2024
Kunstraum Engländerbau Vaduz

This book is published on the
occasion of the exhibition
Claudia Larcher | *HALLUCINATIONS*
curated by Yvonne Rüscher
October 22 – December 15, 2024
Kunstraum Engländerbau Vaduz

Herausgeber/in | Editor
Kunstraum Engländerbau Vaduz
Claudia Larcher

Gestaltung | Graphic Design
Yvonne Rüscher

Texte | Essays
Christian Höller, Ivana Miloš,
Ruth Schib, Klaus Speidel

Übersetzung | Translations
George Frederick Takis

Lektorat | Proofreading
Martina Buder, George Frederick Takis,
Petra Joppich

Ausstellungsfotografie | Photography
Studio Claudia Larcher

Druckvorstufe | Prepress
Marcello Girardelli

Dank an | Thanks are due to
Rosario Caltabiano, Galerie 22,48m2, Paris
Galerie Lisi Hämmerle, Bregenz, Hedwig
Larcher, Helmuth Larcher, Stefania
Pitscheider Soraperra, Werner Reiterer

Erschienen bei | Published by
VfmK Verlag für moderne Kunst GmbH
Schwedenplatz 2/24
A-1010 Wien/Vienna
hello@vfmk.org | www.vfmk.org

Gedruckt in Österreich | Printed in Austria
Thurnher Druckerei GmbH, Rankweil

ISBN 978-3-99153-138-8

Die Deutsche Nationalbibliothek
verzeichnet diese Publikation in der
Deutschen Nationalbibliografie; detaillierte
bibliografische Daten sind im Internet
über http://www.dnb.de abrufbar.

The Deutsche Nationalbibliothek
lists this publication in the Deutsche
Nationalbibliografie; detailed
bibliographic data are available on
the Internet at http://www.dnb.de.

Vertrieb | Distribution
Europe: LKG, www.lkg.eu
USA: D.A.P., www.artbook.com

Die Realisierung dieser Publikation wurde unterstützt von

The publication was made possible through the generous support of

Bundesministerium
Kunst, Kultur,
öffentlicher Dienst und Sport

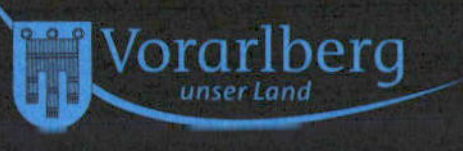

STIFTUNG
FÜRSTLICHER KOMMERZIENRAT
Guido Feger

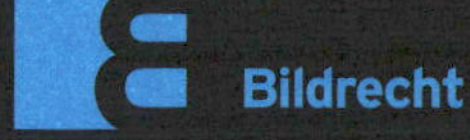

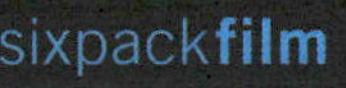

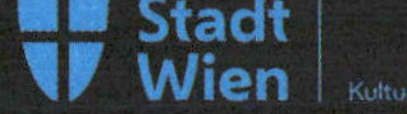

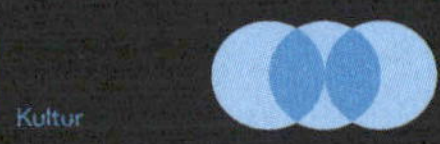

Verlag für moderne Kunst